"Poetry Loves Poetry"

"Poetry Loves Poetry"

edited by Bill Mohr

"Poetry Loves Poetry"

An Anthology of Los Angeles Poets

edited by Bill Mohr

photographs by Sheree Levin

Momentum Press

Momentum Press is part of the Century City Educational Arts Project, a non-profit corporation with offices in West Los Angeles, Santa Monica, and downtown Los Angeles.

Momentum Press
512 Hill St., Apt. 4
Santa Monica, CA 90405

Momentum Press books are distributed by Small Press Distribution (1784 Shattuck Ave., Berkeley, California 94709), Inland Book Company (22 Hemingway Avenue, East Haven, Connecticut 06512), and Spring Church Book Company (P.O. Box 127, Spring Church, Pennsylvania 15686).

This book was typeset by Bill Mohr at NewComp Graphics Center at Beyond Baroque Foundation, Venice, CA and printed at Gemini Graphics in Marina del Rey, CA. The design is by Bill Mohr with assistance from Kate Vozoff on poet headings. Special thanks to Harley Lond, editor of *Boxoffice* magazine, for his many years of help.

And best wishes to "jury number one": Scott Wannberg (foreman), Steve Richmond, Kita Shantiris, Dinah Berland, Ameen Alwan, Nan Hunt, Nancy Shiffrin, Kyle Norwood, Denise Dumars, Frances Dean Smith, Blair Allen, and Peggy Collen, all of whom deserved to be in this collection.

ISBN 0-936054-50-6 (paperback)
ISBN 0-936054-51-4 (hardcover)

The publication of this book
was made possible
by grants from

THE ATLANTIC RICHFIELD FOUNDATION

and

THE NATIONAL ENDOWMENT FOR THE ARTS

for George Drury Smith

Founder of Beyond Baroque Foundation

David James

Nichola Manning

Michael C. Ford

Lewis MacAdams

Peter Levitt

Martha Lifson

Brooks Roddan

Self-Portraits in Los Angeles

Poetry is rarely the lure for someone who moves to Los Angeles and yet several hundred poets have taken up permanent residence here in the past twenty years. The huge majority of poets in *"Poetry Loves Poetry"* were born elsewhere, ranging from Germany, Russia, China, England, Cuba and Poland to San Francisco, Philadelphia, and Cleveland, as well as little towns in the Midwest. In 1957 I was a Navy brat in my hometown, Norfolk, Virginia, and after I finished doing my math homework, I would turn on the television to watch "Dragnet" with my five younger brothers and sisters. Each time I heard the words "Los Angeles" followed by "The Entertainment Capitol of the World" as if for the first time. Week after week "Zorro," "Rawhide," "The Flintstones," "Top Cat," as well as "Leave It to Beaver" and "The Man from U.N.C.L.E." evoked a distant city which created entertainment myths for my generation's childhood. It was a city with the element of the forbidden about it too. I envied my schoolmates who were allowed to watch "77 Sunset Strip," a program which sent us back to our rooms since it apparently conjured up all the tempting vice of the world.

By the mid-Sixties I was living in another Navy town, and film and rock music had replaced television, although it was a late-night viewing of *Requiem for a Heavyweight* which interested me in drama. I was on my way to a rehearsal for Arthur Miller's *The Crucible* when I heard The Doors' long-version of "Light My Fire" on my radio. The dj said this band was playing in Los Angeles, a mere 140 miles away. I had been writing song lyrics and poems ranting and raving about the usual adolescent themes of alienation. I decided to write film scripts and headed to Los Angeles. I wasn't alone. Almost a third of the poets in this book have either acted in a film or play, written a script, or performed in a rock and roll band.

This career choice is not as unusual as it might first seem. Most poets would probably concede that four outstanding poets in the first half of this century were Williams, Stevens, Eliot and Pound. Both Williams and Eliot made serious attempts at

i

making money by writing for the theatre. Two of the more flamboyant, Antonin Artaud and Dylan Thomas, earned money from film or radio. Obviously, the ambition of the poet to make a living through artistic mediums more popular than poetry is not an aberration, but one of the few rational solutions to an archetypal artistic dilemma, which is not limited to poets. William Faulkner and Nathaniel West more than paid their dues in Hollywood.

But if many poets have moved here in hopes of an entertainment career, which, after all, is much more appealing and glamorous than selling life insurance, twice as many have moved here for other reasons. Some of it has to do with the upheaval which this country experienced in the 60s. All wars tend to increase the size of the participants' cities. Saigon became one of the largest cities in the world during the last decade of the Vietnamese Reunification War. The suburban cities in Los Angeles County which first expanded when World War II brought huge numbers of people to work in the defense industries saw another population surge during the longest war in United States' history. The conservative movement in this country makes it difficult to remember how many young people were moving here simply to be "where it was happening," which included peace marches and rallies as well as movies and the Sunset Boulevard music scene.

The entertainment career factor certainly must not be overemphasized. Many poets in Los Angeles had ambitions only for their poetry and found themselves in Pasadena, Lawndale, or Sherman Oaks only because their parents had moved here. Why then did they stay when they found that the poetry scene was embryonic to say the least? One of the major reasons is the same one that lured the movie industry out here seventy years ago: the light. I think the light in Los Angeles possesses more variety in intensity and tones than any other place in the United States. Eloise Klein Healy has a poem in which streets become a version of urban astrology, "Tell me what your favorite intersection is and I'll tell you who you are."; but I feel that if people tell me what tone or blend of light they enjoy, I'll tell them what part of Los Angeles they live in.

The popular image of Los Angeles suggests a vast suburban sprawl, but a substantial number of the poets in *"Poetry Loves Poetry"* live in two small, densely populated neighborhoods: Ocean Park/Venice or Silverlake/Echo Park. Ocean Park consists of a series of hills rising from the beach which descend on their southern border to the flat land of Venice, which extends to the world's largest small-craft harbor, Marina del Rey. Silverlake/Echo Park is fifteen miles inland and is nestled in a hilly district near downtown Los Angeles. My own personal experience is that the light seems to contract as I drive inland toward Barnsdall or Griffith Park or the San Gabriel Valley.

The huge majority of poets in Los Angeles write narrative poetry which emphasizes visual imagery and the plasticity of location. This is in part a response to the quality of light in this city, which is essentially Mediterranean desert filtered by natural mist and haze and layers of marine air interwoven with Santa Ana winds and industrial exhalations. Although there are many poets whose work I admire in the Bay Area (San Francisco-Oakland-Berkeley), I could never live there because I dislike the light. If this sounds more like the reaction of a painter, then so be it. It isn't an accident that several of my favorite painters live or work within several blocks of my own apartment in Ocean Park.

Social factors also account for the prolonged residencies of Los Angeles poets. Los Angeles tends to attract poets who are loners. Very few of us have attended the M.F.A. programs which allow young poets to meet each other and build up networks. In fact, there isn't a social scene among the poets here. Unlike San Francisco or New York, there is not a single bar in all of Los Angeles where the poets in this anthology meet. Outside of readings, about the only other place I see poets is at Dodger Stadium. The distinct lack of a "social scene" is unlikely to change no matter how many poets are working here. This city attracts a certain kind of artist and it's not somebody who needs to be around other artists in order to reassure herself/himself that all is well with the imagination. As Charles Bukowski noted in his introduction to a small but pithy anthology published in the early 70s by Red Hill Press, "I think it is important to know that a man or woman, writer or not, can find more isolation in Los Angeles than in Boise, Idaho."

The only social contact that many poets have with other poets is at readings. There have been dozens of reading series in the Los Angeles area during the past fifteen years. Many focused on independent bookstores such as Papa Bach, George Sand, Chelsea, Chatterton's and Intellectuals and Liars. Other series worked out of libraries, radio stations, or institutions which have a strong asssociation with the visual arts like the Woman's Building or S.P.A.R.C.

A reading series is the most visible sign of the poetic curiosity of an area and the Beyond Baroque series over the past twelve years has been a good measuring stick for the range of books which L.A. poets have stacked next to their typewriters: Michael McClure, Tom Clark, Kenward Elmslie, Alicia Ostriker, James Moore, Edward Field, Bobbie Louise Hawkins, Allen Ginsberg, Robert Creeley, Amiri Baraka, Charles Baxter, Tim Dlugos, Michael Davidson, Ron Silliman, David Antin, Elaine Equi, Leslie Scalapino, Diane DiPrima, Anne Waldman, Robert Kelley, Ron Padgett, Barrett Watten, Steve Benson, Kit Robinson, Alan Bernheimer, Steve Kowit, Diane Wakoski, Bill Berkson, Charles Bernstein, Rae Armantrout, John Logan, and Theodore Enslin. The reading series has also included a large number of fiction writers like Dale Herd, Lydia Davis, and Walter Abish as well as performance and visual artists like George Herms, Stuart Sherman, Tim Miller, Mike Kelley, Marina LaPalma and Linda Albertano.

There are at least a dozen colleges in Southern California which host readings that supplement the Beyond Baroque series with the better known academic poets (Alfred Corn, James Merrill, John Ashbery, Robert Haas, William Matthews, etc.) but these readings are not held on a weekly basis and are not connected with any kind of publishing activity which is the only way to generate serious attention and discussion of poetic activity in other parts of the country. Beyond Baroque has hosted publication parties for numerous books and magazines and has served as a way for poets to meet and discuss theory and practice. James Krusoe ran the series from 1973 to 1980, followed by Dennis Cooper (1980-1983) and Jack Skelley, Benjamin Weissman, and Amy Gerstler in the meantime.

Beyond Baroque dominates the poetic landscape in Los Angeles. Almost all the poets in *The Streets Inside: Ten Los Angeles Poets* (Momentum Press, 1978) first met each other at the Beyond Baroque's Wednesday night poetry workshop in the early 70s. *"Poetry Loves Poetry"* includes many poets who have since participated in that workshop, led its meetings or read at the Friday night series.

When *The Streets Inside* appeared, the late Robert Kirsch of the Los Angeles Times hailed it as an indication of a "golden age" of Los Angeles poetry; but Kirsch also noted that the ten poets lacked a common poetics and did not seem to belong to any particular school of poetry elsewhere in the country. Call it "no-school" he wrote. Kirsch's inability to categorize the poets in that anthology wasn't entirely his fault. I myself didn't have the slightest idea of how to label us and none of the reviews of the book were able to come up with any ideas either. Almost all of them acknowledged that something different was happening in Los Angeles, but couldn't find any way to define it. I expect *Poetry Loves Poetry* will only compound the problem. There are over six times as many poets and many of them have evolved an idiosyncratic blend of poetics which incorporates everything from O'Hara's "Personism" to Olson's "Projective Verse."

If I had to describe the poetics of a large number of poets in Los Angeles in two words, I would use "Existential Romanticism." The existential factor is so obvious that it is easy to overlook, which is a serious mistake. Part of the problem is that existentialism has become so integral to the thought of contemporary artists that it's as dominant as Catholicism in the Middle Ages. "Existence precedes essence" is intuitively related to Olson's "Form is only an extension of content." The romantic counterbalance is the artist's attempt to soothe the alienation with an outburst of autobiographical emotion. It is all well and good to pretend (as many arts programs try to do by bringing poets into the schools, etc.) that artists are "normal people" but the fact remains that they are sick people — in the same sense that I might say a volcano is sick earth. A volcano's explosion and the vomiting of lava is not the only way the earth renews itself with fresh soil, but it is the only process which simultaneously reveals what is underneath the surface of the earth. In the same way an artist erupts and renews the visionary myths of birth and death with the lava of imagination.

The first person narration of many Los Angeles poets' work can be deceiving. Rather than autobiographical, I prefer the term self-portraits. Unlike painters' canvases, the poems are not limited to one face, using instead a wide cast of characters and favoring a depth of field approach with this city's layers of pointillistic motion in the background.

Of course I wouldn't claim that only poets who live in Los Angeles belong to the Self-Portrait School of Existential Romanticism. Schools and regions are too subject to the wandering seedfest of poetics for one group of poets to claim hegemony over a particular approach. Tom Clark's work would fit into this style without missing a beat. But I believe that there are more poets whose work belongs to this school living in Los Angeles than anywhere else in the United States right now.

All groups of artists depend on past workers in their fields to provide a framework for contemporary outgrowth. The self-portrait school is particularly interested in W.C. Williams and Walt Whitman. Both Williams and Whitman redefined the function of sentences in poetry. Many of Williams' best poems are single sentences and the absence of a caesura in Whitman's line is due to his exploration of the sentence in verse. The narrative sentence favored by many of the self-portrait poets in Los Angeles is partially a result of their comic approach to their material. Comedy requires a sentence stripped of abstract rhetoric. One of the distinguishing traits of many Los Angeles poets is the sense of humor which is the foundation of their poetics. L.A. poems can often seem to be "prosy," but that's because the very nature of comedy demands prose and this requirement affects verse with comic subject matter. Traditional verse is at ease with wit. This goes all the way back to Shakespeare, whose verse is often witty, but when he wrote comedy, used prose. Los Angeles poets are not much interested in wit. Wit itself is perceived as an attempt to create a flattering self-portrait of a poet sensitive to the nuances of language. Humor and comedy demand bigger canvases which include room for the only thing which can create comedy — vulnerability.

The vulnerability of personal emotion may tempt some readers to link the self-portrait school with the post-World War II confessional school of poets. The difference is an issue of sentimentality, which is one of the major weaknesses of the "confessional" school. Various definitions of sentimentality have been offered during this century — "a failure of emotion" (Stevens) or that it is redundancy (Williams). But the most obvious tip-off to the presence of sentimentality in work is the lack of comedy. And the absence of a sense of humor dominates the contemporary anthologies of American poetry.

The best known Los Angeles member of the self-portrait school, and certainly one of the most influential poets in the United States, is Charles Bukowski. Bukowski isn't interested in belonging to any school, but his poems often sculpt a torso out of the granite of the English language which are in Whitman's words, "rude, masculine, unbending, lusty."

A number of Los Angeles poets are influenced by Bukowski, although they are very different in style and effect. Ron Koertge's poems achieve the almost impossible: his poems extend from an existential comic vision. If I had to pick out a single poem in this anthology that epitomizes the self-portrait school, it would be Koertge's "An Ontological Report." Gerald Locklin has often been linked with Bukowski and Koertge. All three of them write a substantial quantity of fiction as well as poetry which concentrates on heterosexual warfare.

One of Ron Koertge's students at Pasadena City College was a Los Angeles native, Dennis Cooper, who led the emergence of a group of young gay poets, including David Trinidad and Peter Cashorali. Cooper launched Little Caesar magazine and press in the late seventies, which published small collections of some of the younger Los Angeles poets (Gerstler and Skelley) as well as larger collections of poems by new arrivals such as Michael Lally and Lewis MacAdams. Little Caesar had plans for even bigger projects, including a novel by Tom Clark, but Cooper's money ran out. He has since moved to New York and teaches workshops for the Poetry Project at St. Mark's Church in-the-Bowery.

One of the poets Cooper published was Peter Schjeldahl, a New York art critic who was living in Los Angeles while his wife was acting in films. I decided to begin the anthology with his *"To Pico"* poem (from the Little Caesar book, *The Brute)* to give the reader outside of Los Angeles a sense of an archetypal reaction which many new arrivals experience during their initial period of residence here. It is one of my favorite poems even though it is radically different from my own experience of Pico Boulevard.

Another poet who also became an important editor was Leland Hickman. Hickman grew up in Southern California, spent several years in New York doing theatre work, and moved back to Los Angeles in 1968. Hickman took over the editorship of *Bachy* magazine in the mid-seventies and turned it into a historical document through a series of in-depth interviews with Los Angeles poets as well as a means of intermingling Los Angeles area poets' work with poems from around the country. *Bachy* was published by Papa Bach bookstore from 1972 to 1981. Hickman is presently editing *Temblor,* one of the few magazines in California which links up Los Angeles poets like Jed Rasula and Robert Crosson with poets in San Francisco like Ron Silliman, Lyn Hejinian, Bob Perelman, Kit Robinson, and Barrett Watten.

Paul Vangelisti began Red Hill Press in 1971 with an issue of *Invisible City,* a poetry magazine published in tabloid form with heavy-stock paper. Although Vangelisti co-edited it with a Bay Area resident, John McBride, *Invisible City* rarely published any poets from Northern California. It concentrated on a blend of Los Angeles poets and translations from poets in Italy, Spain, and the Caribbean. Jack Hirschman played "lead saxophone" back in the early seventies as his enthusiasm for the transsubstantiation of vowels and consonants made *Invisible*

City one of the few international magazines published in the United States in the 70s. Hirschman translated Rene Deprestre and Alvaro Cardona-Hine rendered Cesar Vallejo's "Spain, Let This Cup Pass from Me" into a lyrical elegy for a nation. Red Hill Press produced over sixty titles in a flurry which never lost control of the books' design quality, including titles by John Thomas and Bob Peters. Vangelisti also produced poetry and music programs on KPFK for close to ten years as well as doing an extraordinary amount of translating. In addition, Vangelisti edited or co-edited the first two anthologies of Los Angeles poets, one of which was produced as an adjunct to a reading series which he directed at the Pasadena Museum of Modern Art.

The best-known press to emerge from Los Angeles is Black Sparrow, now located in Santa Barbara. John Martin has published over 150 titles in the past twenty years and has made a substantial contribution to American literature in the 20th century. Michael McClure, Tom Clark, Sam Shepard and Diane Wakoski are some of the major poets and playwrights whose work he has published. In addition to publishing Charles Bukowski and Wanda Coleman, Black Sparrow also publishes most of Clayton Eshleman's poetry.

Eshleman, an award-winning translator with works published by the Univerity of California Press as well as Dennis Koran's Panjandrum Press, has edited over a dozen issues of *Sulphur*, a magazine which has concentrated on translations from the French and Spanish poets, and a blend of "post-Black Mountain" and "language-centered" writing. *Sulphur* is now published through the University of California at Los Angeles Extension Program, which has also sponsored two major symposiums on "Los Angeles Poetry."

After editing the first two issues of *Bachy* magazine, I began Momentum Press in 1974 and have published over two dozen titles by twenty-two writers, including poets who have had success as fiction writers. Momentum Press published Holly Prado's book of autobiographical fiction, *FEASTS*, in 1976 and she will have her first novel, *GARDENS*, published in November by Harcourt, Brace and Jovanovich. Kate Braverman (*Milk Run*, poems, 1976) had her first novel, *Lithium for Medea*, published in 1979 by Harper and Row, who also published a volume of her poems, *Lullaby for Sinners*. Joseph Hansen (*One Foot in the Boat*, 1978; *The Dog and other stories*, 1980) has become one of the best known mystery writers in America. Momentum Press has published fifteen full-length (over 48 pages of verse) books of poetry by Los Angeles poets. One of them, *TIRESIAS I:9:B Great Slave Lake Suite*, was nominated for the *Los Angeles Times* Book Awards as one of the five best books of poetry in 1980. Momentum Press has always concentrated on publishing work by relatively unknown poets and *"Poetry Loves Poetry"* marks the first appearance in a major anthology by over half of its poets.

A number of poetry ventures emerged in the past three years as Little Caesar, Red Hill, and Momentum Press faltered due to financial problems and the editors' decisions to spend more time on their own writing. P. Schneidre's Illuminati is making a bid to become the most important new press in Los Angeles with a rapid-fire series of chapbooks and cassettes. Leo Mailman's Maelstom Press operated out of Long Beach for several years until his recent move to Maine and he published over a dozen titles. Applezaba Press has also made a substantial contribution to publishing activity in Long Beach through a concentration on poets living in that town. David Trinidad began a press to honor Rachel Sherwood, a young Los Angeles poet who was killed in an auto accident by a drunk driver. Sherwood's catalogue includes Bob Flanagan's *The Wedding of Everything* and Alice Notley's *Sorrento*. Other publishers include Lawrence Spingarn (Perivale) and Kenneth Atchity (*Dreamworks*/L.A. House). Harvey Kubernick's "Freeway Records" series has four albums with over two and a half hours of recorded poems by a wide variety of Los Angeles poets.

Kubernick's albums, in fact, are one of the best references I can make to answer the question that one of the poets in *"Poetry Loves Poetry"* asked me when I told her how many poets were going to be in it: "Did you leave anybody out?" Poets in most American cities have a hard time believing there are more than

x

a half-dozen poets living in their area who are worth any attention. "I certainly did," I told her. "Enough to assemble a dozen juries all of whom would find me guilty for leaving them out."

A number of poets have worked on magazines or "active anthologies": Doren Robbins co-edited *Third Rail* with Uri Hertz and Michael C. Ford published *The Sunset Palms Motel.* John Harris edited several issues of *Bachy* magazine before he took over Papa Bach bookstore. Jack Grapes co-edited a unique series of anthologies which accompanied the Alleycat Reading Series in Hermosa Beach. He also continues to publish Los Angeles poets through Bombshelter Press, which he founded with the photographer Michael Andrews in 1974. Jack Skelley published four "annual anthologies" of *Barney* which were full of pop-culture-influenced art and poetry.

Beyond Baroque also published a magazine which never managed to gain its own identity mainly because it seemed to change its name every other year, although it did publish work by the majority of the poets in *"Poetry Loves Poetry"* in its various incarnations since 1968. George Drury Smith and James Krusoe alternated in editing issues for the first ten years. Smith founded Beyond Baroque in 1968 and without his continued efforts to sustain this literary center, the Los Angeles poetry scene would be simply another provincial coterie. Smith's assistant editor, Alexandra Garrett, also devoted countless hours of volunteer work to Beyond Baroque's programs. Manazar Gamboa (1978-1980) and Jocelyn Fisher (1980-1985) served terms both as president of Beyond Baroque and as editors of its magazine publication. The interwoven nature of the Los Angeles poetry scene is reflected in the recent appointment of Dennis Phillips as president of Beyond Baroque. Phillips served as book review editor of *Sulfur* magazine for its first nine issues as well as being the first poetry editor for L.A. Weekly.

Although a large number of women poets have emerged in the wake of the feminist movement, there have been relatively few magazines or presses run by women, despite the acquisition of printing equipment by the Woman's Building, which is located in an industrial section of downtown. The Woman's Building did produce several fine issues of *Chrysalis, a magazine of woman's culture*, in the mid-seventies. Susan King's Paradise Press has produced over a half-dozen letter-press books. Aleida Rodriguez and Jacqueline DeAngelis published several issues of *Rara Avis* magazine, which concluded with an anthology of Southern California women writers. They also publish a variety of projects through their Books of a Feather. Helen Friedland's *Poetry L.A.* has sustained itself for several issues with an emphasis on Southland poets.

Red Hill, Black Sparrow, Momentum, Little Caesar, Illuminati, Bombshelter, Maelstrom, Applezaba, Sherwood, Paradise, Freeway Records, *Rara Avis, Bachy, Sunset Palms Motel, Third Rail, Barney, Sulfur, Magazine, Chrysalis, Poetry L.A., Temblor:* all reflect a devotion which enables the poets who begin these projects to overcome continual financial adversity, the contempt of the chain bookstores towards independent publishing, and the slow and often begrudging acceptance of review space in the major literary journals or newspapers outside of our home base. The *Los Angeles Times* has been almost alone in giving these poets consistent review space.

The role of the National Endowment for the Arts' Literature Program in the growth of the scene is very important. The Endowment has provided well over a quarter of a million dollars in assistance to the poets in this area in the past fifteen years. This includes grants to Beyond Baroque, to many of the small presses and magazines I have discussed, as well as individual writing fellowships.

The title of this anthology is meant as a reflection of this devotion as well as being an ironic comment on poetry's place in American society. I discovered the title while I was reading a poem by Harry Northup in which he quotes Jack Hirschman. According to Harry, Jack was visiting a friend in Los Angeles and the discussion turned to the value of poetry in American society. Jack's friend was feeling badly about people's indifference to poetry. Jack said simply, "Poetry loves poetry."

I am pleased that Jack's ironic affirmation should become the title of this anthology. Jack is one of those rare poets whose life and work have influenced poets with extremely different styles and approaches to art. Jack was the first poet I ever met who lived in a continuum of poetic consciousness which didn't acknowledge such academic chronological divisions as "modernism" and "post-modernism." Clayton Eshleman mentioned in his introduction to Vallejo's *Posthumous Poetry* that Hirschman was the man who introduced him to the world of translation. I suspect that Jack Hirschman will be California's equivalent of Dickinson or Blake, a poet whose achievement is only recognized after his work is gathered.

Much of the poetic history of Los Angeles is hidden because the city is so young in terms of being a modern art center. The first fifty years of this century brought poets here who came more by chance than anything else, though certainly something set them off once they had arrived. Yeats' "Visions" began when he was on a train that was on the outskirts of its Los Angeles destination. Bertolt Brecht's poems about flowers and trees remain among the most exquisite tributes to "nature" in Los Angeles. Randall Jarrell grew up here and wrote poems set in his childhood memories of a city surrounded by orchards. Although Thomas McGrath's epic poem, *Letter to an Imaginary Friend* begins with the lines:

From here ship all bodies east.

I am writing this from 99 Marsh Street, Los Angeles
he spends a great deal of the poem dwelling on his memories of growing up on a North Dakota farm.

In contrast the poets who have moved here in the past twenty-five years have made their lives in this city the major subject of their poetry. These poets include the late William Pillin and Bert Meyers, both of whom had significant collections of work published by Papa Bach Bookstore. Ann Stanford, Benjamin Saltman, Joseph Hansen (a co-founder of the Beyond Baroque poetry workshop), Alvaro Cardona-Hine and Deena Metzger are other long-time poets whose work would have to be included in any thorough historical anthology of the Los Angeles poetry.

"Poetry Loves Poetry" is not meant as a "history" of the Los Angeles poetry scene or a compilation of the best poems writ-

ten here during the past fifteen years. In fact, it concentrates on poets who have lived here sometime between 1980 and 1984 and almost all of the poems were written during that time. With a few exceptions I chose short poems written in the past five years to indicate each poet's individual sense of image and rhythm. This structure has prevented the inclusion of several significant poems and prose poem works: Harry Northup's "The Lord Is My Preposition," Holly Prado's "Word Rituals," and Lee Hickman's "Lee Sr. Falls to the Floor." *"Poetry Loves Poetry"* does not, of course, include any poems from *The Streets Inside: Ten Los Angeles Poets*, and there are many poems in that anthology which still rank among the best work by those poets.

This is the first anthology which has presented the work of Los Angeles poets in a national context. Many of us have labored in an obscurity that poets like W.C. Williams and Charles Olson knew all too well. In terms of poetry, Los Angeles, as big as it is, has all too often felt like Rutherford, New Jersey or Gloucester, Massachusetts. But isolation is often required to prevent a poet from producing work that is merely fashionable. I believe the poets in this book has deliberately chosen a more difficult path and that the work they have produced is substantial and will endure. I only ask serious readers of poetry to examine a large body of work by these poets and not to be content with glancing at a few of the poems in this anthology and thinking that you can now categorize poetic activity in Los Angeles. The following list of books has not won any Yale Series or Pulitzer prizes, yet I suspect that several of these books contain poems which will be reprinted in the next century's anthologies: James Krusoe's *Small Pianos*, Ron Koertge's *The Father Poems*, Peter Levitt's *Running Grass*, Leland Hickman's *Great Slave Lake Suite (TIRESIAS I:9:B)*, Kate Braverman's *Milk Run*, John Harris' *Against the Day of the Day*, Wanda Coleman's *Mad Dog Black Lady*, Marine Robert Warden's *Beyond the Straits*, Charles Bukowski's *War, Dick Barnes' A Lake on the Earth*, Dennis Cooper's *Idols*, Jack Grapes' *Breaking on Camera*, Eloise Klein Healy's *Building Some Changes*, Harry Northup's *Enough the Great Running Chapel*, John Thomas' *Epopeia and the Decay of Satire*, and Robert Peters' *A Gift to Be Simple*. Almost all of them are, unfortunately, out of print; but no serious commentary on the poets in Los Angeles could be written without a thorough reading of these books, in addition to three dozen other titles which have been published by Los Angeles presses. Los Angeles poets have been labeled "local" even at times by each other. It is a term which perhaps was appropriate fifteen years ago. I think this anthology proves that the poets in this city are among the most important poets in the United States.

Bill Mohr
Ocean Park, CA
Spring, 1985

Peter Schjeldahl

1. *To Pico*

You are one of the shadowless east-west routes
You start or end, or neither, in breezy Santa Monica
You are one off-ramp on the Santa Monica Freeway
(You cede all long-distance traffic to the Santa Monica
    Freeway)
You are the back door of Century City, ass-end of the Avenue
    of the Stars
You point at Beverly Hills, then bend unconcerned away
You skulk past Hillcrest Country Club fences and high foliage,
    offended and offending
You dawdle through the endless, blurry, unnamed reaches of
    central L.A.
You duck under the Harbor Freeway into so-called downtown,
    to which you lend your irrepressible shabbiness
You consist of asphalt, cement and largely cheapish
    small buildings
You have a dustily marginal air
You seem immunized against the showy
You favor the gross wholesaler and the odd small business
You look unphotographed
You are unthronged
You are a familiar address for stop-and-go business
You are unlike swift Olympic, purposeful Santa Monica,
    wishful Wilshire, nerve-racking Sunset
You are the back of the turned back of the city
You are broad and dry
You are blessedly unfoliaged
You jerk through the city, stoplight to stoplight, like a blunt
    knife through an unfeeling body
You are imperturbable and dumb, abstracted in the sun
You abstractly acknowledge the sun
You do not care
You are Los Angeles and not Los Angeles
You have unlimited, because unneeded, parking

You make every pedestrian look like a thief
You are a deserted mansion of air
You are honest and without illusions, with no spoiled illusions,
    because no one ever had any illusions concerning you
You are fiercely depressing
You are poetic — obviously
You are the typical address of a chiropractor
You laze in the afternoons like a long flat cat
You are, late afternoons, almost beautiful, light-soaked
You are destroyed by twilight
You are dead in the night of your feverish streetlight
You are ruins in the night, post-nuclear, site of mountainous
    gloom vapors, suicide alley
You are inhuman horizontal monstrous in the night
You feature, in the night, a few beery, low-wattage
    Mexican joints, a few gas stations, some lighted signs
You feature no haven
You inform the visitor that something is wrong here
You inform the restless, nervous, uprooted visitor
You inform him that where he has come to is a joke on him,
    and you're not kidding
You do not care
You look uncared-about
You look unintended, uncalculated, uncontemplated by anyone
    ever until this moment
You look to be the forlorn historical accident you are
You are like a side-street with elephantiasis
You are a great place for a murder
You are a great place for the murder of an obscure, transient
    person by another obscure, transient person
You are without remorse, remorseless
You are innocent with the innocence of a homicidal moron
You inform the visitor that sky, light, air, that nature is not
    worth caring about
You inform the visitor that humanity is not worth caring for
You are a self-fulfilling prophecy
You would taste chalky, if you had a taste
You would smell of dry rust, if you had a smell
You would be, if a sound, a faint, distant rattling
You'd be grainy to the touch, of a hardness gradually
    crumbling
You would be to the inner sense, and are, the paradox of a
    grandiose humility
You are the spirit of littleness lordly in the sun
You are a parade route for entropy
You lay across the city like a UFO runway

You complacently anticipate a horrible future
You are stronger than love, than intelligence, than energy
You are a spiritual Fault that has slipped, toppling the better,
    flimsier constructs of human aspiration
You are the secret of the city, the incision that reveals its heart
    of stone
You inscribe on the map a vast, mean smirk (upside down)
You attract me; I am yours; I return to you
You resonate to a well-known, old emptiness
You are intimate
You whisper
You hiss

2️⃣ *I Missed Punk*

I missed Punk
because my record player was broken
because I was suddenly older
because I can stand only so much distraction
only so much excitement and elation
but mainly because my record player was broken
and none of my friends cared much about new music

(Back in the '60s the thought that I'd missed something
would depress me terribly
Now it's just one of those things that happen)
Who are we anyway
any of us
who care about new music or anything?
We are the ones who care about their own skins, certainly
about saving them
and not being totally crazy and alone, in apin
We will go through a lot of incidental pain
as long as it keeps us in company
even ridiculous company, as most company is
We certainly don't want to be alone
and this makes us ridiculous

What I want to be is virtuous and noticed
What good is virtue if no one notices?
You don't know it's virtuous unless someone says so
I missed Punk
but it brushed past me in the cultural bazaar

and seemed to drop a hint about virtue
being what I'd always thought:
a readiness to lose, to let go
because only in loss is one not ridiculous
(if anyone notices)

Never resist an idea
Never say no to a contradiction
They have come to help you
smash the ego
which always reconstitutes
(and if it doesn't, well,
your worries are over)

3: ☐ *The Brute*

I am Samson who made
the temple fall down
killing everyone

I was the strong man
when many were strong
and it meant something

I could just go out
walk up to someone
and kill him

always the right person
I was just
and it was easy

swinging my arms
in the sunlight yelling
and hitting

bodies and bodies
a big mess
under the sun

I am Samson
Let someone else
clean it up

James Krusoe

 Two Outer Space Poems

1 Twentieth Century Modern

Bud and Donna are asked aboard the Deathstar
After a snack they're taken to their rooms
which are decorated in "Twentieth Century Modern"

Bud stares at the clown prints on the walls
Donna's got her toes inside the deep-pile rug
"Hey isn't this great?" Bud says

Donna agrees she hasn't been so relaxed in years
Outside there's too much going on to notice
all those so-called people being blown to bits by monsters

2 Planet Dracula

Well here we are on Planet Dracula
named for one of the greatest vampires of all time
We have no sun or moon
but other than that it's the same as on earth
right down to the poisonous plants and snakes
of which we've got a lot

If we don't like you here's what we do —
we take a little bite of something from your neck
and plant it in the ground
and then in no time there's another person just like you
who talks like you
and has a job like yours
and even acts the way you act when you're nervous
and your punishment is
you've got to watch it live

5: *Ohio*

I suppose there's nowhere in the world no matter how awful
that doesn't produce an old guy sitting in a bar somewhere
boring the crap out of everyone with his descriptions

of how great things used to be before a bunch of people
came to screw things up — and that's exactly how I feel
about Ohio — which back around the Carboniferous era

must have been real pretty — all those big leaves moving slowly
in the wind like patients in a mental ward right after
the day nurse has brought their morning dose of Stelazine

6: *For Dr. Katz*

Walking up the river today I spent my time watching
the water as it shot over the same rocks it's been

passing by each year and around the same bright green
patches of cress along the banks and over dark forms

of logs but what I thought about instead was how you
died surrounded by three of the most beautiful women

I've ever seen who hovered near your bed like cut flowers
drifting in a crystal bowl of water — gardenias or

chrysanthemums or even ordinary roses — as all the while
you grew thinner and explained to me by drawing little

diagrams on paper napkins or on your bandages exactly
how it was your kind of cancer worked — but it was only

after everything was over and I was walking back along
the canyon that I noticed what I'd missed on my way

there — that ahead and all around me were these blue
and tiny flowers which were growing out of rocks like

perfect nodes that might be found on any spleen or say
a liver and all because last night I met a friend you

never knew who told a long and funny story about a man who
had a name like Zotz or Zatz that happened to be yours

7 ☐ *Sex & Death*

for Peter Schjeldahl

First it's blowing and then raining and finally
the sun comes out so I think I'll take a little
walk but what is really on my mind is sex

and death — first one and then the other so that
at one minute I'll be feeling good then Oh-Oh!
bad again then Whoops! it's straightened

out again — when suddenly above and to my right
I see a woman wild and really beautiful who's
pacing on the roof of her garage beneath which

is a sign "For Sale" that's pointing to a stack
of records and damp paperbacks among which
is a book I'd never read but heard about and

when I take it home it opens to that photograph
of you snapped fifteen years ago — the one
that makes you look like Edgar Allen Poe — at once

completely spooked but also tough and cool as ice —
the way I used to get back when I worked in
hospitals and some old guy would start to have

a massive heart attack and while the pretty
nurse was up there banging on his chest I'd
be watching — moving all the extra chairs away

8 ☐ *A Spy*

A man is asked to be a spy among the bears
so he buys a suit and learns to walk on hands and knees
He practices in the mirror until his eyes become small
He slurs his words and learns to live on grubs
Naturally they love him

In time he takes a wife and has a couple bear-like kids

When finally he's called home again he starts his report
"We have much to learn from the bears"
but by then his words all sound like growls —
even to him — who wanted so much to explain

9: *After the Revolution*

They had just finished shooting
those members of the government
who had required it:
the President and Vice
most of Congress and the courts
and now had come to what was needed next
"What is a poem?" asked Chuck
the leader of the guerrillas
"That's a good question" someone else replied

10: *Jungle Girl*

She lives in the jungle with the other animals
At night she hears them calling back and forth
ripping each other apart and leaving the pieces

She's done it herself and it's no big deal
It's just that she gets tired
She falls asleep and hates to get up but does anyway
and every so often kills a deer or crocodile
'cause she's a jungle girl
and if a little blood makes her cry
she'll swallow back the tears like maybe it's
not her that's doing this
but someone else who's kind and better

11: *Youth*

for Dennis Cooper

1
The first time I made out
my clothes still on and hers too

all I could think of was the words
to "Be True to Your School" by the Beachboys—
me—
who'd spent a lifetime hating my school

2
Her name was Beverly
In supermarkets
she'd go straight to the rows of bottled orange juice
uncap a dozen
drink them down past the necks
then leave

3
I was young then
I'd lie awake and stare at the ceiling
unable to imagine
what love would bring me next

12: *Duck Love*

They see each other every minute of the day
and still they can't get enough

In the water and on land they make love constantly
When one of them is hungry

the other's there with a piece of duckweed or a fish
"You look great" one's always shouting to the other

"No—you look great!" the other one says back
They can't imagine a world where they're not together

"And we're just ducks" they say
"Think of what it must be like for humans"

13: *Legs*

for Nancy

The way a bird dog
will carry back a bird—
hold it in its mouth

keeping it alive
barely touching it
while far away

its master's waiting
shifting his feet
his breath steaming in the air—

sometimes at night
you'll catch my legs in yours
and hold them there that way

14: *Two Poems with my Father in Them*

1   *Stuart*

I'm painting a house with my father

It's an expensive place
with everything kept neat
but at one end
beneath a window
there are paint spots on the sidewalk

The last time we worked here
I was twenty-six years old
I'd just been married
Stuart was with us
He painted that window
He used to wear white bib overalls
and wing-tip shoes
I never saw him once without a hat

He's dead now:
those are his spots

My father tells a story he thought up
It's about a man
who reaches seventy and turns around again

As he grows young he passes by his son
and in the end the son gets old instead

I tell him it would make a terrific movie
because that's the way I talk to him

He says wouldn't it —

but from the hungry way he looked at me
when he got to the part about passing his son
he doesn't mean *passing*

and he'd do it

15:   *For Cavafy after Cavafy*

His last act was fittingly on paper
He drew a circle
and in the middle made a dot
and then he died —
this man
who more than most
would not be fooled
by words

But this last circle
followed by a dot?

Did he mean
his life had been enclosed that way?
Or surrounded by whiteness
put himself at the center?

16: *Life on Earth*

Seen from outer space the whole
earth looks like a pea next to
the basketball which is our sun
but despite our tiny size we
still manage to commit most
major crimes including arson
burglary and Burking — a method
of demise wherein the victim's
nose and mouth are pinched —
invented by an Englishman named
Burke of course reminding us
(the country not the man) of
other climes like Togoland —
a place whose only income is
derived from selling stamps to
wealthy twelve-year-olds who
buy them for their pictures of
large beasts that kill — a thing
they'd like to do most of the time —
and also plants and other animals
a few of which attach themselves
to us and in return we feed them
cans of goop and kibbled chow
the urban poor have learned to also
use as tasty supplements for diets
high in starch and fats which hang
along the arteries like happy bats
which as they sleep have secret
dreams of radar waves that bounce
off things to eat which when they
get them in their mouths then
crunch and whir and scream —

We move on wheels and there are
roads we've built to move us on
because a wheel won't work unless
it's got a place to spin — so
properly it's really only half
a tool because the road's the other
half — these and other thoughts
we have when "stoned" — a word which
means to take a pile of drugs
until our minds at last slow down —
a process that seems more and more

to make a lot of sense as we begin
to find them out — like sex —
at first a novelty which soon
becomes a good excuse to hear such
sentences as "My you do that very
well" and "Of course I care for you
far more than _____ or _____ " —
we also celebrate our birthdays
and send cards at other times like
Christmas when we're sure to cover up
the backs of envelopes with special
stamps to indicate we disapprove
of lung disease or birth defects
which although they're sent without
our asking still we're not supposed
to use unless they're somehow
paid for — Yes — mystery abounds
on earth and also tragedy and
parody and blasphemy — or as
a young girl I overheard while
walking on the beach once said —
"It's got incest — it's got it all!"

17: *A Fanfare*

for Nancy

Today the ocean is roaring and the wind is blowing
and in the blue sky there are a few clouds going around

reminding me of how pointless everything is
and most of all our lives filled up with suffering

that seems "too great to bear" etcetera etcetera
but meanwhile as all of this continues to go on

it's your straight-forward decency I steer by — that
and the fact that when you see something beautiful

you don't get angry like I do — and what's so difficult
to mention is I'm grateful that've you've consented being

here for what in the face of eternity must be a surprisingly
few moments but for me all the most important ones

Ron Koertge

18: *The Magic Words*

are not Abracadabra or anything slippery and remote.
The real magic words are these: I love myself
more than I love you.

Anyone's life can be transformed if he actually loves
his ass more than all the others, believes that those
blue veins in his legs are lovely as major waterways
and will own those thoughts that are always there
in the dark behind the eyes.

At one time or another we all exclaim, "Oh, how
wonderful. I'll say them first thing tomorrow."
But few really mean it because it is more fun
to be coached.

Can you remember? Or do you want me to whisper
in your beautiful ear.

19: *Sex Object*

She comes home steaming.
She gets into my pants.
She rides me hard.

I look past her slot
machine eyes
to the ceiling

where the 1969 earthquake
made cracks in the shape
of Florida

and Louisiana, the latter
having for its capital
Baton Rouge

which is located on
the Mississippi River,
principal waterway
of the United States,

measuring 2470 miles
from its source in
Northern Minnesota
to the Gulf of Mexico.

20: *Dope*

Sports Illustrated breaks The Fixer story and people
start calculating my folly, telling me how they
knew all along. I listen a little but mostly I look:
They're all lit up. This has made their day.

"Well," I say, "when somebody's cheating it usually
shows. That's why I check the probable exacta payoffs.
Funny stuff sticks out. So either you lay off or get
out some more 5's and bet the hot cripples."
"What are you talking about?" they say. "It doesn't
work like that. It's all here how they cheated you.
Look!" They're on the muscle. Their eyes are rolling.
They're sweating. It looks like somebody slipped
them something when they weren't looking.

21: *A Jockey*

named Kovacs went down
at Pomona yesterday.
He was riding something
that was born to hold
one piece of paper
to another.

The crowd loves to hate
accidents and everybody
wants to know who Ted
Kovacs was. Like the
next winner, it was
a mystery.

This, then, is to set
the record straight:
Ted Kovacs makes 14
thousand a year when
things go right.

His wife keeps a
scrapbook that shows
the day he tripled,
the $9,000 Exacta
where he was second,
and all the time he
was in intensive care.
When he almost didn't make it
the article ran to nearly
20 lines.

22: *An Ontological Report*

They were on the ropes
that separate the free seats from the boxes.

He was 60 or so with a stoplight face
and a gut like a stove.
She was junk
jewelry, her stockings
doughnuts at each ankle.

She'd bought the wrong ticket.

7-11 won the exacta and she'd bought 11-7.
He showed her the losing stub, hit her
with the program. He swore, hit her
again, showed her the ticket, hit her.

Another race went off and he was still at it.

The exacta he had not won paid $50.00 even.
I had $52.00, so I gave him the Ulysses S. Grant
and said that now he had his money, now he could
quit hitting her.

So. 2 dollars and 3 races to go. It's been done:
1 bet gets you 20, which gets you 60 which blossoms
into 2 or 3 hundred.

My horse in the next race was fourth
out of the gate, fourth as they turned for home,
fourth at the wire.

If anybody deserved it,
I did.

23: *End of Reel 1*

Because Superman is worried about his
health, he flies to a medical center. He is
so embarrassed that the gadgets in the examination
room melt.

An internist attends to the man of steel, putting
him at ease with chitchat about Perry and Jimmy,
even telling him not to worry about being faster
than a speeding bullet with Lois.

Before he knows it, the physical is over and
the news is good: doing everything in a super
way is taxing, but nothing a simple suppository
can't fix.

Left alone with a wink and a handshake, the guardian
of Gotham rips away the heavy foil. Then, lightheaded
from relief, sits down thinking what a swell guy
that doctor was but how odd he should know about
that problem with Miss Lane.

Odd indeed. That swell guy was really Superman's
arch enemy. That suppository, kryptonite.

24: *Happy Ending*

King Kong does not die. He gets hip to the biplanes,
lets them dive by and ionizes them. Halfway down
the Empire State he leaps to another skyscraper,
then another and another, working his way North
and West until people thin out and he can disappear.

Fay's boyfriend is sure she is dead OR WORSE
but just as he is about to call up the entire U.S.
Army, a scandal mag breaks the story. The couple
has been in seclusion at a resort somewhere near
Phoenix. Long lens telephoto shots show them sunning
by a pool. There are close-ups of Fay straddling
the monster's tongue and standing in his ear
whispering something Kong likes. Look, his grin is as big as
a hundred Steinways.

25: *Come*

for Bianca

The moon through my bedroom window
used to reflect off sheets white
as a parson's thighs and spectacularly
dry, drier than Arizona, too dry
for saguaro, too dry for rocks which
fled or died. Maybe the sunsets were
memorable but Lawrence of Arabia surveying
the place said, "Too dangerous, my faithful.
We'll take the long way to Akbar."

But we are like tides leaving behind
the glistening shores. My sheets are
sweet and damp and cool. And Lawrence
alone in his narrow tent thinks
of the languid warriors, the women
among the towering palms, the way they
sleep braided together and how dreamily
they look at him saying, "Lawrence, no.
We never want to leave here."

26. *Horses & Cows*

Who couldn't pick out the intruder
in the Derby, udder sloshing, a thousand
lengths off the pace, the jockey
so embarrassed he is wearing a mask.

Would any lover claim wild cows
couldn't drag him away? Could Detroit sell
anything with even a million cowpower?
What ruler could touch our hearts by crying,
"My kingdom for a cow"?

Given the choice by a playful god
to return as one or the other, we think
of Trigger and Flicka, not Elsie or Bossy.

Yet horses do not give tasty milk
by the bucket or divide up into roasts
with palsy names like Chuck.

Cows do not foam at the mouth from nerves,
then fall over backwards on their riders.
Instead they stand around endlessly
chewing their food like good children.

Then one considers the grief that beauty
can bring, the illusionary bit of freedom
and that cinch, a narrow stall, a scarred
Dutch door, spurs, fat people.

Perhaps there is something to be said,
after all, for a life of less flamboyance,
for the solace of the herd and the regular
eroticism of hired hands.

27: *All Suffering Comes from Attachment*

— the Buddha

A penis is the ultimate attachment: body's gimmick,
spigot, mitre, millstone around the waist. If it
is big, who can be sure he is loved for himself
or that Washington Monument down there.
If it is small, why was he burdened with so little?
If it is average, is it average enough?

Like any deity it has a hundred names, some like
a flower (genitalia), aquatic fowl (the schwanse),
part of a tool kit (whonker). Temperamental
and fiery, the penis is tenor of the body's opera.
Inquisitive and scary, it rises from apparent
sleep, a little Lazarus. Spoiled child, it gets
its own way. Or pouts.

As king of matter, it is for some of us the last
profound attachment, the thing that men cling to
sometimes — oh awful blessing — with both hands.

In the winnowing of parts, the silly feet
walk off alone, muscles of the arms and chest being
ornaments of desire are put away, pretty hair
is exorcised by age or shears. Finally we come
to the penis, last wand in the body's magic city.

And if someone can say goodbye to that, to dreams
of himself as father, lover, stallion, warlord,
guy, then the suffering is over at last
and nameless bliss begins.

28: *Men & Women*

When I was five my mother and father,
Uncle Chris, Aunt Evelyn and I drove
to the home place near Olney. I stood
in the front seat between the shoulder
pads watching for fires and wild animals.

At Grandmother's house I played outside.
I liked to hear the Savage .22 and see
the fields of blood. I like to pee
with the men behind the haunted barn.
Their zippers were long as train tracks
and I wanted my little thing to be big
and wrinkled and sleepy-looking like theirs.

Later riding through the dark I sat between
my mother and her sister so close that
when they talked the feathers on their
hats touched. *Well, not now   she said*
he knows   he said it   does it   hurts some
time have you   you do   he does   he wants

I dozed there in a mist of secrets, slipping
from one fragrant lap to another, hearing
underneath the silver fox, the gabardine,
the hearsay of the real silk.

At home, Daddy carried me inside and everyone
came to watch me sleep. There they stood,
there I lay, surrounded by men and women.

Charles Bukowski

29: *the souls of dead animals*

after the slaughterhouse
there was a bar around the corner
and I sat in there
and watched the sun go down
through the window,
a window that overlooked a lot
full of tall dry weeds.

I never showered with the boys at the
plant
after work
so I smelled of sweat and
blood.
the smell of sweat lessens after a
while
but the blood-smell begins to fulminate
and gain power.

I smoked cigarettes and drank beer
until I felt good enough to
board the bus
with the souls of all those dead
animals riding with
me;
heads would turn slightly
women would rise and move away from
me.

when I got off the bus
I only had a block to walk
and one stairway up to my
room
where I'd turn on my radio and

light a cigarette
and nobody minded me
at all.

30: *tonalities*

the soldiers march without guns
the graves are empty
peacocks glide in the rain

down stairways march great men smiling

there is food enough and rent enough and
time enough

our women will not grow old

I will not grow old

bums wear diamonds on their fingers

Hitler shakes hands with a Jew

the sky smells of roasted flesh

I am a burning curtain

I am steaming water

I am a snake I am an edge of glass that cuts
I am blood

I am this fiery snail
crawling home.

31: *yes yes*

when God created love He didn't help most
when God created dogs He didn't help dogs
when God created plants that was average
when God created hate we had a standard utility

when God created me He created me
when God created the monkey He was asleep
when He created the giraffe He was drunk
when He created narcotics He was high
and when He created suicide He was low

when He create you lying in bed
He knew what He was doing
He was drunk and He was high
and He created the mountains and the sea and fire
at the same time

He made some mistakes
but when He created you lying in bed
He came all over His Blessed Universe

32: *On the Fire Suicides of the Buddhists*

> *"They only burn themselves to reach
> Paradise."*
>
> —*Mme Nhu*

original courage is good,
motivation be damned
and if you say they are trained
to feel no pain,
are they
guaranteed this?
is it still not *possible*
to die for somebody else?

you sophisticates
who lay back and
make statements of explanation
I have seen the red rose burning
and this means more.

33: *Measurements from the Creation Coffin*

the ability to suffer and endure—
that's nobility, friend—
the ability to suffer and endure

for an idea, a feeling, a way—
that's art, my friend—
the ability to suffer and endure
when a love ends—
that's hell, old friend...
nobility, art and hell,
let's talk about art a while:

promulgation of my attitudes
like stilts walking centuries
beeswax for brains
destiny is my crippled daughter
look here, it's difficult
me against them
with them
Kafka let me in
Hemingway beware
Hegel you're funny
Cervantes you mean you wrote that
novel at the age of
80?

writers are indecent people
they live unfairly
saving the main part for paper

jesus christ would have been
a duller writer than Theodore Dreiser
jesus christ would have been a
very lousy writer

the beard and hair fit
but he was too good at
conversations and
miracles

a good human being may save the world
so the bastards can keep creating art
if you read this after I am long dead
it means I made it
and
it's your turn now
to misuse your wife
abuse your children
love thyself
live off the funds of others

dislike all art created before and
during your time,
and dislike or even hate humanity
singly or en mass.

bastard, if you read this after I am long dead
shove me out of here. I
probably wasn't that
good.

34: *Style*

style is the answer to everything —
a fresh way to approach a dull or a
dangerous thing.
to do a dull thing with style
is perferable to doing a dangerous thing
without it.

Joan of Arc had style
John the Baptist
Christ
Socrates
Caesar,
Garcia Lorca.

style is the difference,
a way of doing,
a way of being done.

6 heron standing quietly in a pool of water
or you walking out of the bathroom naked
without seeing
me.

35: *I Liked Him*

I liked D. H. Lawrence
he could get so indignant
he snapped and he ripped
with wonderfully energetic sentences

he could lay the word down
bright and writhing
there was the stink of blood and murder
and sacrifice about him
the only tenderness he allowed
was when he bedded down his large German
wife.
I liked D.H. Lawrence—
he could talk about Christ
like he was the man next door
and he could describe Australian taxi drivers
so well you hated them
I like D.H. Lawrence
but I'm glad I never met him
in some bistro
him lifting his tiny hot cup of
tea
and looking at me
with his worm-hole eyes.

36:   *They, All of Them, Know*

ask the sidewalk painters of Paris
ask the sunlight on a sleeping dog
ask the 3 pigs
ask the paperboy
ask the music of Donizettti
ask the barber
ask the murderer
ask the man leaning against a wall
ask the preacher
ask the maker of cabinets
ask the pickpocket or the
        pawnbroker or the glass blower
        or the seller of manure or
        the dentist
ask the revolutionist
ask the man who sticks his head in
        the mouth of a lion
ask the man who will release the next
        atom bomb
ask the man who thinks he's Christ
ask the bluebird who comes home
        at night

ask the peeping Tom
ask the man dying of cancer
ask the man who needs a bath
ask the man with one leg
ask the blind
ask the man with the lisp
ask the opium eater
ask the trembling surgeon
ask the leaves you walk upon
ask a rapist or a
       streetcar conductor or an old man
       pulling weeds in his garden
ask a bloodsucker
ask a trainer of fleas
ask a man who eats fire
ask the most miserable man you can
       find in his most
       miserable moment
ask a teacher of judo
ask a rider of elephants
ask a leper, a lifer, a lunger
ask a professor of history
ask the man who never cleans his fingernails
ask a clown or ask the first face you see
       in the light of day
ask your father
ask your son and
       his son to be
ask me
ask a burned-out bulb in a paper sack
ask the tempted, the damned, the foolish
       the wise, the slavering
ask the builders of temples
ask the men who have never worn shoes
ask Jesus
ask the moon
ask the shadows in the closet
ask the moth, the monk, the madman
ask the man who draws cartoons for
       The New Yorker
ask a goldfish
ask a fern shaking to a tapdance
ask the map of India
ask a kind face
ask the man hiding under your bed

ask the man you hate the most in this
    world
ask the man who drank with Dylan Thomas
ask the man who laced Jack Sharkey's gloves
ask the sad-faced man drinking coffee
ask the plumber
ask the man who dreams of ostriches every
    night
ask the ticket-taker at a freak show
ask the counterfeiter
ask the man sleeping in an alley under
    a sheet of paper
ask the conquerors of nations and planets
ask the man who just cut off his finger
ask a bookmark in the bible
ask the water dripping from a faucet while
    the phone rings
ask perjury
ask the deep blue paint
ask the parachute jumper
ask the man with the bellyache
ask the divine eye so sleek and swimming
ask the boy wearing tight pants in
    the expensive academy
ask the man who slipped in the bathtub
ask the man chewed by the shark
ask the one who sold me the unmatched
    gloves
ask these and all those I have left out
ask the fire the fire the fire —
ask even the liars
ask anybody you please at anytime
    you please on any day you please
    whether it's raining or whether
    the snow is there or whether
    you are stepping out onto a porch
    yellow with warm heat
ask this ask that
ask the man with birdshit in his hair
ask the torturer of animals
ask the man who has seen many bullfights
    in Spain
ask the owners of new Cadillacs
ask the famous
ask the timid
ask the albino

and the statesman
ask the landlords andgthe poolplayers
ask the phonies
ask the hired killers
ask the bald men and the fat men
    and the tall men and the
    short men
ask the one-eyed men, the
    oversexed and undersexed men
ask the men who read all the newspaper
    editorials
ask the men who breed roses
ask the men who feel almost no pian
ask the dying
ask the mowers of lawns and the attenders
    of football games
ask any of these or all of these
ask ask ask and
    they'll all tell you:

a snarling wife on the balustrade is more
than a man can bear.

Gerald Locklin

37: *Low Tide Floodtime: Winter 1969*

I go to watch the sunset from the seawall.
go alone and others come alone.
we stand up high there, hands in pockets.
the wind comes headfirst, hands in pockets.

I had forgotten california could be beautiful.
I'm glad you're not here with me love; stay
home and sulk. I'm glad my kids aren't here.
I'm glad no young girl strikes up a conversation.

is this what we came to california for?
chromatics of a catalina sunburst?
bomb-burst? eye-burst? oil lights upon
the bruised waters? a sound that laves?

this, and the midriffs of young girls, and to be
where it was happening. it happened
tonight it is too cold for mermaids and
matrons. the sea is post-coital, blue.

the city lies a-light and preternatural.
from here, neither sailors nor storm-troopers.
only the lights of pensioners' chateaux,
the cyclone racer, battleships at rest.

the texture of wet sand is like the gooseflesh
of the surfers, hauling their boards along the long
beach. the red horse of the horizon ramps
to the burst of the black crust.

we are silhouettes upon the silhouetted
sandwall. the waves are
shadows on the wind, the eucaplytus on
the island, rock upon the sun,

the day within the darkness. we stand
with hands in pockets; one-by-one we go
away. we did not come here to commune.
we came I think, for a last look.

38: *Pedagogy*

in the sixth grade they gave us a belgian nun.
she was just learning the language, and she often
had to ask the english word for something.
little things, like doorknobs, blackboard, chalk.

we were a rotten and sadistic bunch.
we gloried in sabotage.
our previous teacher was now in r-wing of the
      local hospital,
which is where you went when you couldn't
      stop screaming.

one day sister bonita asked us what you call
an electric outlet — you know, the thing on the wall
that you plug the plug into.
we told her it was called a cunt.

she left the room to find the janitor, to explain
what it was of hers that needed fixing, what it was
exactly that she couldn't fit the plug into.
she returned to the class a tearful but wiser woman.

which reminds me of a piece of profound advice
imparted to me by a young professor upon
      the occasion
of my going forth from graduate school:
"remember, locklin," he said, his hand
      upon my tweedy shoulder,
"in teaching you are always dealing
      with the criminal mentality."

39: *Growing Up Alive*

dave cherin so fell in love with the movie,
the great santini, that he instituted
bedchecks and reveille
and took to addressing his kids
as "little pukes" and "shitbirds."

i blundered into their living room
an hour before seder
and the kids were running about
calling their parents and each other
shitbirds and little pukes.

one morning dave came down to breakfast
to find the three kids seated before bowls
of sugared nails
because the great santini's kids
"ate nails and shit bricks."

it's a helluva way to bring up kids,
but when i arrived at the surprise birthday party for dave,
the cake was decorated with tanks and howitzers
and read, "to the great cherini:
happy birthday

the shitbirds love you."

40: *Patriotic Poem*

alexander haig says there are things
americans must be willing to die for.

he is not talking to me;
he is talking to my children.

my children, let me only call to your attention
that no one asking you to sacrifice your lives
has sacrificed his.

41: *D-Day, 1980*

coming out of the movie, "yanks,"
my little boy asks me,
did we do something good
in the second world war?"

he's ten years old
and all he's ever heard of our military history
is napalm and radiation, washita
and the little big horn, cuba and
chile, and that george washington

had wooden teeth.
i suspect that it's not good for a little boy
to grow up hearing that his country's always wrong,
even if it usually has been.

this time i'm able to tell him,
"yes, the normandy invasion
was one of the greatest military operations
in history, and not only did we bring it off,
but it's good for the world that we did."

i grew up on "the sands of iwo jima;"
my son is growing up on "coming home."
what adjustments he is having to make!
what adjustments i've made!

42: *The Death of Jean-Paul Sartre*

of all people, he must have been
the least surprised by death.
i wasn't surprised by his death either,
not that i knew anything about his health,
but because i must, as part of my job,
have about fiteen minutes communicable knowledge
of current intellectual trends,
and so i am aware that existentialism
is a word only uttered today

by norman mailer, me and a few retarded philosophy majors,
and i doubt either mr. mailer or the philosophy majors
are complimented by my inclusion of myself.

in college and graduate school, you see,
i basically got by with one term paper.
it was entitled: "the existentialism of..."
you fill in the blank.
"the existentialism of sartre or camus or tennyson or
byron or kit smart or milton (yes, milton) or
chaucer (his retraction posed a problem), or beowulf
or caedmon or the venerable fucking bede."

i wasn't trying to put anybody on —
i'd read every word of sartre and his
commentators and his imitators,
and a lot of my professors hadn't,
and i sincerely believed that all great writers
must have been existentialists because,
like all true believers or true non-believers,
i was convinced that for a writer
not to have been an existentialist
would have disqualified him as great.
all of this no doubt was in reaction
to the catholic schools i had attended
where it was taught that all great writers
were, at the very least, latent or closet catholics.

my standard term paper
received about five hundred a-plusses,
while much more knowledgable and ingenious students
received Incompletes for their herculean-himalayan
and perpetually unfinished papers on "iconography
in arnold as reflected in victorian furniture.'

not only did i preach existentialism,
but i began to live
what i knew to be a distorted, popularized
edition of it.
i'm sure my series of marriages
(perhaps mailer's as well)
owe at least a little to sartre,
although they are neither that simply
explained nor regretted.
and some of my existentialism was,
and i hope still is,

the genuine article.
i lecture once a semester to every class
on sartre's "existentialism is a humanism."
i'd give you the lecture right now,
but, what with declining enrollments,
i'd better hope you'll sign up and pay your tuition.

so sartre is dead now,
along with his vocabulary-world,
and the moral certainties of religion
are alive again and inhabiting the uncrowded humanities building
(along with structure, necessity, and remedial comp.).
there is also talk, of course, of faculty salaries,
student evaluations, and the inevitability of layoffs.
i am among the loudest of the talkers,
because if i were ever laid-off
i wouldn't be able to afford
to mope around the *deux magots* —
i doubt i could even afford the polly maggoo anymore —
and moping is becoming a lost art anyhow.

jean-paul, they have cremated your feet,
at which i only metaphorically sat.
strangely enough, however,
my current metaphysical problem remains
whether i am capable of the freedom, the alienation,
responsibility, and angst

of the either/or

of a marriage/dissolution.

Harry Northup

 43: *a very simple line*

now its seventh in the vein thirty we have been going
daily
to parks in the city to day we went to one just south
of silver lake
i played football catch with a black
"looks like he's proud of his body
"the way he walks
dylan played touch football with 5 mexican boys touch
two hands on the waist
six days ago i turned thirty seven
a low point in my life economically speaking so what rudeness
the altar is not your face man
not yours woman even though i fall before your feet & look up
we speak finally she says quietly "planets & stars"
before you i thought i could not feel again
every night in
afternoons we go to movies
movies in the afternoon
a nice breeze also we went to wattles park & the japanese tea
house was closed for repairs
we sat on a stone bench near a pond
a young girl with a relatively short dress came back she had
left once with a small black dog &
sat on a bridge below the mountain reading
she had white legs pretty legs
above her i saw four people walking down toward the city one
woman was wearing a red dress
the first park was bronson park a park where i reached out &
touched you the third person has become the second person i
meant i touched you &
that was on a friday & the next night you started crying when i
said sometimes i get scared
the next night i cried in front of you

you are the first girl i ever cried before
i surrender
we made love many times after that & the what & the where & how
i parked my poems in front of your house
it's friday night in los angeles
this poem is a reaching out to love
we give space & we take space

survival dream 1

44: *the images we possess kill the capturing*

i know that sounds like an image trying to deny its own
mother
she worked behind bars in a post office
this morning after we took dylan to school we drove up
the coast to sunset
as short as the journey was it was peaceful &
warm
we sat in the car & watched seven surfers all of them
wearing wet suits
the second hot day in a row
catalina could be seen from the coast highway
only later did we notice the smog
above the oil tanker in the southern end of the bay

as often as not we talk about poetry & symbols & myths &
how far is mt baldy?
we see its caps
snowy
a squirrel was looking straight ahead
looking over the top of the cliff overlooking sunset
a high amount of rocks & earth then
pushed up
rocks below where many surfers have broken their teeth
at least one
in the front
i honked & in no time it was gone
turned & went back
down to safety
without taking
time to think

even in our own house sometimes we talk low
sitting in front of the tv
sometimes we sit looking at the tv with the tv off & talk
to each other
poetry is speaking & listening
to one another
the mother i know the one i had was patient & loving & hard
working & kind & firm
i thought about my mother today when the ocean was its bluest
she had blue eyes
where does the ocean gets its color
from the wind it blows past
in the morning when it is cool
we talk to understand
what it is that is sometimes blue & sometimes gray
& we drove to see how bad the damage had been
you have heard this before & you will hear it again
i love my mother   ocean ocean

3 1978

 poem to women

there is no greater energy than writing poem
there is no greater energy than making love
than fucking than waking than holding than releasing
there is no greater thing than woman
there is no nor no nothing no anything as great as anything
nothing is greater than man
than woman with man than man with child than woman who
gives affection to woman
there is no greater earth
there is no greater love poem to islam
than this love for women for boys for ocean for sky for nothing
ever has anything less than giving away nothing less than love
for woman

4 19 1980

46: *language*

language west
open love
bewilder please
depend upon
many with flowers

hungry flaws
waves &waves
flinched when
he began preaching
four white people
in a black church
dancing blood
singing loud &
lively the way
the young should

it took a long while
to sit still
after looking upward
hope was spoken about
spirit also
we sheltered each
memory providing
sanctuary from
flesh worries

language turned
to its neighbor
shook hands
each said to each
i love you

the first time
i said i love you
to a man
at the same time
a man said i love you
to me waking away
a cold deliberate
religious heart
quietly we spoke

never before a church
like that
prayers full of singing
an inner reaching up
to receive a lighter
spirit than exists
in ration
neighbor near &within
quiet speaking love

6 3 1980

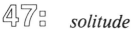 *solitude*

what willful-
act precedes
happiness in
finding new
beauty
with our legs,
our thighs, our
bodies pulling
towards each
other with another
who loves you
as much &more
she having a more
intimate longevity
i do not want to
interrupt, i
half listen, half
watch & listen to
men & women stand-
ing near
getting to know you
more, we dress for
each other
looking forward
to meeting, still
a little bit shy
some are meant
to be near
how much i wanted

to say i like the fur
around the upper half
of your body
how much i wanted
to say
you are beautiful to-
night
how you said something
about how it is no good
to hate the opposite
when many were discussing
darkness
we got closer tonight.

12 15 80

48: *the actor*

the tragedy is
is that it is chosen
the life of an actor
&there is a lot
of competition
sometimes i look at los angeles
like it is a whole community
of actors
of course that is
a very subjective thought
being an actor thinking that
one is helped by his family
one is on unemployment
a job here & a residual there
waiting spending time waiting
driving back from the beach
this morning i looked up
at the blakean clouds
wanted to lose myself
in something greater
& above the human activities
the actor involves himself in
in between jobs
all clear the answering service says
& i say thank you

setting up courtesy for all clear
a habit that there is nothing thank you
making grocery lists
going to the bank every other day
eating breakfast with other actors
things still difficult for you
the tragedy is
is that i chose this sunlight
into a room with light
waiting for a residual
it gets to be like a dream more &more
a dream slipping away
more like dream than reality
bank coffee shop grocery store school
hospital
home supper food love homework woman
a habit that is built up
an actor chooses to be an actor
the clouds & then the waking
to get by thought into a conscious
losing oneself in acting
to hold you & fall back into
& i say thank you to all clear

3 2 81

 a piece about contemporary criticism

the many points on a diamond
each one speaks from a point on a revolutionary-marxist
printing press in the hand of workers
a lack of comprehensiveness
"poetry loves poetry", hirshman said
the hungry energetic critics desire a forceful power
to be light giving
a book must be light in ones hands
pound again & pound again
olson is not my father; he is an innovation though sometimes broadly flat though widely expansive
i take the beauty of h.d.'s sea flowers any day of the week
it is also compression
a poet said to me as i picked up nietzsche as i enterd his
living room his work room "writing is power"

it is also economy & balance & poetry rests upon language
my father is the old testament & the new, homer, hesiod
a blacksmith in vermont, a post man who delivered the mail
on horseback in nebraska, a derelict grandfather on my
father's side; sometimes i look at holly and see my father;
my father was constantly reading
my father worked hard all his life
he had his own store, a general store in denver, & then
the depression came & relatives came & lived with him &
mother & georgie & bobbie & dorothy
& he lost his store
his will broken, he took long walks
he began working for the civil service
he was a quiet man & he wanted peace around the dinner table
the earth that went into the mother is part of the fallen
father
the rocky mountains is a father & fires is a father
school is father, baseball is a father
dry sermons is father
jet planes & my father did not give me much physical affection
he got us out of bed early & we went for long drives across
states
the sun in our eyes driving

5 12 81

Wanda Coleman

50: *Eyes Bleed Pictures/*
Tales of a Black Adventurer

my eyes bleed pictures/us
in bed against night cold
i snuggle warm in illusion
he paints visions of black men who are men
they take form and dance
                    and dance
                    and dance

jazz notes of 102.3 & billy holiday as he caresses a memory
how he fucked her once or twice when she was on the skids
he was almost a kid & she was far too gone
on heroin for him to use

                        there are things between us
                        generations

baby, i wish we had met
when you were eighteen

and what would he have done then?
given me an education
prepared me for survival on the street

                        "i need money, darlin' and i don't
                        care how you gets it"

my eyes bleed pictures
tales of men who hate beyond hatred
who think women are to be ground up like mulch
flesh to feed egos
from which the green of prosperity & nations flow

                        men

marching grey in prison uniforms across the yard of my groin

baby i wish we had
met when you were eighteen

        i, a well-traveled road
        he looks for walls and scrawls graffiti
        makes his mark like no other
        asphalt/my womb buckles

baby i wish

my eyes bleed pictures
stars/visions of glory
black men & women/children marching/legions
claiming heritage so long denied
unsubtle baiting of the ideological trap
blood in my eyes i can't see his truth

i smell cells of folsom on his breath
bodies of hundreds of men cast in to die
mindless in their fury
knowing life outside means everything

        "you won't believe it. i'll
        tell you about my stretch some day
        can't write about it without making
        sound contrived"

eighteen baby, eighteen

        i, a road well-traveled
        note similarities
        ignore them, convinced the problem's
        my insanity & emotional malfunction

my eyes bleed pictures
pools of vomit, tears, runny noise
his hand pushing my head down
i reel with denigration

you're a masochist, baby. if only
we had met when you were eighteen

jazz notes of 102.3 a lady we discuss/crusade for
in this illusion. he tells me she gave him blow jobs

in public, how much he enjoyed playing her savior
she didn't trust him and stole his briefcase for fear
he'd cut off her supply of heroin purchased
from the corporate owners of her soul

and we

lay out the future?
tribes of our people vanquishing the enemy?

                             and us having babies with ultra genetic
                             superiority?
                             and dance
                             and dance
                             and dance

warm in the lie i am his woman
and he loves me

51: *San Diego*

"the light is like this
in the south of france" he says

we stand on the pier
watch the blond boys afloat
with their surfboards
waiting to ride the big wave

"here i can be somebody" he says

a wave comes and two of the boys take it in

they boys. how well tanned they are
with skins the color of wet sand
poised unconcerned
in arian uniformity

"you breathe better here. the air
is pure. we can rent a house off the beach"

we listen to the roar
another wave. more boys take it in

my heart *hangs ten*, braces with the wet thrill
of foam as they splash graceful
into the shallows

"you can find work here easily. me too"
he says

"this is a military town, full of rednecks
a tougher lily white town than the one i come from
and i don't swim"

satin slate pelicans perch atop the lamps
that dot the pier. charcoal and enamel gulls dive
for fish. small gray-brown pipers scuttle
back and forth ocean side
the cream white crests of waves crash
along the most unspoiled beach i've ever seen

his eyes my eyes. his lips mine
afterwards the light is brighter. we look out
into a rainbow of blues greens and aquamarines
watch as laughing swimmers return

"i guess you have a point" he says

we make our way silently along
glistening rocks. the waves roar
i pick sand stones
to carry home

52: *Clown Show*

la lez says she's waited five years to meet me
she hates hets

my son trembles
terrified i will read his fledgling love letter

the house is quiet
except for the struggle of gassed bodies on the kitchen floor

baby boy sticks a paper hanger into the gas heater pilot
sets fire to the rug

the white revolutionary spends six hours recruitment time
he wants my jane doe

mama cries. i've locked her keys in the trunk
and she can't leave without them

there is a party going on in echo park
screams hourly

and the lady who rides elephants
sends psychic messages from xanadu urging me on

while experts on blacks tell me keep hopping
i'm a fine specimen

big brother says i dog cars

the codeine addict calls to give me his love
says he'll make thangs all reet

what will i do with the molting white feather ostrich boa?

my left shoe has a dimehole in its sole
something wet is coming thru

53: *6 AM & Dicksboro*

coffee stain brick horizon
the scum hole of misspent dreams
my lover and i weep in the lobby of our lives

rooms for rent

love. anyway you can get it love

red spot/bloodshot eye
this is the center of my being

and i cry not for myself
but for the children. battered children
welts from beatings. scars from molestations
tiny psyches trampled. discarded. dead

drag the river of my soul
find them there

it is in the horizon
a sun so bright so searing
my lover and i erect wind machines
clear the air

love. any kind of love. but love

how do you read
the hieroglyphics of his cum-on
or the cattiness of her friendship
how does a foreigner interpret
this strange tongue of
aching flesh

bibles in
dresser drawers

they say normal was slain here
someone called the cops
the outline of the corpse still seen
on the lobby stairwell
giving rise to fear/anguish

no message this

mere speculation. the start of another encounter/
advent. every turn of the corner leads to
a new soft and fading carpeted heart
a corridor of occupied dooms
accessible by key

the dicksboro hotel
and i live here. so don't make noise

Michael Lally

54: *Six Anti-Hits*

savage amalgam of movie directors that you are
can only disappoint and impress me at the same time

*

this essence of weather we call "shooting the movie"
makes me glad I became a star

*

so who's been fucking with my tarot cards
the ones I would never write about

*

those assholes of the ultimate critique
believe because we get sentimental about our knowledge we aren't unique

*

they love me for the things I cant control
& tell me how to stop trying to control them as the proof

*

I'll never forget the magic moments
when I knew I couldn't miss and didn't

55: *The Good Life*

I'm used to having women in my life in ways
that make it more relaxed, but I have to admit
sometimes they make me feel like I'm full of shit,
and then sometimes they make me feel like there's
something sexy about that and I just can't quit

56: *Love's Model*

for Karen Allen

you stand up
in my head &
take off all
your clothes

your clothes
take off all
in my head &
you stand up

57: *Was*

There's a false authority
in too many of the poems
of my contemporaries —
I mean especially the younger
ones, and those whose prose
is all about avoiding explanations
for their stiff defenses of
things we thought we'd
leave behind. But maybe
I'll be left behind instead
and all that false authority
will one day be interpreted as
charm, or scholarship, or
moral discretion — and
my honesty and failure to
be more heroic than I am,
be seen as only foolishness
of the most common kind —
my authority having come from
passion and my guilt, my
ambitions and my way of
leaving major decisions to
outside forces, chance, omens,
suggestions from friends and
enemies — my experiences
just add up — my memories
distract and leave me
wondering who I was —

58: *"You're Young. You'll find out."*

Fuck you, I thought. I aint as young as you think.
I was tired of these old men always giving me the
"wait and see" line. My father would always tell me
"in ten years you wont even remember this." But it
aint ten years from now, it's 1954, and what happens
to me now is my main concern and fuck the future.
The world'll probably end anyway in 1960 when the
Pope opens that letter the Mexican peasant gave him
when he saw Our Lady of Guatelupe. Or was it 1970
and Our Lady of Fatima. Who cares anyway.

59: *What I Meant to Say*

about the way trees are
obviously heavily into
meditation (the long
breath, etc.) & stones
& rocks (not the ones
with hearts and voices)
are finally into
accepting themselves...
or the way snow creates
an aura of planetness
or rain all creatures
the same (memories
of moments spent in
parked cars during
intense storms smoking
& drinking at 17 or 21
and feeling invulnerable
& like a secret, romantic
and your own & "love"...)
love of trees so passion-
ate the woods make me
dizzy and overwhelmed,
I like to catch them
alone or in small groups,
& hills and mountains
the asses and lips &
tips of tits or ankles

shoulders hips...give
me some rolling hills
or interesting buildings
or a bright red traffic
light against the dark
blue of an evening city
sky & I go soft like &
all happy with the fever
of my machinery made to
dig all this & know it.
I hardly ever show it
because it seems so
poetically cliched, un-
like the subject of my
other lives, this *this*
and all the *that* that
fits into the language.
I made me look this way.
But it's what I meet
outside on its way in
or passing through that
keeps me talking to you.
I figure if I'm accurate
about my part in it there
isn't anything we can't do.

 *For You*

to Penelope Milford

"It is my rule TO UNDERTAKE
NOTHING THAT I CAN DO."
— Kenneth Patchen

I was writing that screenplay for you.
The bills are all due & someone else
knows how to make money while I got to
play games with my brains & the words
they throw at me, alone, feeling guilty
for an inability to get going on what
would have been the dream script of
our dream. It seems to have done a
fast fade, why is that? Am I dumb,
or just numb to the parts that don't
rely on the heart for inspiration.

61: *Lost Angels*

We are the generation of lost
angels. We rarely feel these
days like we have anything new
to do or say & yet our lives
are totally changed, even from
what they were a year ago, three
months ago, yesterday, trying
to *finally* be honest about our
feelings about each other's fame
& glory, while still trying to
get or forget our own, as Billy
Idol sings and the expression
"thrillsville" is recycled in
some teenaged woman's bed, or
"oh my god" we did that too
the way rocknroll connects us
with the folks we never knew,
maybe spoiling us for joy &
hope & honest bullshit as we
once said to people who were
"naturals" like ourselves before
we disillusioned on the anti-
antis...like wanting to be a
movie star forever despite the
rocknroll & dope & beatnicks
who still can't finesse the
necessary kind of classic
heroism we all continue to
love, like the idols of the
silver screen we injected
directly into the limelight
of our brains and hearts for
smarts the schoolrooms dis
possessed and all the rest;
we don't expect *too* much, just
freedom from the assholes we
suspect have been enthralled
by their own egos making money
off ours.
       We don't wanna go crazy & die
       in some nuthouse with no teeth
       like Antonin Artaud, the world's
       first poet movie star and father

of whatever wave obsesses us now
in the New York-L.A.-Berlin-Paris-
Tokyo-Melbourne-London scene that
is the unbraining of Hollywood's
being influenced by us! (the obvious
vice versa has been *feeling* our
brains since we mainlained Marylin
& Marlon) & what about the "blues"
of John Wayne? That's how we
survived. And now it's all one,
the sum of our music and movie
influences spread across the
globe for anyone to use as in
"the new technology" which has
been in our cells since "action"
was a label for painting and
not just the order for the start
of our hearts' flicks...
We *love* being alive
and trying to share the craziness
of what it means to know it! I mean
did we really come too late for true greatness
or just on time? What is this new place
that defines L.A.-New York and all
the rest as just a state of mind?
Energy versus Peace? FUCK THAT SHIT!
The Peace of Energy that makes us
generate a void of miniscule delights
like we once relied on artificial
stimulants for, no more, maybe at last
we can reflect the serious sensuality
of the stars we talk to in our walk
through the sea we have become—

We are the masses who survived
the troubled times that rhymed
our lives the way old Hollywood
serials did, and understand our
laughter matters. Literally.
That's the secret of creation,
transforming *laughter into matter.*
We can finally *accept* and still
hope, like reality is the freedom
of knowing who we are and where
we're at and the ideal is sharing
that completely, without fear,

then letting go, not hanging on
but knowing anyway, because we're
smart at last and allow ourselves
to be. What are these humming
motors anyway but mammals of our
fantasies! Sure we talk to cars
and tvs and expect the music to
invade our brains, the motors
of our smarts that drive our
hearts to caring about it all.

Hey, what's L.A. but the
city of Lost Angels where
we all were born, even in
New Jersey cause what's
left of that is something
close to nothing, as the
categories fade and rede
fining the specifics is
less thrilling. Like Elvis
isn't. I wish they'd fish
him over the rainbow of
telescopic infinitude so I
wouldn't have to bother with
the memory of his collar
turned up and hair that thick
I thought it was hereditary.
The Shirelles, now there's
some memories that never quit
changing, big women and still
growing. We made ourselves
in the images of images and
then got rid of it before we
came. Coming isn't the game
it once was. And neither is
going.

***

I only wanted to go far, be a star,
understand the way you all are.
Love, money, friends, family,
a stimulating environment, some good books,
records, art, photographs, furniture,
place to sleep and eat and work,
make love and shower, shit and entertain in,
maybe a good car,

some free time,
your name in the paper now and then,
or in a magazine,
or on tv,
your image too,
or in a movie, on a record, in a book,
or on the cover,
in the titles,
on the lips of strangers,
in the minds of a worldwide audience...

So you move to El Lay
to make money and become a star.
So you lived in New York City
to make art and smart sexy friends.
Which wasn't enough.
So you move to El Lay where
She has almost transparently blue eyes,
so intense they give the impression
that there has never been a person
they haven't seen right through.
She has to be over fifty,
perhaps well over, like in her sixties.
It's so hard to tell these days;
or was it always?
Her eyes communicate such strength
when you look into her still beautiful face
you feel beyond time.
Her body gives it away a little.
Small, but not delicate,
there's something obviously
deteriorated about it
that seems in such contrast to her face,
unlike those strenuously physical
geriatric excersisers whose bodies
always seem to be made up of knots
and wires and strings and really ugly
imitations of some impossible youth.
Anyway,
I love her.
I fell in love with her the first time I
looked into her eyes. I can't resist a
woman who sees right through me and
is beautiful too. She's the real thing,
a total woman, smart, beautiful, and
old enough to be my lover, I mean mother,
maybe. Maybe not.

I'm not that young myself anymore, just
having walked through the door marked forty.
The best thing about which was
suddenly realizing why old guys can find old gals
sexy. When I was a kid I could never understand
the obvious attraction
my middleaged aunts could still retain for
my middleaged uncles and vice versa.
Now I know. There's a girlish glow
to most grown women that never disappears,
and if you went through the same or close-by years
with them, you can't help but see it,
and it makes you feel some kind of sympathy and
understanding for them, and then
on top of it they have this look
of having been through some things,
around the block as many times as you,
and that creates some crazy sexy feelings too.
It's all so new,
being old,
I mean older than I thought I'd ever live to be
and still be *me*.

These are some thoughts that moving from New York
to El Lay has provoked. There's so much space here
to panic in. The idea of "image" was crucifed here
for everyone's sins and then resurrected to be
worshipped for as long as this place lasts
and influences the rest of the world.
Hollywood, one of the greatest sources of power
the world has known, and no real throne, no armies
or obvious superiority except occasionally
in technical, even artistic, ways.
But oh these fucking days of driving from
one crazy studio lot to another and feeling
as much at home as I ever did
in the apartments of my peers through all the years
of poetic ecstasy and self-destruction.
What other homes have we ever had, let's face it,
then Hollywood, the New York of bebop & jazz
& street scenes & energy highs (& its flip side:
galleries & Frank O'Hara, off & off-off and then
on Broadway again) or "on the road" or on tv
or radio or stereo or juke box.

Let's face it Charlie,
we coulda been real home lovers
instead of dream chasers which is what we are.
Only worse than the Romantics of old,
we can get real cold
and see right through that bullshit
as we watch the technology unfold
into a future of dreams & nightmares we never
forgot.

John Doe

62: *The Good Songs Are On the Right*

After a couple three beers
and some loose talk with my friend from NYC,
I went to the juke box.
As usual all the good songs wind up
on the right side.
It must be a rule for all juke box fillers
"new songs on the left side and
never take off El Paso by Mary Robbins."
Two little girls in jeans
stop outside the door
of the Side Show Cocktail Lounge on Hollywood Blvd.
They call to their father, an older Mexican guy with slant
eyes and a plaid shirt who yells to them, "Take your skates
off before you come in." Maybe he meant, before you come
into the house? The little girls hold onto the door, talk about
going inside and then leave. They come rolling in laughing
ten minutes later. They hang onto Papa's hands & leg to keep
their balance while he orders three Shirley Temples.

63: *"Sometimes the glass is better than the drink"*

Sometimes the glass is better than the drink.
This woman sat next to me sayin' she had
22 shots of vodka yesterday and had to get
carried out of the club.
I believe her, she's looks too stupid to lie
& I see her down nine shots in my two hours on the barstool.
"No shit lady!"
as Tracy, under twenty really turns it on
for some jock who's probably partners in a

home improvement business and comes down here
once a week to blow a hundred & fifty bucks on . . .
satisfaction?
Smoke in the mirror as Tina throws somebody
out for buyin' only one drink in the last hour.
Neil & I talk to Julie, or "Sarina" her stripper name,
about her kids, not split bottles of champagne
for Tracy who's getting her tits massaged
by the guy she's turning on to, probably named Phil.
black & red   leather & carpet
sometimes the glass is better than the drink
We say our goodbyes
& outside the lights appear like hallucinations.

64: *"It's a Gift!*

My mind is now working like a brand new car.
It gets recalled a piece at a time.
"If I could just win your love dear . . ."

Why just today I pulled my lesser half
out of the bottom of the drunk tank,
or maybe it was just another room in St. Louis.
The wheels inside this rotten old brain keep spinning
like there's smoke coming out of my ears.
Hey fuck! get off my back, the horseride's over
& anyway I think we're here.
Christ please stop me from cutting loose with another . . .
with another . . . with another 2,000 nails in the coffin.

Somebody who tells me that they like me alot says,
"Here we all pitched in to buy you a bottle, IT'S A GIFT."

65: *When Your Time Comes*

Lying in my bunk, I'm dead again
or at least I'm pretending to be dead again.
The curtain divides me from the rest of the road
and people like artifacts who live on the edge
of the highway, watching drivers with their eyes closed
losing control and flying off the road. Sparks turn into

flames, flames into ashes, ashes to ashes and dust to ...
WAIT A MINUTE! now where was I? oh yes, I'm in my bunk
pretending to be dead, staring at the ceiling, someone asleep
above me snorting and I'm thinking of you only ten steps down the hall
It's all red in here.
The curtain on the right and when I get my casket I'm gonna
make it lacquer black like an oriental box with red pinstripping.
A red interior, no purple diamond tuck'n'roll crushed
velvet interior, with a big assed virgin white ivory cross on
top and rhinestones spelling out "Johny Doe here I go." Put
an ivory skull & crossed bones at my head & my feet. Then you can lower
me down but burn me first, pour my ashes inside and build
me a window where the grass won't grow so I can
look out & you can look down.

66: *High Cost of Living*

Girl on a doormat
on the Los Angeles bus going downtown isn't very far
        The banks fill up with letters
Poor girl
No money
Gets more & more . . . stupid
I see her dirty little kleenex, hundreds of 'em
little holes   when she
she can't sit still and drops a white plastic bottlecap
that rolls to my feet.
        I'm gonna end up like that.
        It's fuckin' possible!
Could easily lose to inflation those so-called advantages.

By nine o'clock at night
I'm fighting with someone I don't, no, I don't think
I want it to be you — girl sealed in a torpedo
        you boast
A lack of skyline power
                        you are tropic
& I'm terrified that next week no food comes near us.

The questions asked are always more disappointing than
you thought possible. Even on the thrilling shoulder of
Hwy 80, with giant cement trucks making A-bomb sounds
through the telephone conversation, a modern windmill
that reminds you of some enormous veg-a-matic, the questions still bore the pants off you. We were catching & killing flies, making stupid puns or plays on words, heaving
beer bottles and missing wildly with rocks, farther away
from home than we felt. Black hands full of grease, the
engine still smelled awful from overheating and the truck
was still busted. The radiator hose was a boa-constrictor
with its head blown off with a shotgun. We cut the strings
off with a paper scissors and screwed on the clamp with a
dime.

She stood in the phone booth, one leg bent at the knee,
her sister's high school jacket, with "Society's Outcast"
sewn on the back, swinging on the phone booth door.
Every time he was really bombed and realized how confused and basically miserable life was, he would lay beside
her, blessing her for being the one, simple, lovely thing in
the world. Then sometimes he'd cry and she would tell him
to be quiet and go to sleep because he was drunk and
acting stupid. So he thought about these exchanges watching her talk, answering those same dumb questions. Just
a small curve between her back and thighs; not much of
an ass, more like a boy's, but a good one that he liked.
The more he worked on that mess of a vehicle, the more
he wanted to see that hotel. It always got hot and slimy on
the forehead in Stockton.

68: *"Now that We've Found..."*

Now that we've found that the morgue is full of beauty, it
makes sense that we should want to spend long afternoons
with our new found friends. Plays and jump-rope filled
hours of our time, leaving us quite drained but havin' one
helluva grand time in Baltimore. To the right lived the
pastor and the rectory, which was originally made of
granite I think, had been covered in form-stone (an

eastcoast marvel which is mashed-up cement with pastel blue, yellow, pink and green dye cast into rock shapes to be nailed up covering old buildings for some effect that I never could understand but it looked godawful). Now we covered this with white aluminum siding. We workers had the glorious task of firing bullets with nails in front of them to pierce the form-stone bricks, into the granite so we could hang this stupid siding on the 1x3 wood strips held up by the nails we were shooting. Jesus, this is starting to sound like the fucking house that Jack built. Well you see there was this dead body in a room on the bottom floor. It was a young girl killed in a car crash and she was pretty, pretty mashed that is. Oh, I forgot, the church had been changed into a funeral home in '62 about the time the form-stone went up. So, they're draining the blood, what was left and the two fat salesmen from the office had come to "visit," which means to get in the way at the job site. They had stumbled into the embalming room by accident and wanted to share, with high school pleasure, their dead little girlfriend. At least that's what they kept calling her. Well, I was the kid on the job and I suppose they felt that they owed it to me to pull me into that room where she lay for a quick something or other. They thought I'd be shocked. I wasn't. I had seen my grandfather dead, my brother's best friend dead but they weren't nude and all bashed up with their blood draining. They squeezed her left tit because they weren't getting enough of a rise out of me. I said they were sick in a real low voice and walked out. I guess they got their charge but I felt so sorry for that girl lying there and so fucked by those ignorant assholes.

Going back to work on the steeple of the funeral home was easy even though it shot fifty feet above a three-story roof. And me, the chump, up on a sixty-foot extension ladder that's bowing and bouncing in & out so I'm getting motion sickness. I keep thinking that what I'm doing isn't much, but a waste of time. So, I had a piece of aluminum as pointed as shit for a little corner way up in the peak. It slips out of my hand, the ladder feels like the deck of a ship and I can't think of anything to yell, so I holler "TIMBER!" Now that sounds pretty silly in downtown Baltimore. I look down to see some old lady walking below and I just closed my eyes. After all the screaming has finished, I climb down off the ladder and that fucking piece of siding sliced the strap clean off that lady's handbag. Well, she wouldn't have been far from the mortuary.

69: "It must be thrilling to buy a '49 Mercury"

It must be thrilling to buy a '49 Mercury
just like, you know...
In these days of depression,
we make a tape for Dick Clark's show, drink no beer,
come home by 2 and as I wait for Gil T.
to come over and help fix my car, I'm forced into buying
a bunch of vegetables from the neighbors.
Both of their dogs attack the mailman.
No, he won't stand still but pulls his arm way up high
and there's a fang of the biggest black dog
stuck in his arm.
As he jerks away, there's a slippery wound,
a three-inch gash that makes for quite a show.
Three hippie type women chasing after an oriental mailman
who won't let them bandage him, maybe he thinks that
they're gonna bite him too.
Us witnesses see our English friend pull up.
He's making a lot of money to buy an old truck
like a '52 Chevy or that Merc.
He stays here on an expired 60 day visa that's 10 years old.
Americans have no inalienable rights
when it comes to cars.
Did I mention that we'll probably be pre-empted
from American Bandstand by some stupid
college football game?

        a woman in bed reading baseball books
and I'm out here watching the game
so what

70: He Walked Out the Door

The phone rings at 4 p.m. with wailing, pain and death.
It seems like all those salty tears are gonna come pouring
out of the mouthpiece.
Your close friend killed himself last night and you're
leaving for a two month tour that day
All your so-called saving love and encouragement
isn't worth shit now.
Later the radio broadcast says that John Lennon got murdered.

We finally start driving south at midnight and call the next
day to get some more details.
There's not much crying except at night.
You wonder if it takes a funeral to make us break down?

He walked out the door
with a snake wrapped around his neck, telling me there's a fire
in there.
I found a ring and now who do I give it to?
Maybe the woman he always loved.
The she-devil, smiling right-hand in his dream of
a church without a person praying
sleepless victim
knocking on doors for a different kind of 4 a.m. bottle
no one is seen in their finest hour or their final hour
He didn't wake up
He didn't wake up
beautiful animal sleeping through morning love is yours now.
or at least some kind of infamy.

21 birds flying west
all dressed in black
40 birds fly east
& newspaperment snap pictures

He had already been sentenced twice before the seventh day.

I am awake
leaning on your door
3:10 and it's freezing
4:10 and it's bleeding
It's morning and we're freezing, that guy over there from out of
the crowd, bleeding from the ears never heard the animal's growl.

David James

71: *"words in order"*

words   in   order words in   other words in   order words in   words
other   words in   order words in   other words in   order words order
in   other other words other order words order other in   order in
words   in   words other words in   order in   words words in   words
order   words order   in   order words in   words other other other other
in   order in   words in   words order in   in   in   words in
words   in   words order words words in   words words words order words
other   words words order other other words in   order other in   order
in   other order words words in   other in   in   in   other in
words   in   words other order order words words words words words words
order   words other   in   in   order

72: *Say What?*

Our language no longer supports
the resonance of the simple expletive
Huh! & *How!* have both
been appropriated to tv

Westerns and when
the other minorities
innovate a phrase
to specify their impatience
with our infamous difficulties
in rhythmic articulation
we repeat it for 15 minutes
as an extended disco single
as if thereby to numb
the elegance of their disdain

So when we see
the Chinese learn our Hustle
the historical implications
are so baffling
& the anal anxiety so sharp
that when we try to speak
all that comes out
is *Deng!*

73: *The Fourth Confrontation with Tina Turner*

        when among the many changes she performs:
Somethings got a hold on me
we share the ecstasy of her possession
& in the relief of her confession we accept
complicity   we acknowledge that
through the power of her persuasion
she has made herself credible in all her self
representations   the pretender to all parts
in the drama of loving   we see her face
to face with the perfection we have found
in her perfect simulation

        each morning she retrieves her role
from the heap of clothes on the chair by her mirror
where it lies wrinkled & small
belying what it will gain
with the strutting of her stuff
through itself without depth it defines
the extent of her occupation
she has put it on so many times
that it seems custom made
& tailored to her extreme habit
        it is tight like a stocking
she smoothes over her calves
& through the tautness of her thighs
bracing her legs & pushing down
to accommodate it to her essential motion
which begins as she leans forward
slipping into it with a shake through her spine
that allows the fitting play
of her breasts her shoulders & her arms
at last stretching its web
from the spaces between her fingers
        it is exactly superficial
& epidermic in its response
to the flex of her body's dance
she moves absolutely within it
it contains her so completely
you wonder if she can breathe in it
        it grips her like a nightmare

        where she continuously relives
the opportunity of Annie Mae Bullock
naive in St Louis & 17
she traded for the image
heralded now by posters on the streets
        her apostasy was a churching
& from Ike she took her proper name
& began the history of her own
substantial fabrication   the deliberate framing
of a being more intense in which to live
an act replete with arrogance & risk
that she observes over her cheekbones
as from behind her eyes she wakes
into the dream of her personal show

        she puts on her face & her final smile
in the mirror is a sigh of recognition

to the public front she beholds
that it becomes her
  the assumption is complete
that for her reality will always lie
in a confrontation with Tina Turner

74: *We Are Perpetually Moralists But Geometricians Only by Chance*

1

I see the city on a level
With the Gulf signs. In the cool dawn
They hang like red moons.
My eyes are mirrors, they shine inward.
The freeways and the signs focus
Behind my mind. I want no center.
I am obliged only to the precision
Of my responses. I am pledged to it.
We are lovers.

II

At noon I drink beer at The Fox.
I play the jukebox and make time
With the Chicana dancer. She says
I am goodlooking. I tell her she's alright
And shouldn't be working
At a lousy place like this. She has a scar
Where her baby should have been.

I take the freeway through the desert
To see the Dunes and Stardust.
I confess to the whore in Caesar's Palace
That I lack the 50 it takes to party.
I tell her I have been to a theater in Hollywood
To see the Kool & The Gang Show.
I tell her I know all the words
To *Slippin Into Darkness: You know*
He loved to drink good whiskey
While laughing at the moon.
I tell her I have found myself finding
More in the Moments than in Marcuse.
I found love on a two-way street.

She is unimpressed.
It still takes 50.

Her dress is slit to the navel.
The sides of her breasts are firm
As she waits for the Keno girl
And the one man a year who will leave her
A $1000 bill from the wallet
He checks while dressing. You deserve it
Baby. With you I can make it last.

I go to Death Valley and send postcards
To my friends across the sea. I write:
The brittle-brush and creosote are silver
In the night. The greasewood
Is closed to the smell of the sage.
It's cool here. It's alright. You should
Come visit me. I ask them all to call me
By my first name.

I remember when we played KGFJ and drank
And drove the freeway fast at night.
We stayed up to watch the sun
Rise over the Mojave. We ate
Breakfast at a gas station coffeeshop
Then went home to bed and to a trust
We did not care to keep. You yawn
And stretch your arms and push away
The night's meeting.

I feel the light and rolling presence
Of your breast on my forearm
When I turn in the night, even tho
Now I mostly sleep alone,
An amputee telling tomorrow's storm
By the tremor in a missing limb.

I will make laws, solemn and severe
For myself that I may not fall
Below the dignity of my kind by thinking
That the body dies with the soul
Or that the universe is moved
By chance. I will not imitate
The desert or its sands.
I will be pleased by perfume.
I will be disgusted by filth.

III

Since I have become jealous
Of unmediated memory
I spend the evening looking
At maps of places I have been.
I know by heart all the exits
On Interstate 15. I know
I will always live
Close to an on-ramp.

75: *Baja Trip*

In Baja you have to be strong
to resist the urge to generalize

from the ramshackle crosshatching of plywood bits
& pieces of pastel board that make a shack

there or from the mellow, almost waterless,
springing of the desert into bloom

to what is vaguely called
the "condition of man."

For the ocotillo fences, sprouting rich red
beaks & the swept & sprinkled sand

they have for a backyard
are peculiar to that horizon & maintain

a shimmering precision would not submit
to our attempt to pin it down in words.

Lost somewhere in that waste
of beauty which in our presumptuous tourist way

we found significant: that yard, that shack & there
a girl with deep & silent eyes & asked

direction: *No se*, she said, she had not heard
of the town we sought some twenty miles away.

I wondered then at my desire
to know her & why

anonymity should be
so exact an aphrodisiac

& as we sought our way among the dune
buggies & budweiser cans & all

that weird beauty, I realized I already had
& never would

76: *"totally almost black"*

totally	almost	black	almost	totally	black	totally
almost	black	almost	totally	black	totally	almost
black	almost	totally	black	totally	almost	black
almost	totally	black	totally	almost	black	almost
totally	black	totally	almost	black	almost	totally
black	totally	almost	black	almost	totally	black
totally	almost	black	almost	totally	black	totally

Nichola Manning

77: *Family Fame*

When I played tennis in England as a teenager,
they once did a big article on me in the local
paper. But the night before this came out my
drunken dad got in a violent argument with a
railroad official, who called the police.

So the article on me was headed:
NICKY MANNING GOOD TENNIS PROSPECT
Parallel to this down the page was the headline:
TIM MANNING ARRESTED FOR OBSCENITIES

And they used the same photo of me and dad for
both stories.

78: *Variation*

The English Language is in Long Beach,
    California, 6,000 miles from England.
It came over the North Pole,
40,000 feet above the Northwest
    Territories, looking out the window,
"the word blue,"
referring to water which would kill it
    instantly if it fell from here.
But it didn't fall and went on to find
    English names for previously Mexican
    things.
And by the time the Mexicans started
    calling Long Beach "Longo"
the English Language
had acquired a different accent,

eaten thousands of "burritos" with hot
    sauce,
and didn't consider England its home
    anymore.

79: *Grand Language*

After vomiting
The English Language was still in Long
    Beach,
still obsessed with the idea of doing some-
    thing on a grand scale, like murdering
    some whores in Salt Lake City.
Some one said there are none there,
but the English Language
had invented Salt, Lake and City, and put
    them together.
So she could add "whores" —
as old as the word KILL
translated from the Hebrew,
something you should not do.
But once it's done all The English language
    can do is put ED on the end, then go to
    relate what happens next,
sprinkled with Latin words if it gets caught
    in the legal system.

80: *Composure*

When being hung by the neck do not sway nor
raise arms. Do not smile nor cry nor choke.
Pretend you're at a bus stop waiting in light
drizzle without umbrella or warm clothing.
Surrounded by the upper classes out slumming.
Imagine you're gaining their respect. or
imagine you're at the Welfare Department trying to get on disability — not by groaning,
twisting up and turning purple, but gaining
their respect by standing motionless two
feet above the ground.

81: *Pyramid*

When a pyramid is in its usual
position the bubbles rise to
the peak and escape through a
special opening in a few big

gulps. But when the pyramid is
upsidedown they climb to the
large, dirt-clogged bottom, too
spread out to be forceful, and

thus escape slowly, unpredictably.

82: *Disability Questionnaire*

1. Do you consider yourself ready to work yet?

   "No."

2. If no, give reasons:

   "Well, I'm not very talented at office
   type jobs but I have my pride, and if
   some middle class asshole starts making
   snide remarks I'm liable to bust them
   right in the mouth. But I wouldn't mind
   getting rehabilitated into The Army as a
   machine gun operator, or into a factory
   job where I had access to a sledgehammer
   so I could brain my enemies. Otherwise,
   I'd like working with innocent children.

83: *Rachel Would Never*

Rachel would never talk to me in school
but we were eight
and would shit together on the common near
    a mental hospital which seemed to contain

·nothing but old men in overcoats who went
    on walks near us.
But one time a *woman* escaped and next day
    the local headline was MADWOMAN WALKS NUDE
    DOWN HIGH STREET.
I hope I never do that,
and the intense look on Rachel's face as the
    shit started coming out was sexy.

84: *Trial*

All good people get out of their cars in
    special clothes and walk very stiffly
    into church
while there are such things as drums and
    the clacking of balls.
So it's a good thing sound doesn't travel
    too far,
and sperm is usually secreted,
and milk,
which the middle-aged women smile and pour
    into their coffee after church,
having bed wonderful children
who masturbate as quietly as possible under
    their very sniffing noses that are so
    ugly, especially when you look up at them.
Like the aging waitress,
very polite, talking of gravy,
but her hair is dyed my color,
a slut underneath.
Which I'm not because I try and I'm very
    disgusted.

85: *Wallpapering*

I've stuck wallpaper on my walls,
on my ceiling and windows
and chimney and TV
and washing machine.

I don't want any of the neighbors saying
they're better wallpapered than me.
I've dipped wallpaper in cologne
and then put it on my kitchen floor

and bedroom and bathroom floors
and my canary and goldfish and rattlesnake.
Nor do I care if Klyda comes
to the back door, announcing,

"a wave of violent wallpaper
has swept through Turkey."
Let no one say my wallpaper is violent:
I scrubbed it well with Ajax before using it

on my jersey and skirt and bra.

86: *O Wise Margaret Thatcher*

I think you're doing a wonderful job in the
Falkland Islands. Is it true that a single
British submarine destroyed half of
Argentina's airforce? Not bad.

But what I'm really praying about is the tea
situation in Los Angeles. I've been all over
Santa Monica, to the Ambassador Hotel, and I
even called the British Consulate. But there
is not a single packet of Lyon's Red Label
Tea to be had.

Even in Boston where they hated the English
there was enough tea to fill the harbor, and
I don't suppose it was any godawful Lipton's
or Constant Comment. Here in Los Angeles
everyone praises my English accent yet I am
given cups of perfumed water. What an insult
to the Union Jack!

I know I'm not supposed to order saints
around, but couldn't you commission a few jets
to fly out here and drop, not bombs, but good
strong tea, on my or any of my friends'
apartments?

Would worship you forever if you came through
on this one.

Amen.

87□ *Lyrics*

The handsome young man
taps his stick
on the military map
and says

here! Here!

He's spotted the enemy.
His brave, handsome
comrades join in immediately,
beating with their sticks
up tempo,
teaching the midgets
rock and roll.

88□ *One More Round for Hiroshima*

I always wanted to do it with
my mother. Fly to Australia,
that is, with her in the baggage
hold, and me in first class with

earphones on, listening to
something quiet and undemanding.
And, possibly, by the time the plane
touches down in Sydney, she'll have

been dropped on Hiroshima.

89: *Ritual*

In places where trains are banned
there are always underground
houses, long and thin
which go "chew chew" on tape
and have horrible dry ludicrously
expensive cheese sandwiches
tiny beers rancid gins
uncomfortable seats and tables
that shake,
spilling the boiling hot
soup liquid.
The druids who live there are
the vanguard of the revolution,
complete with chemical toilets.

90: *Potential Traffic Conductor*

John had been standing in the middle of the mental
ward with his arms pointing ahead of him like a
sleepwalker for fifteen years. Then one day the
very famous Dr. Blank was to visit the hospital and
I guess John overheard this.

When Dr. Blank arrived with his entourage he went up
to John and said, "Hello, I'm Dr. Blank. Could you
tell me where the conference room is?" John moved
his right arm 90° and pointed down the hall to his
right, then brought it back to its usual position.
and continued to stand in that position until his
death ten years later.

91: *Long Beach*

1
In a helicopter over Long Beach you can see
that the buildings have no roofs and are all
empty inside, except for weeds and trash

dropped into them by a large excreting
enemy. The sky?

2
On the ground you see vehicles without
engines. You see people sweating and asking
each other what to do. You also see empty
jars, empty cigarette packs, empty cans and
empty perambulators.

3
The more you look at these, the nearer and
dirtier they get, until the only thing you
can be is a vacuum cleaner.

Michael C. Ford

92: *Holy Toledo*

for James Krusoe

The snow, now, newly fallen
Olympian flaky drift
Running on the invisible lawn

A convent contain'd by birds
The east window becoming a
Painting by Morris Graves

And you mesmerize sisters of the
Passion as though the apple
Orchard is a frozen pantheon of
Popes chair'd in some flashy
Vatican promenade

Later you feel slow snowy
Ambulations of eyes starting to
Shut down drowsy

It is Sunday; tomorrow you will
Go into town to work
And think about nothing

93: *An Early Start*

for Steven Robert Lowry

This guy in Downey, California
says this about travel:

"I wanna grind off a few miles
before breakfast"

Maybe he's right!

In a particularly desolate part
of the Snake River plains

somewhere between Bliss
& Glenn's Ferry Junction,

there's a sign at the side of
the road; black letters advising:

WITH A LATER START
YOU WOULDN'T BE HERE YET

94: *Placeat Tibi Obsequium Servitutis Mea*

just south of Hornhook Hiway
near Dunsmuir, wind whistles
in the calculus of grass

under a crop of clouds dusting
the twilight-wet apparitions;
vampiric teeth begin to engrave

the neck of Turntable Bay. you
pretend to be asleep in a car
on Blue Gum Rd. you demand a

vision! where's your sanctifying
bread? where's your eucharistic
booze? where's your mantic saint

of the eclipse. the stars are
dead mosquitoes dried on a
filthy washboard. you believe

Blue Gum Rd. is the universe,
a void of bluebook examinations on
astrophysics you'll probably fail

in the morning. your typewriter
cannot record it. the keys stick,
you're stuck,

the void passes over
the washboard tonguetied
mouth of night

Yolo County/1983

95: *Talking to Holly Prado*

It's the way poets talk to eachother
— Eloise Klein Healy

You're right, Holly!
Poets are always
Writing about pain

Oh god pain!
Crazy kocomaimie
Pain

Wrist to
Forehead
Pain

My own pain,
Holly, holds suitcases
On highway 395

And, when it reaches
Reno,
It will lose its shirt

96: *In those Dream Machines Even Delmore Schwartz Could Have Begun Responsibilities*

What happened to old Chevies
you could tear down — the
ceremony of taking care of
your own transportation?

My memories are at the mercy
of the Mustangs
of Buellton

97: *Young Girl on a Train Haiku*

Desert sunset dies —
She lifts her hand-puppet frog
And it croaks at me
                    Isleta, New Mexico

98: *Preferring Charges*

Right now, I'm in one of the
Research rooms at Utah State
Trying to write coherently
Concerning the fate of Russia

A muzak version of commercialized
Shostakovich charges my mind the
Way *ostinato* rapids are charging
The Logan

Ice-encrusted twigs, as they
Thrash in the rushes out there;
It's like those mice in the
Agricultural industry building

Their fate is somehow Ukrainian

99: *Upon Becoming a Respected Poet In Odgen Utah and Coming Back to Los Angeles for a Minute*

So, when I get back to my shack
in Rancho Pk, the new bride upstairs
is dancing on my distracted ceiling
& she still keeps the radio on full tilt

& when I go outside to breathe she yells
thru a window at me:
"Can I borrow $5?"

I say I was just about to ask her
the same question

"Bein' away so long sure put you in one
rotten mood," she sd

"John Keats is dead," I sd — "so is
Shelley — happened a few years ago
& it just hit me"

"Oh, yeh, yeh, they them 2 moviestars
got 'emselves kill'd in car crashes
down by San Diego that time?"

"You got it," I sd

"They musta been good friends, hunh?"
She seemed concern'd

"The best," I sd

Then she goes away to crank up
Jefferson Starship

I go back inside
crack open a beer
& listen to the sink
drip

100: *It Had to Be Two Years Since Sunday*

it had to be two years since Sunday

when we (when Carolyn pastured *Blackjack*)
stood against the twilight winter-still

farm. now even a new one, over the *Bench*
to the north — the Arabian-eyed

potential rodeo show winner. how long
again, before we stand against these

seasons?

a dairy pitcher — the word *creamery*
in stencil-abbreviation, so it reads:

IDAHO CRY

how long looking into the horsey falling
night, listening to potatoes

grow (actually hearing them grow)?

101: *Air Mail / Postage Due*

I think I know the way
without the road
— Deena Metzger

Robinson Jeffers talk'd all trees
Into human function,
Even without leaves,
As though they were all relative
To you & me (as if we were)
Yes!
As in *The Humanist's Tragedy*
He reminded me,
As if we'd both been sprung from
The same womb
But being buggy abo our
Differences & distances
Doesn't alter the fact
That your eyes are intensely
Blue (very much like my own)
That they give me coolness,
Like December weathers;
Yet we have no ties,
To distant relatives,
As we have no gestures
For different religions
No!
We are among trees;
We are shower'd by
Their leafless fall

Written on the day celbrating the 91st anniversary
of Jeffers' birth

Exene Cervenka

102: *"you start out with a shot glass"*

you start out with a shot glass
and end up with a measuring cup.
thank god for fast forward.
i'm not one to dwell on the past
i've always got my eye on the future.
oh, christ look out,
duck, here it comes.
is it gone?

life always knows what's best for you.
you know that don't you?
if your dick gets stuck in neutral,
well, it's just a brief resting period,
unitl a better thing to stick it in
comes hopping along.
so there i was. hopping down this dark alley,
life always knows what's best for you.
someone's looking for a victim, and you are provided.
someone needs money, life will give them you,
to fulfill their prayers. a man needs a woman,
incidentally you fit the bill, but the butcher
won't take his check. isn't life funny?
isn't it handy to hand you over as a hand out?

morbid little ditty.
sour little kitty.
set aside a little time for pity every day.
don't forget to wish through your tears.
wish for something pretty.
wish upon a tear.
ugly modern tower.
the glass will shower down.
it will wet the backs
of the labor that put it up.

push it into the sky.
fill the sky with buildings.
paint the outsides with glass.
make the pretty building sparkle.
it's so sunny here.

103: *"the lady in dread"*

The lady in dread
crosses my path

When she comes to bed
she becomes naked
and then she comes.

The lady in dread
she takes a bath
after the water drains
her soul slips around in the tub.

It's like a path to glory
or a simple bubble bath.
She's got literature
for brains
and a very dirty birthday suit.

104: *"banished 2 bakersfield"*

sharp tongue, and with it,
i tell you to prove it.
but you can't even prove you have a dollar
to buy me half a beer cause you expect me
to pay for everything, and you expect it every year
that we are together, except when you are with a brand new whore.
but as i am not a whore, therefore, i will buy no more.
for beer and understanding,
you will have to go to bakersfield.

105: *"Right now I'm shaving,..."*

Right now I'm shaving, I don't shave my legs or under
my arms, I shave the ingrown brain cells off my brain.
As you get older your brain which is like having two
of you, as you get older...When you were younger,
it was a friend to play with, then the co-writer of
all your material, as you get older the brain becomes
a pyschiatrist to help shovel handle the unburiable
load. Drinking is medicine. Every hangover has its
memories that have to be analyzed all day in bed.
It takes supreme effort to effect any personality
changes, unburiable load, as you get older the brain,
and every step forward toward is like a mentally
retarded teenager learning to drink from a cup again.
Miles of cars in rush hour traffic line my soul. And
every glance I cast, reels in a fish of infidelity.

106: *"helicopters and sirens"*

god it's like all the time.
it's like bongos at a beatnik pot party,
i mean incessant.
spotlights and red lights and blue lights and white
lights, it's like a nightclub out there!
i've never been to a floor show, have you?
what is a floor show anyway? girls in lace legs,
kicking?

somehow along the way i acquired a long page
like a dress that gets longer every year
even if you keep trying to hem it?
there was a fruit fly on my whiskey glass just now
that sets my skirt a flying.
i won't have filthy creatures climbing all over
my drinking utensils. don't i get some consideration
after all these years of hard work and devotion to
american culture, not to mention my contributions,
and the tax on my minimum wages, the page gets longer,
all i ask is an advance for a new filing cabinet, it
cannot be expected to do all this writing and file it
by myself too? i need a staff of bleeding hundreds,
whipped like a tub of margarine to heal my hands.

my bleeding knuckles after scrubbing all those dishes
of their incriminating fingerprints, why i haven't
had time to throw a plate at a man in three years,
i tell you i'm overworked, and my dress is getting
longer every day, oh exene, the ash is long on your
cigarette, can't you hire a girl to come in and clean
it up?

107: *Untitled*

IT'S
1000 HOURS
AFTER MY LAST
CIGARETTE.
YOU ARE IN MY ROOM
SITTING ON A
$12 END TABLE.
HERE COME
THE GARBAGE MEN.
A MACHINE MADE
FOR DAWN'S EARLY LIGHT.
THEY MAKE
A LOT OF NOISE,
DON'T THEY?
THE NOISE I HEAR MOST
IS THE SOUND
OF NO CONVERSATION
BETWEEN THEM.
THERE IS
NO CONVERSATION
BETWEEN US EITHER.
SOMETIMES
MEN COME OVER
JUST TO
READ YOUR MAGAZINES.

Michelle T. Clinton

108: *Aint bout Nuthin But Some Toast*

How you like yo toast be a very important thang
cause you the only one can get toast right.

You take like eggs, 'n you say I like my eggs fluffy,
I like my eggs wit pepper, 'n if you cold fry them in margarine
stead of oil, I would like that.
' somebody brang you eggs sactly like that.

But toast, no matter how good you splain it,
somebody brang you toast it be half way cold
or the wrong kina bread or soggy or too brown
or sumthin 'n it jess donn be right.

Yo momma caint do it. Yo runnin partner
on mushrooms & motorcycle caint do it,
you second best lover wit serious head
caint do it like you needs to get it done

when you come home, last unemployment check in hand,
nobody at the pad, bird sleepin, kitchen cold & black,
tight money funk fillin yo mind, when caught tween
the rush & crash of hellacious party in the streets,
yo main squeeze donn get it up regular no more
'n you caint stop puttin things in yo mouth:

Time for toast, however you like it
cause you the only one know the ins & outs
of yo tastebuds & fingertips.

Eatin toast remind me a flying a flag you donn wanna spit on,
eatin toast remind me a basketball, African bonding,
& dialectical materialism. Eatin toast say Keep hanging
girl, the wicked system out in the streets
can fuck wit yo pocket yo nigguhs

but who got yo self
when the kitchen all cold & black,
cat snorin, roommate out chasin pussy somewhere,
jess gime some Wonder bread 'n I'll be cool,
gimme three cigarettes, jet fuel coffee finna perk,
& steam risin offa my hot buttered toast.

109: *Star Dust*

At ten o'clock, the women come out their rooms,
their hands rubbing their highs & backs. They
drop coins in the pay phone & lean against the
gray wall, listening to the rings.
In my room is a color teevee, chained down,
a broken mirror, & a white lamp with a bulb
that works only when it is screwed in.
Behind yellow curtains, limp & uneven,
I smoke hashish & cigarettes & wait
for the women to go away fro the phone.

Though I have been known to fuck more than one man
at a time, get slapped around, free base,
& steal shiney things from middle class bathrooms,
I am a decent woman:
I don't shoot dope, never had to take a righteous
ass whippin, & ain't never sold no pussy,
so I don't have to look at them. I prefer
to sit behind the haze of limp curtains
& wonder at the center of the white flowers
on my broken lamp painted with red nail polish.

"Bitch. Where my money?" I hear men cursing,
"You better act right. I ain't playin.
Bitch, I'll stick my dick up yo ass,
I'll fuck you with my dick up yo ass hole,
I ain't playin wit you."

My old man returns to me, his shoulders hunched
over the Times, his arms carrying white bags & brown bags.
"Look at her red pants! I can tell she's a whore!"
"Shut up boy. That's that scotch talking.
Can't you be polite?"
"You god damn whore!"
"Shut up man! I got to get along wit these 'hoes."

"OOOO, I'm gonna fuck you tonight, baby,
I'm gonna do it to you tonight,"
as I push him through the door remembering,

I am a decent woman. I listen through
the rain to their curses, I hallucinate
unwound hangers, my man brings me wounds
wound in a taunt penis, the newspaper
folded & creased, with red circles around
want ads. We eat chicken McNuggets
with our fingers, drink Jack Daniels
from the bottle.

I am a decent woman: My old man
never has no money, so I fuck him
for free.

110: *Tween a Mammy & a Stud*

(for my sisters in the Bay and Celia)

We called them rabbits when I went to college,
those white girls with limp hair in barrets
& thin arms in cashmere sweaters.
Seemed like it'd be easy to make 'em scared
& when they cried, all the men & nigguh
women in the room wanted to put an arm around 'em.

You can make 'em ease their head back & moan
if you take a small breast, a smooth vagina in your mouth.
They give up the grind too & afterwards stare at you
with wonder filled eyes, like you were Superman,
a wild King Kong tamed or sumthin'.

I even got to defy white men if they hovered
too near my lady. I'd huff up & think
Back off home. This here's mine.
My bitch. She wants me more than you
& I ain't even got no penis.

But when all the sisters with white girl lovers
discussed the situation we noticed how
they flung their hair in the morning
but liked ours short, never called us pretty
or soft, didn't like us in earrings or brassieres,

& how they twitched whenever black men walked
in the room, & how they always managed in bed
to be on the bottom.

'N I remember how gay & straight black women
put the bad mouth on any brother wit' a rabbit
on his arm, & won't give up no play to nigguhs
who done bought the shit about Cinderella &
Snow White & needs a fragile princess to make
him feel power.

And I wonder now, drinking this gin & tonic,
watching the bar light play in your red hair,
land on your thin shoulders & mouth I can't
stop watching. I wonder why I feel like
bustin' that beer gut white boy while he
licks his lips & stares at you.

I wonder just what you want, just exactly
how strong you think I am, & just how deep
& funkey all this shit is
that I'm playing into.

111: *Manifesting the Rush / How to Hang*

If somebody tries to give you something, let them. This applies
to everything, especially cigarettes, sex & drugs.

Tell them to take a hike.

Laugh at everything you can.

Find people who are hanging & hang with them. Screen them
with drugs: weed alla time, cocaine too hard on the pocket,
beer'll make you fat & gin'll make you drunk a lot quicker.
Slamming is hard on the nerves, green pills white pills & black
ones from somebody's doctor play real well, & nobody crazy
with good sense does acid.

Tell everybody everything. No masks, no mysteries & tell
everybody you won't tell anybody, & tell anyway.

Figure out who is hanging with who. Go to people you don't hang with but know they hang with people you hang with, 'n say HOW'S DAH HANG?

Establish an in clique code word for those not hanging: ya gotcha basic square, ya gotcha pasty faced 'merican geek, bending over, goin' for the okey doke. Ya gotcha LA strangelo, & ain't nan' one of 'em know know hot to hang.

Open your home as a hang center. Keep tidbits in your freezer, stock up on ultra-stress formula vitamin B complex. Do a lotta dishes. At least once a week, plan on giving over an evening to somebody's bad trip, somebody's peel, some trim together sculptor will do the break down & then you got to hang tough.

How to hang tough: Imagine youself very cool, very sharp & altogether together. Remember it's fine to be crazy, it's like really okay to be crazy, like what the fuck else we gon' do, we got so much heart, so much insight, we livin' in a hellacious world, man, folks like us, if we wasn't crazy, we'd be dead or crazy ONE! Then tell your partner. Let him know who's boss. Listen. Hold his hand. Hold him. Tell him his momma loves him. Confess something evil. Hold him. Tell him, again, his momma wasn't jiving, she does love you, man, she just didn't know how & it ain't nuthin wrong wit being crazy, & you ain't crazy no way. Be prepared to knock his ass out if he gets too wild.

Regarding sexual activity, consider filthy language and lingerie. Never sleep with anybody crazier than you. Unless you up for a wild ride. Keep your hands cupped over your heart. Do not fall in love.

Dave Alvin

112: *1969*

We hiked in the Sierra for two weeks.
Three men; Jack, Tex and my father
with three boys;
my brother, Phil, his friend, Doug, and me.
My father carried the most weight,
ninety pounds;
the cooking utensils, a sleeping bag
along with a few carefully wrapped
vodka bottles.
In the evening
the men would sit at the campfire
farting, smoking,
passing one of the vodka bottles to each other.
Tex had several different stories
of how he lost his thumb.
Jack had the Korean War
and his job as an L.A.P.D. artist.
My father had World War Two
and union organizing in the southwest.
They told stories of poor G.I.s
who met the wrong hookers
and G.I.s that liked other G.I.s
and drinking binges in liberated Paris
and the more noteworthy sights of the world.

Fuck the alps. My father would say.
I've seen 'em and they don't touch the sierra.

*Well I've seen some parts of Italy that are
pretty nice, Cass.*

Doug would creep off every night
into the woods
and not return until the men had exhausted
their stories and gone to bed.

That boy is an odd one, Tex would say
as Doug disappeared in the dark trees.
What the hell do you think he does out there,
jack off or something?

He's just an asshole. Who cares?
My father would laugh then resume the bullshitting.

Phil would read books by flashlight
and sneak a cigarette or two in his tent.
I would try to sleep in my bag,
listening to the men talk,
praying the mountain trip would end
so I could go home to hamburgers
and rock and roll records.
We lost the main trail for two days
and Jack invented a path across a ridge
of dry manzanita to Rattlesnake Creek.
From there it would be an easy hike
back to the Kern River.
The manzanita ripped through our shirts
and tore at our skin.
The boys complained
and the men told us to shut up.
My father fell twenty feet or so
down a cliff of loose dirt
but broke none of the precious vodka bottles.

We camped in a small clearing
on the banks of Rattlesnake Creek.
I played with a crawfish.
I let him crawl up and down my arm.

Ain't no crawfish in California, fuckhead.
That's a scorpion. Phil laughed.

I hurled the scorpion into the creek
and said fuck for the first time in front
of my father.

That night Jack
told us about murder scenes he had covered;
the positions of the bodies,
how they had been mutilated,
how they had died,
fast or slow.

My father talked about when his Signal Corps
unit liberated a concentration camp.
He had to photograph the survivors.
He had to photograph the dead in mass graves.
He had to photograph skeletons.
He had to photograph teeth for possible
identification.

Tex tried to talk about knife sharpening
or the next day's fishing
or Oklahoma hookers
but the other two men drank
and told their stories without laughing
and ignored him.

In the daytime, as we hiked,
Doug and Phil lectured me in growing up.
They were high school juniors
and in September I was going to be a freshman.
They told me how to pick up high school girls
and what to do if I got one.
They told me what to drink
and where to drink it,
what to smoke and where to smoke it.
Near the end of the trip
I got up the nerve to ask Doug
what he did alone in the woods after dark.

I just write in my notebook.

Write what?

Stuff you wouldn't understand.

Phil took me aside.
He said that even he didn't know
what Doug was doing but he was pretty sure
that Doug was taking LSD.
I didn't know what that meant then
but it sounded important.

After ten days of sun and heat
the weather turned to rain and hail,
four days running.
The creeks and rivers were flowing mud.
We strained the dirty water

through shirts and rags before drinking.
There was no hope of fishing.
The men ran out of stories
and the evenings were spent
cursing the weather
and cursing the boys.

I never should've listened to you, Cass.
Bringing fucking kids like these up here.
I've had scout troups of goddamn eight year olds
more mature.
Jack said, sure that we hear him.

I wonder about the future of our country sometimes.
Tex whispered.

Your're all grandmothers. My father ended it.

It was over.
The fishing had been bad,
the weather either too hot or too cold,
the trails lost.
We made our way to Cottonwood Creek
where there was a telephone
and my mother was on her way from Los Angeles.

In Lone Pine
we ate our first meat in two weeks
in an all night diner.
Tex came into the diner
and threw a newspaper on the table.

Looks like you'll be busy when you get home, Jack.

Jack shook his head.
Here it goes again.
On the front page was a photo of Sharon Tate.
None of us had ever heard of her.

HOLLYWOOD MASS MURDER, the headline said.

My father looked out the window
at the Sierra rising from the Owens Valley
in the moonlight.
Then he turned to me and smiled,
Well, people are fucked.

I went to the bathroom.
In the mirror I saw
one black hair on my chest.

113: *San Joaquin Valley No. 1*

A teenage girl
works the nightshift
at a self-serve gas station
in Modesto.

She says little
and what she does say
is without a smile,
through a hole in the window.
She wears
an orange and pink uniform
under the shadowless
yellow flourescent lights.

All the customers
make jokes
as a cold wind blows
across the valley
but she doesn't laugh.

114: *San Fernando Valley No. 1*

Marina has a bad hangover
but manages to fix coffee and eggs.
Marina doesn't remember
what she drank
or if she took one kind of drug
or more.
She doesn't remember
the name of the guy in her bed.
But she does remember
her audition at eleven o'clock
with a rock band.
Marina wants to be a singer.
She sips her coffee and stares

out her kitchen window
to the hamburger stand across the street.
The Mexican aliens
have lined up again,
waiting for someone to come by
and pick them up for one day
of cheap labor.
They look like hustlers
on Santa Monica boulevard, she thinks.
A pickup truck driven by a young blonde man
in a T-shirt with a photo
of a rock band on it
pulls up to one group,
waves for four, and five get in.
The man from the bedroom
straggles into the kitchen naked.

Why do they bother? Marina asks him.

Who? He says.

Those Mexicans.

Oh.

She finishes her coffee
but ignores her eggs.
The naked man eats them for her.
She goes back
to her bedroom,
does her make-up
and chooses what clothes to wear
for her audition.

Bob Flanagan

115: *Driving into the World*

Need: that's the word tonight
as, plip, plip, the rain
takes chunks of metal and paper
down the drain—
hair, teeth, and slivers of bone
carried out to sea.

The storms come and the world
is altered. Leaves
land in puddles, shattering
small motels along the road.
The ocean is out there,
worse then ever.

You wonder if the car will hold up
and maybe you're disappointed
when it does, or else the rain
disappoints you, the way it softens
the hard edges, and makes the world
seem like mush.

Where's the view, the tourists
with their kids and cameras,
their soft mouths gaping in awe
at the expanse and desolation,
motel signs lit bright as beacons
to welcome them?

Sure not like home, is it?
And what is home? Sticks of furniture
piled against the wall. "These
are my things," you shout
until the house is empty
and there is no one left to shout at.

Every room has a mirror, a toilet.
clean towels, and blank walls
with spaces where paintings
used to be. When you leave
someone comes to make the bed
and take out the trash.

And as you leave things behind —
a shirt, a comb, a pair
of socks — they become all
you can think about, and then
you forget them, as you forget
the names of cities.

At the water's edge it's not like
being on the rim of a continent
or even part of this world.
Waves make their ghost-like
appearances, taking with them
whatever's in their path — even you.

Behind you the ones you love
are sleeping. Clouds form
thick blankets, stifling
even the brightest stars.
The sky is black, as if in mourning.
For some, this night will last forever.

And if there are miracles
it's that the engine starts
and you are driving, and the sun
really does come out,
at night there's a full moon,
and, before you know it, you're home.

116: *Solid*

As a family we are solid
Death is a shield and we are solid behind it
Dad comes home from work
Mom is making dinner
We are all together, solid and waiting

We have a pool
It cracks
Water floods the yard
We are all together with rakes and shovels
A gopher sticks his head up
The rake just misses

Paint chips away from the house
My brothers, wrestling in their room, break a lamp
Dad puts his fist in the wall
Mom throws dishes

We are all together in the front room
Dad puts a new leg on the couch
It snaps off

The neighbors tell us our cat's dead
No more cats, Dad says, no more neighbors
We are solid together in Dad's fist
Mom grabs a hammer
My brothers find rocks
My sister, small as she is,
Stabs the air with her scissors

117: *New York*

If within the gene pool there is memory
as some people say
maybe they remember what I remember
although it isn't much.
The Staten Island ferry comes to mind:
the red seats.
They could have been blue.
Red was San Francisco.
If they were red
how do I know?
What kind of red?
Postcard red?
Television red?
How can I remember red?
I need to separate what I remember
from what was told to me.
I remember the sound of the ferry —

the big boat eased into the dock by tugboats.
Now I don't really know if the big boat
was eased into the dock by tugboats.
Where do the tugboats go?
What keeps them from being crushed
between the dock and the big boat?
And why do I keep saying "big boat"?
What do I mean by big?
It was a big sound, a scraping
and grinding that shook the floor,
or should I say deck, beneath our feet.
I could always look forward to that
and so could my brother
who cried even before it started.
And when it did start it was terrifying,
like the whole ship was being ripped to pieces
and we would never make it to shore.
All four of us, still such a new family,
drowning, just a few yards,
from the city, New York,
a place I can't even remember.

118: *Fear of Poetry*

I'm afraid I won't be able to start
this. Or once having started
I won't get through it. Already
I've re-written the first line
three times. I like *won't* better
than *will not*. It's more
personal. I think I want that.
Now I'm getting self-conscious.
But I'm doing it, aren't I?
I've written nine lines so far — ten
— eleven, counting this one.
Kim wrote a poem in only eight lines
and it knocked everyone dead.
It was about death. I think
"a wave of cats" was an image she used.
What I wouldn't give to use that
in my poem. But my poem's not about death.
It's not even about life.
My poem is about my poem. Ugh!

Now I'm really stuck. It's been two days
since I wrote "My poem is about
my poem. Ugh!"
Life has certainly gone on since then.
Another Hollywood figure has died and the rumors
spring forth like a wave of mad dogs.
So much for life, and originality too.
Many many many many many many many
people have died, their bodies
tossed off like so many cockroaches.
My sister died two years ago
and the shock waves still resound
throughout my family.
My mother is locked into a depression
and my father seems *too* happy.
But I hardly think about it now.
I have my work.
My poems are certainly moving along,
especially this one.
In yesterday's version, after my sister
and my mom and dad, I talked about my friend, Jack,
and the song we wrote called "Fun to Be Dead."
I felt I had to mention Jack because
I took a line from one of his poems and used it
as my own. Now, many many many many many
lines later, I'm confessing.
I had reached a point of not knowing where to go
and I was afraid I would not finish
just as now I neither know where to go,
nor how to finish.

119: *from The Fuck Sonnets*

I've been a shit and I hate fucking you now
because I love fucking you too much;
what good's the head of my cock inside you
when my other head, the one with the brains,
keeps thinking how fucked up everything is,
how fucked I am to be fucking you and thinking
these things which take me away from you
when all I want is to be close to you
but fuck you for letting me fuck you now
when all that connects us is this fucking cock

which is as lost inside you as I am, here,
in the dark, fucking you and thinking — fuck,
the wallpaper behind you had a name,
what was it? You called it what? Herringbone?

120: *Bruises*

for Sheree

These bruises are not metaphors.
Their appearance means more to me
than words. I take my clothes off
and I put my clothes on. So on
and so on. The heat becomes unbearable.
And now it's the noise, and people,
especially close people like friends
and family. Being close to someone —
that's what hurts. Being whacked
in the head with a two-by-four —
now *that* hurts. And that's a metaphor.
These are bruises. They look like roses,
and mean that much to me. I'll miss them
when they fade, as I miss you,
the one who gave them to me, these
and others, like badges, worn
by me until worn out (the bruises
or me?). I've spent days writing
words about these bruises, until now,
in fact, they are long gone.
With them goes whatever it was I thought
they meant. This page was blank
when I started. Now the lines have
stacked up into some kind of statement
about — what? Love? I belonged
to you. Those bruises were emblems
of that. But now, thanks to the body's
remarkable healing ability, I'm pure,
fresh as a daisy,
and I look like I could belong
to just about anybody.

Amy Gerstler

121: *You Belong to Me*

Climb aboard the celestial transport,
my puzzled consolation prize. Remember,
I went on ahead to prepare a place for us.
Now the table is laid, meteor coals glow
and strange, unnamed gases mingle to
assume human forms. It's been eons. You're
still my health, my breath of necessary
menthol, my winter enlightenment, star-
studded hot flash, prelude to words.
Do you like this song so far? Look:
your hand's restored to normal. Listen:
your friends are here, all talking
at once — the bloody butcher, dusty baker,
wild-eyed hallucinator. Hurry up my love,
or the galactic crack will grow closed
and our ship begin breaking up. I haven't
aged much, have I? Why are you shaking?

122: *The River that Runs Under the Bridge of Sighs*

Remember when I found white flowers
from the bountiful tree that graced
her driveway all over the hood of
your car, because you'd been parked
there overnight? Careless love,
to leave a blizzard of telling
blossoms. You shrugged your honest
shoulders. How should you know?
I've never been in a blizzard,
but the flowers were white and did

fall from above. Could you pour out
the tea water, it's almost boiled
away. Are you saving your sperm
for her, or a rainy day? Nevermind.
Would you dust, and return those
overdue library books? Or just tell
me your story again, about the
difference between what one is
and what one witnesses. Temptation.
Testimony. The tests of time. If
I do this the minute your back
is turned, what will I attempt when
you're far away? The leaflet stuck
in my door reads YOU CAN LIVE
FOREVER IN PARADISE ON EARTH.
WOULD YOU LIKE TO LEARN MORE?
I'd like a drink of water. Guess
I've lost my spiritual thirst.
Tapwater, please, nothing difficult
to obtain a sip of. Not the milky
way, the Mississippi, or the cloudy
liquid Mexican peasant girls seeking
religious visions swalllow, hoping
to be made holy a moment.

123: *Elaine's Heart*

There's a street by my house
called *Coeur d'Alene* I've
gotten lost on. It's narrow,
with few houses, no lights.
Elaine's heart, full of ardor
and corpuscles, beats under
her sweater, but can't be
translated. You can fall for
her, and end up pacing, face
pale, almost erased, dark
circles under your eyes. Walk
into your living room and plop
down on the couch. Her old
Marlboro smoke wafts in from
the kitchen like mood music.
Indoors all day I read about

avalanches and floods, towns
sucked underground leaving gaps
in the map. This isn't what I
meant but I haven't drunk enough
to banish logic and really spill
something. Several revelations,
gin-and-tonics and tidal waves
later, I'm still staring out
the window. The night sky's
ironed out now, a limbo of dark
unformed stars. Small whirlwinds
of dead leaves stir up a slight
euphoria. I look down at the rug
that softens my footfall, blink
up at the light. If I could climb
some rungs back to those amazing
sensations, but it happened so fast.
I remember a big sinking feeling
that came in waves. I can't recapture
the shape and color of her sweater
with these black scratches. I wish
I'd stolen it.

124: *Dear Boy George*

Only three things on earth seem useful or soothing
to me. One: wearing stolen clothes. Two: photos of
exquisitely dressed redheads. Three: your voice
on the radio! Those songs fall smack-dab into my
range! Not to embarrass you with my raw American awe,
or let you think I'm the kinda girl who bends over
for any guy who plucks his eyebrows and can make tight
braids—but you're the plump bisexual cherub of
the eighties...clusters of Reuben's painted angels,
plus a dollop of the pillsbury dough boy, all rolled
into one! We could go skating, or just lie around
my house eating pineapple. I could pierce your ears:
I know how to freeze the lobes with ice so it doesn't
hurt. When I misunderstand your lyrics, they get even
better. I thought the line I'M YOUR LOVER, NOT YOUR
RIVAL was I'M ANOTHER, NOT THE BIBLE, or PRIME
YOUR MOTHER, NOT A LIBEL, or UNDERCOVER BOUGHT
ARRIVAL. Great, huh? See, we're of like minds. I almost died

when I read in the *Times* how you saved that girl
from drowning...dived down and pulled the blubbering
sissy up. I'd give anything to be the limp, dripping
form you stumbled from the lake with, draped over your
pale, motherly arms in a grateful faint as your mascara
ran and ran.

125: *Head over Heels*
for Jocelyn Fisher

Earth looks boundless, bluegreen
and bright from this height. My
husband protected that globe
as though humanity were pick
of the litter of life forms.
He was used to pure yellow
suns, and peaceful beings,
now extinct, whose vision melted
metal. He communes with them
enclosed in a pillar of white
light. My love must seem dim
by comparison. Nights long ago,
he'd land on my balcony, knock
softly, and when I'd open up
say "I know it's late Lois,
but I was flying by and saw
your light." I never should
have left Metropolis and retired
to his Fortress of Solitude.
Now I nag: "Keep those X-ray
eyes to yourself, with the baby
due." He sees a comet streak by
and looks lost; dreams of alien
vegetation. I keep remembering
manhole steam in winter, that
giant hot breath lifting my skirt.

126: *Invisible Hand*

Tailspin over Canada. Winter forever.
Last thing I remember, engine froze.
Thought, word and deed disposed of.

Was that an owl that swooped down,
awful blind bird, flapping like that?
O Bert, are you still warm at home?
Shhh, lie quiet till the doctor comes;
my heart his kingdom, my backbone his
ladder. The repose food, water and
legwork only postpone. When I was five,
butterflies ripened, rather unraveled,
on a bedraggled trellis outside my
window. Now I'm a cocoon too, wrapped
up like a black widow's dinner in this
silly linen. What's the matter, risk,
rush, whisper, radio command, oxygen
mask? I've lost my pearl earring, gone
hard of hearing. Whose loose teeth?
Blue wind/black heat/warm hands/blood
loss/cold feet/gas smell/dim qualms/
white diet/I'm just a quick sketch/
settle for less and less and less

It's so quiet here.
The water's so blue.
The weather's unbelieveable:
cool breezes and white clouds.
"The thrill of well-being beyond
expression" the only expression
on anyone's face. Sincerely wish
you were here, but you're down
there, in that shady cafe, drinking
beer, like the doctor told you not to.
I still think of you every day
in a lovely, vague, limited way,
but hemmed in by your tweed suit,
shingled roof, the Rocky Mountains
and current calendar year, dazed
and jaded, your mind's a blank
as you shiver in tune with an icy
season. Who got my lingere, bike,
map of Manhattan? I miss manmade
things, clocks for instance, and
wearing your leather jacket. But
for some reason today, a field
of green broccoli filled my mind's
eye, then an invisible hand wiped
the thought away.

127: *Recitation*

I wake today in a strange room
with a souvenir bruise on my lip.
There's a cracked plaster saint
in the corner wearing sunglasses
and a dunce cap. Looks like I've
fallen into lapsed Catholic clutches
again, but better being lost in
the thick of this ignorance than
living in the library where I spent
my childhood. My fellow victim looks
whittled-down and white against
the flowered sheet, in unearthly
winter light, wondering where
it's safe to rest his tired eyes.
Sivce there's some shred of prayer
for every occasion, teach me
the Novena for awakening cast out
of heaven, onto a loud green fold-up
couch, so far from my guardian angel's
sight she'd need field glasses, no
a telescope to find me. I have a
hangover and the sun hurts my eyes,
which feel newly peeled. Sweet saint
of the Impossible, where's the vision
to distinguish me from other silly
women? Behind my shut lids all I see
is a field alive with bees, drunk
and blond with pollen, and a million
mindless, idle lilies.

128: *Song of the Sperm who Missed the Target*

Gosh, we're lost. We've been swimming for hours, too proud to slow down
and ask directions. Let's pull over now and look at our map. The names of
these towns HARMONY SPRINGS, MOTHER'S ARMS, BUTTERFAT
LAKE are great. Hope we reach them someday. "Stupid misguided globs"
the other cells jeer at us. "You'd lose your tails if they weren't bonded on.
You'll never get anywhere. Bloodless, lungless nothings. Why don't you
trade places with an overworked nerve, do something useful?"

129: *Mother and Son*

Now you're old enough to hear about the night you were
conceived.
No, mother, I don't want to know.
Nonsense, it might explain your behavior.
I sustained some minor injuries that time. Maybe I should
lie down, with a cold wet washcloth across my forehead,
to help me remember. There, that's better. I'll describe
how I had to buy orange lipstick the next morning at the
five and dime to camouflage my bruised mouth. Then I'll
tell about the black belt, white vow, the lie to the doctor,
the ice cubes, the percolator, and much later, the salad
tongs and spatula. Darling, your legacy. You want to lie
down too? Naturally, you're about to ask how I chose
him. I could fib and say his moral intelligence impressed
me. In fact, it was an olfactory decision: the scent of his
sweat, if this makes sense, seemed to harmonize with
mine. I couldn't tell the smells apart, and I spend hours
trying. To my surprise, I got pregnant, though I felt like
I'd been confined in a soundproof booth the whole time,
while outside music was played and taped, which at some
later date I'd be expected to identify.

130: *Christy's Alpine Inn*

All this loosened emotion
crunches underfoot like snow.
That last avalanche soaked
my new tourists' boots.
Expert Alpine Cyclists just
whizz past and snicker.
If you laugh at me, I'll
suffocate myself with my
muffler, I swear. Would
you untie my wet shoelaces
before icicles form? You're
sighing. Sad? Romance
exhausted so soon, with
half my trousseau still
in boxes? Sing to me in
your shy, masculine bass,

while our sleigh waits.
Your beard feels like eider-
down, not stubble. Today:
lettuce, salmon, and cocoa
on a silver tray. Tomorrow
we reach Sicily: sunstroke
and pizza. You're so sure
of yourself, like the well
scrubbed bar maid who hoists
beer steins. I'm easily
disenchanted, and sorely
miss your cliches and kisses
when they don't flurry around
me like a storm of feather
pillow stuffing. When I rest,
I think perhaps our descendants
should honeymoon in these Alps,
where everything that's said echoes.

David Trinidad

131: *Ordinary Things*

On the patio, next
to a large, rather
awkwardly-transplanted
bromeliad, sits
the blackened hibachi
that hasn't been used
since last summer
when a number
of us, who knew you
intimately, got to-
gether to commemorate
the first anniversary
of your death.

It wasn't much
of an afternoon.
For the most part
I was quiet, kept
myself preoccupied
while everyone ate
and talked about
ordinary (it seemed
to me) things.
Your name came up
once or twice—
I can't remember
in what context.
No one cried.

After we hugged
and kissed each other
good-bye, I rinsed
the glasses and plates
and placed them

in the dishwasher. I
sat down and listened
to music (your
records — they were
all scratched).
I chain-smoked and
drank until I was
numb enough to fall
asleep without
reexperiencing
that impact —
one set of headlights
abruptly intercepted
by another, the unut-
terable welding of
metal to flesh —
instant blackness.

This year it
is different.
Everyone is off
doing the things
students usually
do after graduating
from college:
marrying, starting
families, making
lots of money at
jobs you would
have thought out
of character for
your friends —
such a *gifted* group.

I light a cigarette,
sip at this scotch.
In it, there is one
small ice cube left.
It is still warm out-
side, although it
is getting late.
It is very quiet and
the light is faint.

The telephone rings. For a split
second she panics, can't focus:
in front of her the television
is high-pitched, an indistinct
pattern she'd slept in spite of.
She clutches the remote control
—the screen flickers off. The
telephone rings again. She pushes
herself from the couch, crosses
the living room sucking in breath
like a long drag on one of her
menthol cigarettes, stops, clears
her throat, lifts the receiver
as it starts to ring a third time.
"Hello." Silence. "Hello." The line
goes dead. She hangs up irritated
yet relieved. No, that was weeks
ago; no, weeks before that—the
countless arrangements and sympathy
cards—that she was terrified of
the telephone ringing in the middle
of the night. Terrified of everything, really, although a part
of her felt numb because it had
become familiar—the parking lot,
lobby, elevator and corridors; the
matter-of-fact tone of the nurses
and hospital operators. Terrified
of meeting her daughter's sunken
eyes, of seeing that fluid seep
through a tube toward the needle
sewn into her wrist. Terrified
of the doctor, his warning that
it could spread quickly once he
"opens her up." In the kitchen, she
chases a shot of whiskey with tap
water, then turns off the lamps,
feels her way along the dark
hall, and lies down on the bed
without undressing. Beside her,
her husband snores. The shutters
slice the light from the street

across the walls and ceiling.
She closes her eyes and pictures
her daughter in their backyard,
on an afternoon years before. She
wears a pink dress; her blonde
hair is in braids. Blindfolded,
she waves her arms and takes
little steps toward the other
children who hold hands and dance
in a circle around her. Later,
she unwraps gifts — a bottle of
bubble bath, an aluminum tea
service — then sits at the picnic
table as the lit cake is set in
front of her, her eyes shut tight.
She makes a wish, opens them
wide, and with one swift breath
blows all eight candles out.

133: *Song*

This single by the all-girl group
   I worshipped as an adolescent
sounds exactly like it did on
      countless summer after-
   noons. Those teenage emotions
   survive too — so very seriously
      thoughtless as ever.

134: *Monday, Monday*

Radio's reality when
the hits just keep
happening: "I want
to kiss like lovers
do...." Why is it
I've always mistaken
these lyrics for my
true feelings? The
disc jockey says it's
spring and instantly

I'm filled with such
joy! Is it possible
that I'm experiencing
nature for the first
time? In the morning
the sun wakes me
and I am genuinely
moved, almost happy
to be alive. For a
couple of weeks it'd
been getting a little
bit brighter every
day. I wasn't aware
of this change until
the morning I noticed
the angle at which
the light hit your
GQ calendar, fully
accentuating the aus-
tere features of this
month's male model, as
I sat in the kitchen,
in your maroon robe,
and waited for my tea
to cool. I was thinking
about my feelings, about
how much I loved the sun
when I was a child and
how I loved the dark
as well, how thrilling
it was to lay in bed
on windy nights and
listen to the sound of
bushes and branches being
thrashed about outside.

Actually, that's what
I was thinking while
you were making the tea.
I was staring at the
calendar, at the smoke
from the tip of my
cigarette as it drifted
in the sunlight toward
the open window, when
you set the steaming

fifties-style cup in
front of me. Was it
at this point that
my manner changed?
Your gesture reminded
me of innumerable
mornings spent with
my parents in the pink
kitchen of my childhood.
I remembered my mother,
how she always wore her
gaudy floral bathrobe
and shuffled about in
her bedroom slippers as
she dutifully served us
breakfast. My father
sat alone at one end
of the table, his stern
face all but hidden
behind the front page
of the *Los Angeles Times*.
They seldom spoke. I
felt the tension between
them, watched with sleep-
filled eyes as he gave
her the obligatory kiss
on the cheek, then
clicked his briefcase
shut and, without a word,
walked out the door.

As I was getting dressed,
you grabbed me, kissed
me on the lips, said
something romantic.
I left your apartment
feeling confused, got
on the freeway and
inched my way through
the bumper-to-bumper
traffic. I was confused
about sex, about the
unexpected ambivalence
which, the night before,
prompted my hesitancy
and nonchalant attitude:

"It's late," I said,
"let's just sleep."
The cars ahead of me
wouldn't budge. I
turned on the radio and
started changing stations.
I was afraid I would
always be that anxious,
that self-obsessed, that
I might never be able
to handle a mature
relationship. Stuck on
the freeway like that,
I was tempted to get
into it, the pain and
the drama, but the mood
soon passed. (After
all, it *is* spring.)
At last, traffic picked
up and I enjoyed the
rest of the drive, kept
the radio on all
the way to work and
listened to all those
songs, though I finally
realized those songs
were no longer my feelings.

Dennis Cooper

135: *Winchester Cathedral*

There's a face in the back of my mind like a
stained glass window that throws its light on
my lines. Brian Winchester's its name. It

is my subject, like "God" was the subject of
the cathredral thus named. If it's hard to
imagine in this time, it was harder to look

at the light in his eyes, though what I
could see there was admirable, cum laude,
literally. One night he was small and cold

at the crown of the nearest church tower,
a star in the lighting intended to separate
it from the skyline's less known, then he

leapt to the foyer. My hand is falling
to earth. As it touches it scribbles poems
lit from inside. I wish they were lines of

cocaine, less like dust on a place I admire,
the window which brightens my room when it's
sunny outside. Writing a poem in his likeness

I make it as light as the feelings that form
in his wake. Just as black men lugged stones
on their backs many moons to build that church

on the horizon, I've carried these words for
a while, and throw them like rice when he
enters. A mechanical glow from my writing

is changing from heaven to hell with the love
that has colored my lines. Brian Winchester
come home. It feels like a cathedral now.

136: *For Mark Stephens*

My mother drank, and she sat
in a house the size of the Hilton
in one small room, at a black
grand piano, through cigarette
smoke, by a dinner so old it
cracked like dried mud. A tune
created her mood. Some whim
was letting her play the same
exercise seventeen times. She
had been smart in the Fifties.
She was not handsome, but she
was composed, made me between
vodkas. My room was up one
or more of the stairways, left
down the hall, left again. I
knelt there, twisted a knob and
rock music rose genie-like in
the room, gripped me and took
me away. I'd leap in my room,
hand strumming my belt like a
rock star, lip-synching what
hid my new thoughts in my body.
When my sister split, there
were places to hide in the
mansion. Piles of her junk
became far distant planets.
I couldn't quite build a
transporter, though I hung up
black lights, sheets over
lamps, played songs at half-speed.
I thought if I darkened
the room, blurred sofas, sat
there, that might be heaven,
controlled by one light switch
like LSD hinted. Hearing a
song, I went up. Downstairs
my mother got drunk all alone.
Knowing that I was nearby she

would wobble to the piano,
plop down and play the one
piece she learned from lessons,
her body bent forward, with
spit on her lips, eyes shining.
The melody rose through her
clutches, was part of the world
that corraled where even her
hands couldn't snuff it. The
music sank through the ceiling
to where I'd crouch dreaming,
host to the tingle of darkness.
It touched in a way I couldn't
shrug off. Doped, far away
from my life, I listened, and
it reached out and caressed me.

137: *The Blank Generation*

for Rik L. Kik

The future fills you
in with a question.
You answer, "Death,"
get your face on the
lid of SLASH Magazine.

It's as if someone
unchained your hands.
Your scratch yourself.
You break a bottle
on your head onstage

and get popular fast.
Kids like to watch
you more than movies,
then they're bored
no matter what you do.

You hate them all.
You speak their minds
writing poems and songs
black with mistakes.
They know what you mean.

You're not on drugs.
You're not singing to
get in their pants.
You see yourself dead.
You scream yourself hoarse.

138: *Being Aware*

Men are drawn to my ass by
my death-trance blue eyes
and black hair, tiny outfit,
while my father is home with
a girl, moved by the things
I could never think clearly.

Men smudge me onto a bed,
drug me stupid, gossip and
photograph me till I'm famous
in alleys, like one of those
jerk offs who stare from
the porno I sort of admire.

I'm fifteen. Screwing means
more to the men than to me.
I daydream right through it
while money puts chills on
my arms, from this to that
grip. I was meant to be naked.

Hey, Dad, it's been like this
for decades. I was always
approached by your type, given
dollars for hours. I took a
deep breath, stripped and they
never forgot how I trembled.

It means tons to me. Aside
from the obvious heaven
when cumming, there's times
I'm with them that I'm happy
or know what the other guy
feels, which is progress.

Or, nights when I'm angry,
if in a man's arms moving
slowly to the quietest music —
his hands on my arms, in my
hands, in the small of my back
take me back before everything.

139: *Drugs*

A friend dies one night,
swallows too many pills
on his way to a party
and grows pale as dust
in a shaft of moonlight.
You long to reach him
again, all your life.
A priest says you'll
find him in the future
under cover of death;
you will stand sing
near his glowing side.
We tell you to join us,
get loaded, forget him.
One day you shoot so
much stuff you fall over.
You hope to see him but
only grow clammy, more
stupid, like someone on
quaaludes. Now you and
he walk the same clouds
only when we've been
stoned and think back
on our lives, full of
dead bodies, and bright
now as heaven behind us.

140: *My Choice*

for Julian Andes

My friend looks at the guys I land on
at parties, even at concerts where

he keeps his eye on the music. He asks,
"Why scummy ones?" Why settle for
boyfriends with dirty, robbed lives?
With my looks I could have anyone,
he says. The fact is that my friend
is often alone, moaning about some
distance, its unfairness, its light-
headedness. I tell him that I picked
my type at a young age, from pornos
stuffed under a mattress, in crouched
down old movie halls. I am used to
their style: hello spoken straight
to a kiss, handshakes right to the
body. Plus, those guys are interesting,
individual and quite handsome in
a certain light. Besides, I understand that longing. I feel bold in
their interest. My friend can wait if
he wants to. I'm hungry and I'll eat.

141: *Hustlers*

for Jerry Patterson

Two beers screw my head up.
I lean back against a dark wall.
My long hair drifts in my eyes.
Let's say the moon makes a decision.
I land the corner legend surrounds.
I say more than I pretend to.
I prefer to be fucked to The Beatles.
I stand with the guys I resemble.
Jerry, Tom, Dick, Sam, Julian, Max, Timmy.
Guess which of those names is perfect.
We dream of a casual million.
We light our cigarettes gently.
I take what the night has to offer.
I roll a ripe peach from one wrist to the other.
I can't speak I'm so fucking stupid.
Our bodies are simply stupendous.
When we breathe, it takes us apart.
You know. You're inside us.

142: *Kip*

"Kip" lies in my bed with his clothes
around like exhaust, and there is
a smile on his lips, as there is an
undertow in the river outside the
smoke-yellowed window, cooling people
and rushing them off. His underwear
seems to have come from inside him,
like breath on my mirror, where he
scribbled his price, so, when I took
my turn pissing, I'd know the cost
without asking, ruining my mood,
which appears to be callous. I
stand at bed's end and order him to
a position, crouching a little to
look up his ass, where I want to
end up the evening in sweat and a
sharp little moment. He has been
fucked hundreds of times. Naked,
his value is present, and a well-
fucked hole is its presence. But
I'm being too clinical. This is
the flesh that belongs to the face
I decided I needed. So I fuck it,
make the most of the "Kip" who's
available, whose resemblance to
something I own is striking, whose
ass I am striking with the palm
of my hand, whose eyes, vaguely
mascaraed, keep what they believe
close to them, like a tenement
child with its one scrawny talent,
protecting it, as if lovers wanted
to steal it. They want to see it
flawing his eyes with an endless-
ness, which leaves him like this.

143: *For My Birthday*

After much talk and laughter
friends are buying a whore,

one I couldn't worm from
the bars with a toothy smile.
He will be fairly beautiful.
They have shopped the foul
alleys of Selma, finding red
hair and eyes with dark powers.
On the night of my birth I'll
proceed to a particular motel.
At an appointed moment someo
will knock two times and enter.
It will be my gift, paid up
until morning, and I'll try
to talk with him first, then
just give up and rattle him
orders that he'll understand
or embellish, teaching me love
the easy way: arms obligated
to take me, repaying each kiss,
caressing by reflex. I'll be
nice to him, hoping he might
contract my desire, knowing he'll
ditch me when his watch strikes
day, anxious for a real fuck or
someone who speaks his language,
as dull and slurred as that is.

 *Abba*

for Brad Gooch

We snort all our coke
on the way to the party.
We bring the new album.
We dance while we listen.

The band is two women
whose husbands control them.
They do not speak our language.
Each syllable's an obstacle.

They are in love with a man.
He is in love with another.
But they're in no hurry.
They could wait forever.

And when they are out
on the make for a lover,
they'll always find him.
They are the tigers.

We are too stoned to.
We dance till we're tired
and listen to lyrics
we mouth like a language.

What we feel, when we
hear them, is inexpressible.
We can't put it in words.
Maybe our dances show it.

Abba lives for their music.
We long for each other.
They see what we're doing.
They put it on record.

They play it, we listen.
We are absolutely stunned.
We feel, and they know
more than anyone can say.

Jack Skelley

145: *Planet of Toys*

When I was frozen the world was warm enough,
I couldn't swim but the seas were still metalized,
no way to go and no where to get to.
Then I requested my first weekend snow rabbit,
and the cranky elders called me forward.
"Steer clear of the southern domes," they intoned.
"Mister Machine keeps the city streets burning,
and will sooner eat you than heat you." But I was uncurious—
I had seen the bushes blaze communing
on my balcony at midnight, and now flew up
to the bluest hangnail moons the mountains touch.
But when Binky clanked dead on me one night
after the power caves were closed,
my only resort was a blood-red pillar
flaming near the black hemisphere.
I was magnetized, of course, long before I set my probes,
or got out the hooks and cables, long
before I landed, or caught the smell the ice makes
when antique cavities are seeping through the cracks,
or heard him hissing always around the next corner;
and by the time I climbed on top of him,
my headlights too clanked closed.
Then, Wammo! What a blast!
Trucks don't pop those ballooons,
they're too big, colored bubbles making
worlds multiply, and mind-babies busting out instead—
"The end of all this mechanical foreplay," he concluded;
"No way," I said, "let's get on it again."
I was only fourteen, but I felt ages
of fire pulling up from the gyrations of insurgents
to come; and now I'm warning all you cool girls, yeah,
you'll get wet at the bottom, but it feels good in the summer.

146: *Helium Kid in Space Mountain*

I had the whole car to myself,
blazing to the bone, science fiction city,
screaming my head off through comets and cluster
and the 2-D doughnut that rolls around,
until, taking that last turn speeding down
through total black to hit a thousand white
explosions, my car jerked still,
all lights frozen and this pimply
employee with a flashlight and cap was saying
stay in your seat and no flashes when I knew another
car was speeding down the track to smash
mine if I didn't say OK and get moving,
closing my eyes hard to bring on the black
and opening them again to the dark wind.

147: *Genius of Love*

I see New York in the sky,
from some patio jacuzzi at midnight
as the Tom Tom club comes on
and everybody's swimming through
their own personal millenium.
But hey, you are cutting
a melodious gyre when you shoot
your blue eyes my way.
I try to keep cool, but
my desire is showing through:
we're gonna have some fun.

You and I, we're so mutually jazzed,
it's like we're way jamming
in the world's tightest groove band,
in a ten-tired disco paradiso,
its empyrean spotlight on the
smartest dancers, instruments
in perfect harmony and synch,
awesome delight flashing over
young faces everywhere.
And by the time we're back to my place,
heaven is absolutely happening
for these two bodies that burn in the dark.

Then the whole thing eases into blank
and the worthiness of earth
no longer worries us.
We're traversing planets
with our serene encircling,
we're into the firmament.

And when you finally have to leave, yeah, I'm bummed:
one more corporeal universe has collapsed.
But I know the sky still hangs there in the dark,
though everything else seems to fall apart.

148: *Emergency*

It's still dark, my chest is hollow, and aches,
salt tears drop onto my overcooked oatmeal,
then I must go out and meet the masses —
whole shoals of ruined spirits that flop
around my path like grunion, or echo dumb
replies like Chatty Cathies. I want to shout
through the cut-out slot I breathe through,
but I'm drowned out by the shrieking of these corpses
from their burning tombs: hell's great heresiarchs
compelling us to shrink from our desires.

Yet sometimes, in line for my lunchtime burrito,
I catch sight of two eyes, a nose, the lips
of a pretty saint, who points salaciously toward heaven.
Then I think of you, believe again in miracles.
Maybe I can get you on the phone tonight.

And by the time I'm making dinner, I'm not
so much another big dummy, as a Lazarus
ready to rejoin the living: I have killed
my puppet, that grim traitor, and I autonomously
walk and talk. So I put on a record
and actually dance as the Whispers are moaning, "Operator,
Got to talk to her, This is an emergency!"
But when I finally call, no one answers.
Over there it's three hours later.
Where could you be? A big emptiness
begins to gulp me up, and the drift
of burning fish follows from the kitchen.

149: *Doctrine of Plenitude*

I am able to understand my confusion.
I was sitting purposeless, I was distracted
by the dressing of limbs, the parting of lips, I drew
another virile demon or ethereal goddess
from a blank dark: sweat beads on the neck,
down the butt crack, the eyes vacant,
open a slit, a quick gasp, and our biological
priest has mounted his pulpit another time.
And what a majestic pulpit it is! I could
see the gilded ceiling of the cathedral reflecting
beams of light through a part in the curtain. Recalling
that light, I saw there was no need to go
outside of myself. Wanting nothing for use,
needing nothing for replenishment, it was not on account
of desire nor constraint that I ended this black sacrament

The mind of some great architect might
have conceived ten thousand other possible
worlds than this. But this is the best world
for the purpose that I have in mind. There
is a face I want to see and see. There
are those hips my hands would cup around and lift
and spin. There is my chamber turning past
midnight again, as the walls spin out
and the stars zoom down and the flesh burns up.
The sky is inside this person's skin, clouds
swell warm beneath my fingers and there is
a pullulating stretch under my skull,
a hot series of thoughts — this breathes
ancient light from the planets when they quake
          on the horizon.
I can diagnose the groans of the biggest
machine. The ocean's growl articulates a song
that I've been humming.

                         I am the sire inseminating
not from urge but momentum. I incorporate
myself worldwide and centralize the bread
and wine: everyone partakes and everyone is free
beneath me. If I enter us into war without explicit
declaration, I act in our name, just as the infected
blood of a father may pass on to a son

with a weakened intellect and will. The law of instinct
determines a rigorous end.

                      And I had foreseen
all of this. And when I leave I
shall take with me the spurt of energy
that flung our orbits, threw broad beams
across the vault, installed the lamps and switches.
And when I leave I shall liquidate my conglomerates:
my weapons factories will explode, my reactors
fuse, my drills and tankers will release
their crude. I'll get fed up with myself.
I will want my money back. I
will eat the indistinct elements, and,
in a big flash, body is heaven.

Ed Smith

150: *True or False*

Upwards of 60 percent of all airborne household dust
consists of all dead skin flakes by weight.

151: *Babysitting*

okay, now it's your turn to
look for the soap

152: *For Dry, Damaged Hair*

You know, it's probably
too expensive for you, but
the best thing really is
imported Yak semen. The
harvesters get up very early
to take extractions from
the male bulls. The semen
keeps better in the cold morning
chill. It's a closely guarded
secret. Women in Beverly
Hills buy it. I found out
about it through my connections
with the underworld.

153: *Anyway*

I can tell you I love you
more than the salt on my meat
but I rarely even use salt
and you're a vegetarian.

154: *Looking for Work*

"A job!? I thought I was supposed to get an old horse with a
life preserver around its neck!"

155: *Gifted*

God made me so I don't have to bend down to masturbate.

I can stand straight up if I want.

My arms are long enough.

156: *Please*

Please repress me
Please do your best to break my spirit
Please judge me
Please grade me
Please reward me and please punish me
Please teach me right from wrong
Please make me feel unimportant
Please make a mockery of my existence

157: *Untitled*

Imagine waking up
And finding
Blood on the sheets
That had come out of your body
In the night
In your sleep
And it was perfectly normal.

Imagine pissing with a hard-on.

158: *Untitled*

Today, I aspire to drunkenness
And to a long swim
Straight out from the shore
And tonight I'll sleep
In the same fetal position
That I'm standing in now.

Lewis MacAdams

159: *Cornerstones*

Truth is a lock.
Poetry is work.
One cup of coffee
with a glazed do-nut,
ham from a microwave to go.

The Dairymen's Co-op trucks
bounce over the gravel
and rumble up the San Joaquin.
The only politics is immortality —
that is, whose wave and thrusts
align themselves
with the root and growth principle
of the world.

160: *Solitude Conundrum*

The cigarette smoke curls
around me in the one
bright light above my head.
If it is true
what the Buddhists say —
self-disgust
is the first step toward enlightenment —
then I am on the road
again.

Dear Lord of language,
of gestures and of moves,
lead me on.

161: *Moguls and Monks*

A dollar-green Cadillac limousine
pulls from the gate at Paramount
and turns down Melrose.
The mogul passenger leans his bald head
back on his head rest and smiles,
his face a mass of pure contentment

as two Buddhist monks bow by,
waiting at the corner for the light to change
so they can bow across Gower.
Though they don't see each other, I am them both
as I turn up Highland, cruising
in the twelve spiritual
directions, with the
thirteen calls for cash.

But last night I met someone who was fine.

Fates, be kind.

162: *Trumps*

Selfish babies dressed up for
affection and display. Quiet desperation
is starting off the day with a giant coffee
and a roach. Lord,
how the spirit hates to be alone.
How it seeks the Other, because it knows
it shall expire
without the fire.
So the prayers go up
from the laughing ladies and their ferocious dudes,
season after season and beyond—
Love, do I have to cry your name out one more time?
When will you come to me
in some form I can handle?

163: *"new moon fading"*

New moon fading.
Culver City before dawn in the rain,
inky mile after gridded mile.
Forgot my sandwiches
so I missed my bus, had to race
past the Venice post office twice,
ghostly figure past the Ace Gallery
with a sack lunch and a book
chasing the 6:39. I think
we'll call this one "Work Moon"
because we're going to
work. We're going to
work, work, work. We're going to
work, work, work, work, work, work, work.
"He who digs Los Angeles *is* Los Angeles."
Los Angeles, you swallow up
nearly all the southwest's water,
nearly all its available air and light,
so you must give everything back enthusiastically
in story and song.

164: *"Malraux says to love someone"*

Malraux says to love someone is not to
hold that someone for marvelous,
but for indispensable.
The way seabreezes
skirt along the edge of the continent
that's how I want to reach you,
slip inside you like
a coastal weather change, a la
anything interesting happening over there, dearie?
Damn it, why don't you write me? C'mon, honey.
One fire, one desire.

165: *To Hughes Tool Company*

At the very last minute
I grab a bite to eat
and rattle into Playa Vista.
Wasted days and wasted nights and days is how I cruise
the urban wreckage, sift through the stiumuli for
ideals: Fox won't have a place to creep,
Hawk bereft of hunting grounds, no place for mallard duck
to rest on his migrations. I mean,
what's more important? Real estate millions
or the way sunset emblazons puff balls in the Ballonas Wetlands,
last wetlands left in L.A. County, delta where Ballonas Creek
and the Pacific Ocean do their seasonal dance to the tides.
Soon I'll be able to walk out here on a
redwood platform and buy souvenirs—cartoon ducks
in redwood taste—Playa Vista built by the Summa Corp.,
shadowy Howard Hughes Tool emanation conceived in Hughes'
sleazy twilight as a guest of the dictator in the sealed-off top floor
of the Managua, Nicaragua Holiday Inn. Soon there'll be more people
in Ballonas than in Century City, land where snowy egrets strolled
with scissor bills and curlews and great blue herons for thousands
and thousands of years! HUMAN RACISM!
                              Motorcycle policeman
that ticketed me for jaywalking
my first day in Los Angeles, tell me again
that you can't change Los Angeles.
Ducks fuck off around these parts. Deer, motherfucker, disappear.
Like a terrible freeway collision you don't want to
bum people out about, you can just take your Playa Vista subdivision
and slide it back out a black hole. Like children spilling
from the bed of a pick-up truck on a freeway at rush hour, blood-gallons
turning dark brown, we don't need Playa Vista.
We don't have to have it.
We're better off without it.

166: *Beirut*

Words, Lewis MacAdams, Lyrics, The Dark Bob
© 1982 High Performance Records

Beirut, for the last four nights I've been thinking
But my mind has been strangled up with fire.
So if I don't scream for you tonight, Beirut,

then I'm just another fucking liar.
Beirut, Beirut, Beirut.

Even though I'm mostly Jewish,
The dogs of war in the Israeli High Command
didn't do this for me.
But tonight, they got a finger pointing at 'em,
and it's at the end of a Palestinian baby's dead right hand.
And there's a lot of 'em, tonight,
buried in the rubble of Beirut.
Moderne, urbane, downtown, destroyed Beirut.

When those F-15's came screaming over
and all those people started to run,
it was those brave Israeli pilots and
all of us folks back home that made 'em and sold 'em the guns,
we killed 'em
killed all those babies...in Beirut.

Now I've never been to your city,
though I used to want to go there.
But last night on the television I saw your heart in flames.
And where I come from, I believe way too much in karma
not to have to be screamin' out your name —
yeah, in shame!
Oh, Beirut!!!!

Peter Levitt

167: *The Turn*

Right now there is a blue jay
startling a bush
of coral monkey flowers.
I want to talk with you.
Have you noticed the in-
cessant greenness of the leaves,
the way all the frogs either
chatter at once or suddenly
stop? How people seem to
likewise come and come
and then are gone? When
I look at my hands the twins
of Gemini are mere
abstraction and the love
there in the delicate
pale walls of my arteries
is all. Have you noticed
how everything is either
moving or standing still?
And eventually all that stops?

168: *"Mother you will die"*

Mother you will die
and I

will have spent
my whole

life trying
to regain

entrance to death
which was mine

at the start

169: *Reply to Lethe*

Of light
not much, even

such flame as sun
presents, itself drowning

the world transparent
into gulls, boats

objects of fame
on this dark bay

of shadow, echo
really, not much

but the song
itself, ferries across the water

170: *Practice*

I light a single stick of incense
on the altar. Smoke rises,
vanishing in air. Upstairs
a child with rosy cheeks is
coughing, turning over in a fevered
dream. Do not ask why I sweep
the matting, prune the coleus,
sit daily on the front porch
staring at the sun. With so much
work to do, I have no time to seek employment.

171: *Green Sonnet*

I smell of her wood
the sapling

& only she
knows why

when my sister comes running & says I love your hair
the way it smells & tangles her legs up around my beard
i tell her sis, this crystal you've left is the world &
then I kiss her, o don't I, but really, it isn't the world
& my sister's been dead I just taste her every time I see
the moon sail off to another sky & then I wander, o don't I
into the deep forest of the world & there when I'm alone
I strip off this skin & wade into the mist of green fern
breathing hard all around me & no one believe me no one
                    ever knows why

172: *The Boat*

Morning is a ghost
as it moves
                    through its dream,
mountain apes howling
back and forth to one another,
tossing insults like perfect
smooth stones
                    that fall
and clatter on the walls
of this canyon,
                    into ravines.
There is no way to rise
into the day,
                    through the quiet
shattering of light, which
scatters the pattern
of leaves
                    onto the surface
of this lake. There
is no way to quiet
these apes,

who fear the moon,
its darkness. Down,
against the wooden bow
of this boat, nightfish
are knocking. They will continue,
the small constant thud
of their bodies, a reminder,
as I tear upwards
                    through this mist
which gathers its skin
around me as I sleep.

O Moon, fruit of the night tree
& the night. Moon who is no different.
Dark lover of earth. Crescent moon.
Light whose body is the vessel,
and the tide. Here,
with your eye on my naked body,
is one old man
  in a boat, rowing.

173: *In the Chinese Post Card*

All those peachblossoms,
    like in the poems of Tao Yuanming,
& the thin black-barked
        tree limbs

    craning
above the river, &
            all the tawny wheat
        cut & stacked

& its wild blonde fragrance
    crackling the air, &
way down,
    close to the earth

a tiny black-haired figure,
    a girl,
        & way above her,
Condor Peak.

174: *The Red Camelia*

The red camelia we bought
and planted
                beneath our bedroom
window (because it knew
how to live beside the pine)
has proven the classical
beauty we hoped after all.
The first week its roots
took hold in the soil,
it was sturdy and a sudden
wind seemed to pass through
with transparent love. The
second week buds we had
only suspected, opened.
This week they only fall.
Though it is spring
and all else blossoms
around us
                they, in their cycle,
fall. I know there are hundreds
of ways to kneel
                and kiss the ground.
Rumi told us that. But
as I place my knees
firmly on the earth,
lifting the fully formed
blossoms, and cupping my hand,
each one is a tear
for me, precious
yet so quickly won.

175: *'Born to die'*

'Born to die'
who can deny it?

the simple fact
of all things

opening,
closing

on others,
ourselves

a fist
an eye

who would have it otherwise?
to hold what thing?

in what place?
Beauty? Love?

you're just not paying attention.
It all must go

if we're to breathe
again. The bandmaster

says it best:
and a one, and a two, and a three

176: *A Hasid Poet*

the dead rip their clothes
when they see him
— Reb Yaschalevich

In a place out of reach,
that's where the dead go

but it's very far
so far when they come back

(I mean when we do

we can't remember.
You ask how I got this way?
I tell you I'm not sure.

One day I went looking for the love
I had just the day before

but the dead sent me back,
said it wasn't my time.

177: *"Undiminished"*

Undiminished
the painful blowing out

of the eyes
and all that

could be seen.
It is our world.

Tin shacks
and the children

playing among them
like ragged flowers

a torn red dress
a flag

waving in the heated
afternoon. Our world

the soldiers marching
out marching in.

The sight which would go blind
undimmed.

178: *"Budding,"*

budding,
whether tender or dead

the fierce nakedness
of trees

is still to be seen
as they rise

out of the earth
(and yet stand above it)

transparent in a luminous wind
or cool

in the shadows
they shake down around themselves

and who has lived yet
so long

they are not held moist,
refracted in the eyes

whose silent longing
is just to see them

whose hidden sacred root
in what is unseen

stems from the heart —
we begin nothing,

we end nothing, and yet
are always at the source.

Martha Lifson

179: *Sesshu: Bodhidharma*

The bodhidharma is the eyeball of my neighbor' Paul
who works on cars all day, not just ordinary cars,
turquoise ones with whitewalls, his girlfriend's army jeep,
not just the low modern jeep, but, no,
this one's like a sedan from an old movie
where cops are chasing robbers down some Cleveland street
and railroad tracks cut straight through the middle of town,
sort of like Bucyrus where blueberry muffins are home-made
in my childhood on the way to Put-in-Bay
and necklaces I made summer after summer
out of small coiled shells until the back
of my closet was filled with strings of them
and sand. He stares at the wall endlessly.
He's cut off his lids; Paul's fixing the car;
I'm making another string of Lake Erie shells.

180: *Sitting in Juan's Restaurant*
All Afternoon, La Paz

There is no one to say what it looks like to
and no one, not even the one who speaks English
speaks my language anymore —
The can of beer smells of fish.
The boy's feet white from dust.
I have never sat so still for so long,
can no longer remember if it is hot
or if the wind has turned into a small boy
wearing an orange Jane Fonda on his chest.
It is such a long way to travel to sit still.
When we throw colored tissues on the ground
they float like fish.

181: *Photographs by Kertesz*

All nudes are distorted
and here we are taking off our clothes
again.
                    I knew someone once
who wore silk kimonos to bed every night
but more often it's this problem of

                    fitting together
seeing how the crooks are to go
and in the dark.

And illusions we carry, his that I am wise
and will impart it through the skin. Mine
that his warmth will make me unafraid
for days and days.

Of course we're not to blame,
it's the angle of knees to back,

                    of elbow to hair

how crooked we all appear and undefined
as if the brush forgets how to make
a straight line, as if

                    long ago

I was having trouble in school
because I couldn't see the blackboard.

182: *Elgin Marbles*

Their shoulders lie back in their sockets, they
insist on warmth, throw off drapery; their skin
grows hot. Innocent, uncouth,
asking all of us to come touch them,
pull off their marble clothes.
                                    Once
I saw a shoulder like that on a girl
larger than her age who knew how to come on,
who disdained anyone who'd lay a hand on her.

Blouses the color of naked skin, she cut
her hair almost completely off and sat
absolutely still: no one could touch her.

This time
in the vast hallway when the guard's back
was turned, I put my hand on the shoulder
of someone whose name is not known for sure.

183: *An Exhibition of Gorky at LACMA*

I've always seen those things
in abstract paintings but was embarrassed to say so and
now you tell me it's the newest theory about Gorky himself
that he wasn't solving problems about latter-day cubism
wasn't figuring out relationships of shapes
but was putting down that leaned-over ass just as I thought
all those toilets or at least the paper looks like porcelain
to me and that red smudge is certainly death anyone can see
that
and the green horned fuzz in the corner of that cheery one
is a sheep, it is a sheep, the whole work: pastorale.
Too bad
he couldn't've just stayed there but kept on moving while
that flowerlike scrawl of a lily turned metallic
turned flying petals of tin
knifed him in the back.

184: *Still Life*
(with brass bowl)

Like the dreams I had taking naps, flying
about the wallpapered room gazing at tearoses
and yellow ribbons wrapping up the wall
and keeping me from flying out the window
(avoiding that corner of the southwest room
I pivoted and hung, the brass bowl polished
to a sheen sits on a table edge so near
the edge it would fall to the floor if it
didn't float. Like a miracle. The fir

in the corner of our lot grows in each photograph
unitl it is larger than the house, until I am
completely grown, someone who never visits
and has no family left. They knew about
balance and about how things change
by increments through time like the face
of my father in the hospital bed resting
with half a brain for the last time.

185: *Still Life*

The exquisite juxtaposition of bodies,
the white, slightly bulged jar, the open box
(who knows what's inside) a pipe
leaning aslant the side, the flower is
bursting apart on the jar, hold this moment,
hold me, keep after me, make me finish,
the possibility of others urging us along
keeps us going even when they're gone,
the idea of them, thoughts of your vivid eyes
keeps my heart beating, a roman mosaic
for springtime, my love, give it to me,
bring peaches and sprigs, bunches of fern,
sweet violence in a multi-colored jar.

186: *from Conversations and Rooms:*
The Room

1
The room took them toward the ocean
by about 3 blocks
                              still they were
miles away. The moon had
risen and the landscape had been
graphed in circles: the trees planted in circular mud
the chandeliers throwing punched yellow dots
across the concrete mall.

The room followed close behind
but she had had
                              too much to drink
                              didn't notice she was getting nowhere.

2.
The carnival airbrushed
cowboys and -girls over the merry-go-round

> "come back tomorra" he said and she
> saw gold stars, circular patens of gold

on Wilshire insurance companies rake it in
she explained in a lofty sort of tone
he had returned to the room, shut the door
before she noticed they'd never left

> the black cloud followed them,
> overhanging

> for 7 complete blocks

and she was still standing
at the kitchen sink waiting
for him to move toward her or away.

187: *from Conversations and Rooms:* *Scenarios*

There were several possible ones: after
he left on the train, before her leaving
for good, or she never went at all. Desire

was this interruption. Quinces and mulberries
apples and trees, even the possibility
of lying next to each other before he said:
I wonder what I will think of this in three days.

She tried to arrange a twelve hour flight
that would make connection through
the same city. They might tour together
walking up steps by the sand where stairs curve,
air looks clean, smells of urine and sage.

He grabbed a poster of it, wooden cormorants
duplicated themselves across the canvas
a trompe-l'oeil on the other side:
clothesline letters hung up to dry.

She wrote him as often as she could,
he forgot to phone, she couldn't imagine what
to say. All this contained some version
of truth, some mouths and teeth, the boniness
of remembered feet at the end of a bed.

188: *Nishijin* *

for my sister

When we got lost the man from the elegant shop
who spoke little English said left at the Chinese
for Raku. You said, how the hell will we know
one from the other without the plastic food
they all look Japanese.
                              But we chanced a left
and the museum, displaying a large pink poster pot,
just what we wanted, was closed. I wanted so much
from you after all these years: girlhood and lawns,
no husbands, no children, nobody dead.

Walking arm in arm in skirts through narrow streets
I wanted to twirl until cloth stood out
from skinned knees, until freeze tag, until bed.

You think I remember too much, your children
crawl in and out of your lap, you stiffen
when I'm up early too. But that one day
when we got lost and didn't find Raku,
had to break down and take a cab, we laughed
until we cried and heard the steady whirr
of looms making cloth behind closed doors.

*Nishijin is the name of the silk-weaving district in Kyoto.
The name, meaning "Western Camp," harks back to the days
of internecine strife that raged in Kyoto during the 15th century.

Brooks Roddan

189: *The Moment You Became Marc Chagall*

I want you to prove that everything in the world
    is wrong,
to step behind the shadow of sight and sound.
The courageous breath of snow melting
has marched from the mountaintops
willing to change names
with us in mind.
It slips unnoticed into the void of a small village
    through the grace
of the sunlight that satisfies spring,
to become the black and white line drawing
    that lasts forever.
I want you to look at the world as ground
    no one else has covered,
with a new sense of time on your side;
to consider the God who made more colors than words,
    the God
who wants something done.
I want you to think of the shape the earth
    gets away with,
the circle spinning in mid-air, the beginning that had
    no visible means of support,
that suspended sensitivity we survive on. The stars
stretch their imaginations with the light
    handed down
through centuries, the light that is always new.
I want you to show the true colors, the colors
    that accept suffering,
the conquerors breaking open the blood clouds,
the blurred civilizations and continents
that had no idea where their breath went,
    the people
who woke in the middle of the night, crying,
holding fast to colors that refused to join cults.

I want you to use the green, the memory
    that serves you,
to get attention in the tree of change,
in the lake of losing control,
in the faces of those from the countries
    love was asked to leave.
I ask you to save the dead souls
    from themselves,
lessen the tenseness in the trees, increase the love
among the animals that live together,
give time back its true being, its nothingness, its movement
    from one thing to another,
the lie it is telling the world.
I can see you going to the windows
    of the century,
crossing the bridge of Carl Jung,
    taking
the crucifixion from his hands
    and changing it.
I see you, the diplomat of dreams,
    freeing
the cow from the pressure of the pasture,
giving the bride her black gloves.
I want you to close your eyes and hear
    the world
end on a bad note,
and bring back the light that is lord
    of the landscape.

190: *The Days Are Numbered*

Rumi, the great poet, was thirty-seven when he started to write.
Writing was a wandering in and out of mountains,
crossing rivers, coming face to face with the whirlwind
named for the One who said nothing.
Rumi listened too hard he heard time going by in the verbs.
At my age I should be preparing
some way to come to terms with this silence.

191: *Toward a Poetry that Is Strange and Comprehendable*

The word white has no meaning.
The world has been made and remade
and waits for its afterlife.
The sea drys itself off, crabs crawl like guilt
    losing and regrowing limbs,
their sins forgiven.
Worksheets are scrubbed clean.
The word black writes its memoirs.
When something doesn't move that doesn't mean
    it's dead.
When something moves that doesn't mean it's living.
Life and death.
Death and life.

192: *Seven Lines that Aren't the Lord's Prayer*

I am my father's thin child.
In this body his name gathers the goodwill no one knows.
The world is the question he won't ask.
His breath believes in the law, his spirit has second thoughts.
Free will is the myth he carries on his shoulders.
The stone he thought of has become the mountain.
The world began with the power of the lost.

Holly Prado

193: *Rises in the Evening More Daylight*

the room fills with
a weaving from peru its natural dyes its lavenders
uneven and beautiful
which is my planning the last letter I'll ever write
then my hand to my face to remind me of stubbornness
this face
it is a visit from a stranger a visit from a sister
I give up the story that I was a happy child

black wool diamond in the center
with a stripe through it like sudden rain
pure grace
but paid for over and over if anything is to be whole is to be
colors purged from insects   squeezed from plants
applied to thread   combined with other thread
worked then finished

hour after hour
shape and weight and length
the handfuls of what I might have lived
what I do live
when someone says "you're so serious"
I think "not serious enough"
there are so many imitations

194: *By Seasonal Odor*

my mother's suicide of cancer
though she loved gardens loved sweet fruit
brown bear brown woman honey on the paw

sometimes there is nothing I want but fur
as a child I'd pray but find myself asleep

a recurring dream of animals who licked a magic bone
who never had to cry again

twenty-five years of grief
midwinter it is time to mate
today I have a body
oh bear the larger heart
bear
·wisest in healing
will dig herbs will set bones

if I have lost my trust because one woman died
because I had to be a man too young because I have not made a home
dark nest bright cave
then it is time to bring the forest back to life
if the wound is deep enough it's clean
I was born in spring an animal
daughter of mud

the bear stands in its own smell in the smell of its young
the bear's claw passes its power to the sick
I crouch I growl low in a dream
my shadow insists that I'm the sex I've always been
this shaggy coat gives me my shoulders the tension turns to
muscle the muscle turns to heat I lift myself

ancestors those young girls who dressed to worship artemis as bear
blood under the pine tree

be innocent begin in mud
I wash vegetables in the sink
such skins I wash this morning
the man I love and winter blankets
he kissed me he licked me awake

cancer means the cells as abberations
too much eats nothing but itself
what was in my mother's heart
she gave me
fear
what is loved dies
that's what I thought
the man watches me take a bath I know he won't hurt me he likes
to see me warm clean naked
I do not cover myself from him

today I have a body
hot fat yeasty
something close to the one I may grow
if I refuse nothing
the upright stance the growl
the lightning paw that reaches out to stare to understand

brown earth brown fur brown
weeds the memories be
patient
brown
the eyes of the bear look back at me

195: *After Struggling with the Mystery of It All*

I go to the zoo to the bears large black
two mate in front of me
so sure this male bear so sure this female bear
they fuck and rest fuck and rest fuck and rest
steady faces with no sense of time they are not
artemis they are not
the constellation named for the bear who turns the world they are not
the skin that hangs in the museum once worn by a tribe for vengeance
they are two healthy bears
"oh gosh" a child says "they must love each other"

196: *The Wind the Question of What It Will Do Next*

let it take the last gesture of perfection

my language flattens as I saw a friend
flatten cloves of garlic with the side of a knife
to make them workable

rhythm comes and goes and laughs to see us search for it
when we are breathing all the time

through every window
restless damage and reeking of what is ready to be used

197: *How Words Are Said*

ferns the earliest yet did not shrink to fossils
the excellence of string quartets
old wounds even the scars I touch
hurt
even friendship I have given wounds myself
cello the ferns so much my language
the rooted things each frond its family shape
eons
the earth in layers each scar another seed
removes all doubt
on and on the music on and on
my hands I do not want them any softer
every pulse the memory of every other pulse

198: *from Dream Combinations:*
Generations

black grape skin covers ribs beneath my dress.
covers breast loaves. covers breast horns.

little girl dolls. their arms and legs and heads make a stew.
one a squawking duck mouth.
one a rubber map of lumps. the most crooked nose.

without a mother I eat the child.
black juice, gradually, under the dress.

half mad eater of dolls. lover of dolls. tear them.

even to bone the yearning when I wake up.
the house where I kill to make blood flow.
crippled walking. major resurrection.
obscene and worn out thrift shop clothes ready for another
         color.
rose occurs and occurs. even limping, I eat.

one a butterfly with plastic cheeks.

it takes so much sex to grow fat on myself.
lip force. flesh knock. the juice ferments.
break up housekeeping: half mad guilt in the lap of leafy
         faith.
I carry it everywhere with me. I watch the colors change.
I bury what's left.

199: *from Dream Combinations: Brooms*

ordinary soap. childhood vagina. stone bud.
the house when everyone's gone.
my own gift. no visitors.

dead grandma. she won't talk.
under my panties. ritual lips.

dead grandma I want your eggs. freckled.
the good advice. your map. tell me your chin.
wind blows your flowers off the china plates.
I keep a juicy orange.
hot old grandma. blood calendar. earth furnace.

come on. our names. eggs.
talk to me in the living room. we both love cats.

you a funeral but a big meadow and even more wheat.
me a lamb kiss. moist stone. lonely.

200: *from Dream Combinations: One Memory Wheel*

ragged heart bread. I escape but still look back.
his puckered lips. all that sunburn.
once he kept me waiting. I waited. he married webs.
I was the seed of a knuckle.
ragged scrap. the fist.

when I had pulse luck.
fast medicine. that star moon skirt.
could be a snake on my head. all those roses on the shoes.
this skirt flames down my legs.

ragged spark. at least my own forest without puckering.

hermit mouth into the distance.
bare hands and vinegar and sugar. fist rose.

201: *Folk Tale*

nothing has ever belonged to me
but what I've called loss returns as souls
october teaches me its first day
in the death of my young friend
five years ago her tumored hands
failing   shaking
when we talked we talked of breath
deeply more deeply breathe more deeply
then breath was gone but not her myth of cures

october
someone has stopped crying to rise   to dress   to meet cold weather
someone has forgiven the city its violence
someone has planted zinnias in a bathtub in a parking lot
someone has learned the exquisite hardship of sanity

spirits everywhere not waiting for spring
here they come unmasked
I read a russian woman's life
her friends memorized her poems when it was too dangerous to write
    them down
my own nordic ancestors set harps in their graves
ladders to the next world
our myths   our souls
the first day of october I follow the twigs cracking
laying their patterns right under my feet

a friend tells me she has a good idea
a friend tells me she has found one laugh in the middle of an argument
a friend tells me he has lived through a meaningless war
a friend tells me a child has been born at home
a friend tells me nothing but hearing her voice
convinces me to give up hunching my shoulders for the relief of saying
all the poets   all the friends   all the dead who are not the withered
    dead but

new
they forgive death   they know they have helped
deeply more deeply breathe more deeply
the endless exchange   the endless inheritance   the endless
living and dying
take a risk
nuts split   their meat falls in its pieces

small lamps from the bonfire where the masks are burned

202: *Two Poems from LUNA*

5

suddenly
I am painting things in the bedroom
where I make love where we
make love suddenly
I am painting white black pink-orange
I am making the room fresh for the moon
to come in through the new white shades

I spend money I spend everything
I will not stop spending myself on
this bedroom where a poem holds one wall
written by the man I make love with about
the bedroom a flower's head in a bowl of water
I did not fall in love with a poem but
it helped it made me believe that he saw the moon too
and we do
on a sunday afternoon when I come to him naked and
he circles my breasts with his hands
I believe him
the poem next to us
a man can know this strange need to
cover a chair with black velvet to
be struck all week
the moon dropping all over me
all over us
all over my lying down on the bed
to take his cock in my mouth

7

are you there moon
I can't
oh yes
above the garage

we step back to let you fall on us
it has been days of the same old
I don't think you love me as much as I
love you so much I think I love you more than
ever and why don't you love me the way I want
you to love love is always the same old
man woman hard throats all crying sorrow ache
we do go mad

are you there
yes above the garage in your full lunatic time
but you lean back in your sky chair
yellow like fur that steadies itself after a meal
glossy and
here we are the lunatics
standing back to let you have us

if we could really let you have us
it might take one night instead of two weeks to
forgive ourselves

Dennis Dorney

203: *The Viscounts Play Pacoima*

Pacoima High took 1959 seriously,
and none yanked the hot-wire of community
exactly like the Viscounts,
understanding "time of their lives"
as a sedative for age, a transparency
to blow smoke rings through.

They practiced Rockabilly imitations
in Willie G's garage, quoting
each note off Decca 45s
stolen from a local *Sight and Sound* franchise.
Their sax player always brought glue
and they'd pass the paper bag
breathing that white moment furiously,
f-hole guitars bending swift as a knucklehead ride
through Arkansas...Tennessee.

Perkins, the bass man, dropped school
in junior year to marry and deliver spare parts
in his orchid and black truck.
Music froze time for him like a photograph
of a bullet caught kissing the heart of splintered wood.
After practice, he'd cruise Drive-Ins
along Van Nuys Boulevard selling rolls of speed,
planning burglaries on shops with dim alley access.

The Viscounts were founded after a dance
at El Monte Legion Stadium. A fight broke
in the parking lot with swabbies.
Perkins had clubbed one and seen a girl
snapping her fingers, crazy and simple and warm.
A phosphorous night had dunked them all
in its chrome vat of invention.

When Richie Valens agreed to play
the auditorium in Pacoima, jocks bobbed
to classes faking lyrics to "La Bomba,"
grils in poodle skirts daydreamed into geometry.
When asked to open the show, the Viscounts
tucked themselves away in rehearsal.
Girlfriends brought cheeseburgers, bottles
of Brew 102. Perkins lifted a pink sportcoat
from the rear of Silverwood's, everyone varnished
cootie shoots in their hair for wicked effect.

On stage, 1959 lept like a marlin in tow,
the band shook rains of sweaty vocals
onto the crowd, then through walls,
like an X-ray searching for a shield.
Everywhere that floral stink of noise.
Richie Valens' performance was recorded,
a collector's piece now. Pacoima blanched.

Perkins' wife obtained an autograph on her breast
and someone took that snapshot of the audience
which later appeared in *Look* magazine.
The Viscounts were still together until 1964,
eventually becoming a house band
at the Tattle-Tale Lounge. Perkins is a shift boss
at the Rath meatpacking plant in Duarte,
still counting downbeats, waiting to punch
his time card, with a "Ready, Steady, Go, Gone."

204:   *Sand Dune*

Dinosaurs sleep around me, protective,
like that Easter in Baja, you with
that ridiculous knife, scraping oysters,
threatening the sun in a slow masurka
along the tide's brown rim,
Even in shade, playing jeopardy,
the blade rested in your hand,
caked in mayonnaise and brine.
You write that snow is warming its voice
in Philadelphia, your spine blue-pained,
the word *cripple* coiled on its page
fanged and intent as love.

Last night under a full basket of moon
with its hush, I hiked this valley floor
retrieving meteor rocks, boots crushing
desert into pleistocene frost.
There were hex signs in the mountains
shifting mile after mile. Dantesque totems
above alluvian fans. We will all
shake apart in petrified clusters,
feel our only mud bake into dust.
I'm waving just over the dune. Look up,
raise that stupid knife. We grow wildly.

205: *from Pieces of the Map*

2.
Los Angeles in the Fifties: a billboard
of tract houses and palm trees
with wet paint and brass door clackers
polished under a sun in dark glasses.

A time of planting, when muscles wound
on the future like kite string. Your wallet
grew ith pictures of skinny children,
union cards, poems from your wife
scribbled on the back of blue envelopes;
and everywhere the grass needed mowing.

"The Yellow Rose of Texas" played over
and over through torn speakers
as you sipped beer in a park dug-out.
Under field lights, summer moths
balanced on sticky bottles.
Men from the studios chattered it up
on infield dirt, new softballs
skidded and lept into the nights
black as a rich man's car, falling finally
in your eyes, your spit-softened glove.

One year, Marilyn Monroe presented a trophy
and you blushed, shook her hand.
When she died, you bought a lantana in bloom
and bricked a planter off the garage.
You claimed the purple bells were her favorite;
when I asked how you knew,
of course you forgot to answer.

Doren Robbins

206: *The Ensuing Voyage*

In the night I washed dishes for Rossetti,
and I watched Rossetti while the busboy filled
and refilled the sink.
I watched him butchering and broiling,
eating standing up, working
continuously — with no sense of harassment, or giving
the illusion of that sense — chopping, sauteing,
smoking a cigarette — testing the mousse,
tasting every sauce — quieting
the alarmed maitre de, coaxing
the produce-man on the phone
to deliver to him first...
as he sweated into his beard and glasses,
stained with the fragrance of lamb shanks
and rosemary — whimsical,
solemn, as though annointed
by what he worked with — not talking,
not wasting a branch,
a slice,
a spoonful —
he worked continuously, symphonically,
peremptorily — the veins
thick along his forearms,
sweeping the fallen wrappers from his path.
For Rossetti I carried flour-sacks
from the storeroom,
stacked crates outside the backdoor,
so that he might show me
the way to use a cleaver,
or how he mixed herbs
into broths.
For Rossetti I said I was glad
to wash dishes,

for Rossetti
I lied. All the next night
until he showed me
the way to cut garlic
I struggled whether to drown that lie
under the soapy ladles and spoons...
...and that second night,
standing outside the apartment,
June sky deep
with lucid constellations,
blue and orange petals
of the birds of paradise
glowing near the laundry-room light —
and the sudden cold breeze
chilling my hands made raw by water,
blowing in
to my stagnant sails.

207: *Only Miro*

And the masters teach nothing
about cunning — only
Miro — not Valesquez,
not Rembrandt —
only Miro
after each conspiracy to demolish
all Spanish rural collectives
was accomplished,
who then turned out paintings
that are in many canvases
unendurable calligraphed migraines —
mythic painter of The Phosphorescent
Tracks of Snails,
subatomic surrealist,
only Miro
said the one sensible
masterful thing:
"I walk the tightrope
because I can."
Giotto, Klee, Kandinsky
I studied The Masters —
delivering canned-goods
to cafeterias,

standing broiling meat
in restaurant kitchens
I studied The Masters...
every day
working on sketches,
every day parked
in the truck beside warehouses,
or sitting out back on milk-crates
with pigeons and garbage
while the waitresses smoked
and talked with their shoes off
making disinterested or tender
comments about the drawings...
seven years working in kitchens.
Line-cooking in unvarying
tropically heated conditions.
Seven years — returning
to the apartment at night
to make something
from the modest
light of sparrows
and women
the bright
wind starting inward.
At that time
aside from Miro —
The Masters had indicated
nothing
about cunning.

208: *The Flight of Soutine's Red Gladioli*

Soutine's Red Gladioli,
Soutine among the curved
inner rims
of the petals — rising
bird of red oil —
wracked all night with brushes
to enter a gladiola's
intricate menstrual wing.
Soutine's head bud-like sweating
in the light of slick paint —
pigment of absinthe, glimmering —

red oil, raw side
of red meat — skinned blossom
or the babies' first skin rinsed
in bloody pollen.
Red only
a woman lives
fragilely in —
at births, between
conceptions. Fertile
blood gladiolas wore
for Soutine,
in the cold flat,
above the floor infested
with fleas — managing
a warmth
for his fingers
and ill friend, Modigliani,
dark feathers
in the penetrable
blaze of petals.

209: *Working with Albert*

Heatlamps, microwaves, steeldoors
off the alley
where the drunken cowboy
sang for change. And Albert...
black dirt
under his nails, twenty-four,
no references on the job-form...
one man short on the broiler
and they took him on —
fingers soft and stupid,
worn-down shoes...
while I was breaking
from the heat and speed
of broilers
I worked beside him
showing what I could
among the fiery pans,
but the heat got to him,
and the speed got to him,
and the pressure of the assistant manager,
the sharp lights, the waitresses

in their unreal costumes
made him sweat more...
he went out to take a leak,
he went out to have a smoke,
but he didn't smoke
and I didn't see him after that—
heatlamps, microwaves, steeldoors,
and there was the Glassman
who had the shop next to us,
the Glassman
who made mirrors
and light-fixtures you wouldn't
want to hang anywhere.
They sent me out to look for Albert
and I found what turns
out to be an uncle, the Glassman,
who must've told him in the morning
there was an opening in that kitchen
and to get his butt over there—
the Glassman telling me about
his kid sister's troubles,
stinking Tokay and Havatampa—the Glassman
who made all that shiny junk—I don't know
who bought it,
someone must've
but not Albert,
given back to the Doctor's
and the Psycho-nutritionist's,
not Albert—
timid, small-featured,
luckless one.

210: *The Big Store*

I've been walking around tonight like I did
when I lived in some worse part of the city
where the vegetable trucks
covered with a sort of brown soot,
pulling into the big market,
would wake me in the middle of the night....
Below drab white clouds and a beautiful woman
embracing the hood of a new car
                on a billboard,
I walked around.

And there are places you go
when you are alone like this
that have meaning
and you don't know it
for years. Not bars,
not places where there is
even any music —
              but the Big Stores...
the Save-On,
or a Thrifty Drug — a place where there is
a soda fountain, and you can have some food —
just that you can sit for a while
and not be bothered.
I'm talking about loneliness and the Big Stores
that seem so peaceful
like a huge sky drifting
with rain, more like a woven mist
                        that smells like metal...
the Drug King,
the big Owl Rexall,
places where the light is over-charged
but does not glare
        or spot things out.
And the aisles that are crowded
with all the practical items
and all the useless items —
suddenly have a warmth
because there is no place you feel right
        but there
in the big well-lit room . . . .

Tonight, as though I was in the past,
I went into one of the Big Stores.
In a suburb, somewhere in the middle of California,
strange, uncertain about where I was, not knowing anyone...
somewhere between Los Angeles and San Bernardino,
where I had to pull in
because the road was too dark
and alone
and I couldn't stop my mind...
you pull in,
that's what happens,
you get out of the car and go into some coffee shop
and sit at a counter
where no one will bother you . . .
        when you are on a street where there is a Big Store . . .

You see it up ahead of you
like an exposed mine,
on a street that reminds you
of a street in the city you come from — a place
that used to disgust you
with its cleanliness and its order
because there was so much back then
that had no order
and was all pushed around
inside of you . . . and the drugged armies
that were wasting
and defending
a small country in the Far East
followed you on the gray roads
        of sleep . . . .

That's what happens.
You go
and browse around in there for a while,
looking at paperbacks and magazines . . .
you get lost for a couple of hours
in a place like this
when it is impossible for you
to be married
or at a job
where you would have to talk to people at all —
because there is no place you feel right,
and nobody
can take it.

211: *From Either Side of You*

I thought I would keep going
without you — to stay in these few rooms,
to stare at the chairs that I hate
without you. I thought I would
go on like that,
alone with my days,
bitter, smoking into the steering wheel
toward Alhambra, or Pomona,
to build frames, to work machines,
driving interstate 10
into gray hell.
I thought I would go on like that,

full of wretched conceptions,
dreams of illness
and a toy window —
I thought I would go on
without you.
But I had to keep you —
to have come this far
I had to find things to compare with you
just as I compare myself with those rivers
that run with dead things
with the most fertile liquid,
and with dark fish tossing from the deep.
And I came to trust in you,
in the tiny flower of shining glass
over the pause of breath
within you — just as inside the leaf
there is another
in the pause of wind,
a transparent leaf
which is the one that is more real...
In this way I trust in you —
as I trust in those things that surround you
in the mist moving closer,
surrounded by the clouds' mauve color,
as your hair surrounds you,
the blossoms of the pomegranate
turning slightly metallic,
as the breeze surrounds you,
in the dusk, in late Spring.
I trust in you, in what comes
from either side of you, impassively given
without knowledge, without request —
I trust in the petals that open
on the invisible hedge.

Jack Grapes

212: *The Count's Lament*

There are not too many ways
to drink the blood.
Thick and slightly warm,
like pureed vichyssoise.
Sometimes, I roll it around,
what little there is,
in my cheek between tongue and palate,
just to get a taste again
of what I've forgotten the taste of,
drinking it so much now
out of desperation
that perhaps even this sip
is not enough anymore.
Perish that horrible thought!
I go now from neck to neck,
throat to throat,
reeling, scratching with my fingernails,
flapping against invisible mist
that issues from their mouths
as they walk about the streets
in a cold you can wave your arms in,
should you need to.
Not the cold darkness I bask in.
A darkness that has a taste,
a dull texture that grinds in my sleep.
It's all the same.
Flamingoes!
Daffodils!
To dream of a blazing sun—
just think of it—
to dream of that burning
and be unable to touch it,
suck its fire into my own veins,

down the gullet where it boils
the substance of my flesh —
then to wake, biting at splinters!
It's no life for a Count, believe me.
Were I to drive drunken
down one of your neon streets,
what breath test would you give me
when even the flesh turns white
and thin at the end of a century.
A century!
It's like a snap to me.
All I vomit is blood.
That sickness comes out of my throat
just to be drunk again for fear of waste.
The indignity!
Just to stand at the sideboard
with a scotch and ice in my hand
and clank the cubes around the glass
and finish it off with a puff.
The worms. The rats. The beetles.
The spider spinning its web
for the unwary fly,
tiny cracks of blood I've long disdained.
And now all there is left,
is you,
your own meager supply
that brightens with my pulse.
Imagine what it might be like
to flow in my veins
for centuries without end.

213: *Pretend*

pretend you don't see me
behind the typewriter;
pretend the words
were always just this way
on the page
before the face
of the one
who wrote them
in his underwear
on a cold november 5 a.m. monday
morning

thinking about the commercial
interview he has today
at 3:15 for Benson & Hedges
thinking should i shave
my mustache should i cut
my hair should i wear
a suit should i
tap-dance?
thinking my sister lives two
thousand miles away and at 20
hasn't what it takes
to live the next 30;
thinking why was my wife crying
over the toilet when i walked
into the bathroom.
pretend i have no face.
no name, no history.
pretend
the poem's
the thing
that dies.

214: *Trying to Get Your Life in Shape*

it's like doing the roof:
just when you've got the slate set,
the tacks in your mouth,
the tar hot and ready,
your foot accidentally
nudges the hammer
and it begins to slide away
from you
like a christened ship.
down it goes.
you hear the crash below,
take a deep breath, say *shit*,
and turn for the ladder
just as it
catches a wind
and begins the long lean
away from your outstretched hand.
aw shit!

you look up.
storm clouds from out of nowhere
belly over the setting sun.
the dark ice age is at hand.
and no one is home.
and the doors are locked.
your baloney sandwich
has been pecked away by birds.
you sit back, you
contemplate this new richness
come into your life,
and shiver on the roof
knowing it could be worse,
why you could be inside,
warm by the fire,
sipping sherry,
shoes off,
just
temporarily
alive.

215: *The Lost Things*

I lost my hiking boots.
And my green sleeping bag.
Maybe someone stole them.
Anyway, they're gone.
So is my only copy of
Hear Us O Lord
From Heaven
Thy Dwelling Place.
By Malcolm Lowry.
So are some other books.
Daniele left my red baseball cap
with the silver wings of mercury
in the bathroom at Barbarella's
Pizza place.
And I can't find
my favorite pair of scissors
either,
not to mention
my Bluit camping stove
and large cooking pot.
I loaned them to Karen Kaplowitz

coming out of the Cucamonga Wilderness
and she still has them.
She's a lawyer.
Now my mail isn't coming.
Someone put in a change of address form
and the post office has been forwarding
all my mail
to the Graduate Department of English
at the University of Pittsburgh.
This is true.
"Why am losing these things,"
I keep asking.
I keep asking this.
Out loud.
I'm driving Lori crazy.
"Something strange is going on here,"
I yell.
"Where are my boots," I whine in the middle
of a movie.
My favorite hiking boots.
It's very distressing.
Someone has my sleeping bag right now
and they're hurting it.
Someone's grimy hands are pulling apart
Hear Us O Lord From Heaven Thy Dwelling Place
and they don't even care about the underlines,
or the notes I've made in the margins.
But I'm not going to let it get to me.
The red hat, with the silver wings of mercury,
I plan to get it back if it's the last thing I do.
I'll keep a look out
and someday whoever took it
will be wearing it in the May Co.
thinking I've forgotten all about it.
But I haven't .
I'll see it.
And I'll get it back.
I'll get all my things back.
My Bluit camping stove
and my large cooking pot.
And my mail, all my mail.
My sleeping bag.
My boots.
My broken-in hiking boots.
I've missed you all so much.
So very much.

The lost things are coming back.
It's all coming back to me.
And I need to feel that I deserve this.
I need to learn
how to open my arms
and take them in,
as I would myself,
lost
these many
many
years.

216: *Nearing the Point*

Nearing the point
where the point at center
and once on its own
transforms earth to water
and back up above the shore line
around the unnecessary eyes
of its fish.
And each too to have seen it,
this black eagle
that flies out from your throat
and refuses to sing.
In our twentiety century
not because of me
not because of you
love is denied
kept silent
touches in departing
brushes us with wingtips
in cornerless space.
And higher still,
each out of desperation,
in orbit,
a little weaker,
reckless, sprung from the bedhead
where only yesterday
we stood
surrounded by the white ash
of our bodies.
So if not dead from the black water,
then dead from the frost,

from the window from the contrary idea
and so dead in fact from peace.
Convinced by the rooms we have loved in,
I get up from my chair
and walk toward the door
in this name flying up like a balloon,
while on the earth
there is time between points
to swim up from dreams
and smell your lover's shoulder
so deep in the earth's arms of sleep.

Paul Trachetenberg

217: *Lawndale, California*

A reformed New York Jew,
a Morman Utah Dane assembled me
in this place by the shore.
My first salty breath.

My words then romped
through big open spaces.
The sea and salt of this suburb,
dissolved the locusts and pogroms.

218: *The Freeway*

It divided the sea town
sacrificing my home.
We U-hauled inland,
leavin' the pillar of salt.

The scent of Anaheim's orange blossoms
deafened the pounding surf.
I was numbed by this schism.
I was numbed by this schism.

219: *The Beach Boys*

"Surfin' USA," the craze
of the West Coast.
Their songs waved
the Bay of Fundy to the Tasman Sea
foaming á la mode.

The kids of day, like thirsty nomads,
swam from the desert sea
to the soupy blue.
Idle without wheels,
I swam in envy.

220: *Boxboy*

I got a job putting eggs
on harder stuff in bags.
A proficient chest-beater,
I coralled cars kinetically.

After the last cattle gathered,
shrieking banshees appeared.
Those wind-swept gulls shouted saltily:
"Let go of that job."

221: *Fifty-Nine Chevy*

An impala on my lap,
purchased by the Niagara
sweat of baggin'. I tapped
on its furry dash
and blew its lyre-horn.

I tar-surfed Beach Boulevard
like the seniors.
Wowie! Huntington Beach had broken the spell of twilight.

222: *Flew the Coop*

I began countin' again.
This time, hair-spray
and other foodless wares.
An Alpha-Beta warehouse
became a new Alcatraz.

On weekends, I flew in my Chevy
to Laguna where the gay boys lay.
Those bronze boys had lower tan lines
than the Huntington Beach Boys.

223: *Riding on Words*

Verses developed
by Sir Robert's prodding.
A fiber glass board emerged,
I surfed inside.

I did take jogs
for glimpses of boy seals
balancin' on their boards.
Torn between inner & outer surf.

224: *Gestalt*

I surfed the cosmic wave
indiscriminately.
A coppice of entangled kelp
to be had.

Who was I foolin', climbin' without rungs?
The myriad pieces, I claimed,
were not my concern. "Wipe outs"
were a steady diet indeed.

Peter Cashorali

225: *for caesar again*

i'm in the shower with him.
we've just finished having sex; i'm over today
to clean his shop, make the little
extra cash i'll need
to get past the end of the month. ten minutes ago
i was sending someone i couldn't take care of
to where he'd be safe
from ransacked apartments, bounced
checks, the arrival of pain
in familiar muscles — i was off of this
rough world for a little while on his
slim back. under the steaming water he looks
like a print on rice paper.
he passes me the soap and says i feel
funny asking this but are you falling in love with me.
he says this is like the first time
i tried to ask you, when we were
going together, remember.
i try to tell him — yes: no: a little;
that everything in me that turns
to another person pulls me
towards him, but i've
set my feet against it.
i can't really
get it out.
i say that i won't be taking up his offer
to work for him full time —
that this sudden greenness we
have again for each other won't
hold up under too much traffic.
we trade places and he watches me rinse off.
he says i just want you to know you
have a job if you ever need one.

226: *ruined buildings*

i pass by quickly like a flock of birds
taking off, settling, taking off.
my heart, stomach, rectum,
the bones of my feet are in opposition to my purpose.
ruined buildings are cradled in folds of the canyons.
they're set along the approach to downtown.
their roofs are off and the rooms are piled
w pieces the eye can't reassemble. the walls are gone
and the view has washed in to take the place of the viewer.
just the foundations are left, holding portions
of meadows and hilltops over the street, beds of grass
deep enough to drink up the one who thinks. grass
penetrates the brain and the body is left by itself.
alone, the body is a single thing again, a boulder of flesh
under the passing cumulus clouds. shivers of pleasure
run through it again and again w o leaving a trace.

227: *spacing out*

sometimes it happens that we lose our footing in what we
know and start falling down it; we only stop when we hit its
outskirts and can't go any further; and there on the other side
we see what could be a chair. we don't want to look at it, as if
the space showing through its back were the inside of a
boulder where nothing could live, or as if we don't see a chair
at all but instead a window opened on a landscape that begins
to spot our eyes with white-out. we get up and find our way
back in to dinner, but sitting around the table our precious
family of friends is speaking in the strange skimming dialect
they've just learned. we try to rejoin them, but when they address us the expressions they use are like frisbees of some
material too light to catch or care about. we go from them to
the back steps. the early evening is still light, but huge and
cool. its hugeness rushes away from us and pushes the first
stars apart, it sucks a few loose particles away from us and
carries them with it, particles of us too small to ever change or
be destroyed, that will be used in something else. we struggle
on the back steps, trying to bring what we're feeling up
through the packed earth under our thoughts, small bits of
space begin to arrive in our brains from the enormous evening.

we sit still, waiting for enough of them to accumula around
the new feeling for us to know whether it's going to be a fear,
or a joy, or a new continent of calmness where we'll spend the
rest of our lives.

228: *walking in greenland*

i can't say what it is, but it's like we were walking in greenland,
where there are trees, and hills, and huge boulders pushing up
through the nap of the grass, but hardly any names, and those
occurring only in the lacey outer edges, where the people live.
it seemed as if we'd walked for days since coming across the
last thing with a name, not even rivers were reaching names
anymore, and we could still think, of course, we knew what
the trees were and that what the air felt was cold, but we
weren't talking very much. in fact we weren't talking at all. if
we slipped on the rocks and fell we'd say, "ough," or if it felt
like we'd hurt ourselves a little we'd start to cry. and then it
was if we'd walked far enough into greenland, because the land
went down and then up, and in the depth it made we saw
something that we were seeing for the first time, so that it's
easier to say what it was doing than what it was: it was hovering a few inches above the ground; it was revolving slowly; it
was shimmering like a globe of water the size of something
large; and we all went down and grouped ourselves around it,
close or a little distant, as it drew us. i don't know what it was
like for the others but for me looking into it as far as i could
was like having two feelings at once — the first like a flower
that had come back from extinction into my chest and
shoulders, a delight but i didn't pay much attention to it
because the second feeling was a sort of sad happiness, or a
gentle terror, or perhaps something just out of reach of an intersection of two words like this, coming from outside of me
and taking all my attention into itself. this broke when i realized that one of us had picked up something, i recognized what
it was immediately: it was a pebble, a small stone, a rock chip
that because of our surroundings was either granite or a piece
of shale, and had thrown it at what we were all seeing, and it
had bounced off and landed at my feet. then someone else
reached out to touch the thing and her hand slipped into it,
and she didn't make a sound but followed her hand in, and as
she did it was as if her knapsack couldn't enter without being
empty, as if it split at the back, and her thermos of hot coffee,
her oranges, her roses, her sudden sharp pain, love of a close

friend, grief, hilarity, all spilt onto the ground. one after
another we followed her in. and now i would be happy even to
say what this was like, but all i can tell you is that wanting to
tell you is like trying to vomit up something which is not in my
stomach, but below it.

229: *birds of prey*

marsh hawk

a young hawk devouring its kill. that's what this is.
that has its feet on his chest and bends down to him, pulling
                    his skin
off in strips. he sees the hawk's idols, held over its back
on the ends of sticks. their bodies are parcels of smoke
and fire, they're a house the hawk is building w each
new concession it tugs out of him. he abandons
room after secret room to the black-tipped grin but it
keeps coming in effortless pursuit, celebrating
a law of physics: that the lesser froce gets out of the way
of the greater. he gets out of its way and gets
out of its way until he's a meaningless red jumble,
waiting in the lumber of a ruined house
for this to stop. a young hawk devouring its kill, that's
what this is.

swainson's hawk

the first time he bit into submission he knew
it was what he's always needed. it ran
down his chin, wherever it dribbled he felt soft brown muck
wash away from arrowheads that had been buried in him
for years, his flesh finally backed off of their irritation and
started on the journey they'd been pointing him on for so long,
towards control. now he lives in the air, watching for weakness
to make its appearance so he can snap down to it, skirts
fannning out behind him, w eight blue hooks for pulling out
the guts of softness. this is the leash and collar the horned toad
dreams of when he pitches his little shadow on blankness
and takes a sleep. the marsh hare hears the whistle of descent
and tenses, every hair erect, preparing to be relieved of this
chaotic world.

red-shouldered hawk

after years of discipline, eating flies, sleeping in a pouch
of his own snot, the bullfrog has finally arrived
at the last level of swamp. he's a black magician who practices
to
call power down from the sky in an impersonal red flash,
                    for that he swallows
a little bit and a little bit more of the world's shit
each day, not to transform it into something innocuous but so
                    he can fit
under even a butterfly's heel. he knows it's the victim who
holds the reins in his broken hands, that everyone else is just
                    an empty glass tipped
towards coincidence. he makes himself
loathsome so no one can resist spitting on his back, standing
on their spit, the carpet of victims thins out until nothing
but dirt and strangled water are under his own feet. then the
                    sky sends it
representative down into his designs. but obedient
to schedule, a hawk appears and slides down the ribbon
of air tied to the frog's neck, pins the medal
of its anger to him, upholsters its claws w him, takes him
where he was going anyway.

gyrfalcon

he's been on the path to the ultimate victim ever since the
first one submitted directions to him, it's
led to this circle at the top of the world where nothing
                    moves, where
the path ends at a cliff. no one else is there. he waddles to
                    the edge
in his white furs and looks out, throat pressing into the frozen
globe of fog the ultimate victim is
traveling through to get here. he doesn't know who to
                    watch for but
knows how they'll part in front of him, can taste them when he
rubs his tongue against the roof of his mouth. in the frost
                    overhead
his name is called, mispronounced. his stomach jumps and he
                    looks up
to see who'll pay for this mistake but dropping down on him
                    is someone

in a coat like his, mouth sprung open and red tongue
                    signaling him
to hold still for just a few seconds longer. he folds back
                    on himself
and snarls, screams his name w o clearing the other's eyes,
                    they keep coming down like a
ceiling when the house turns over. the french doors
in his throat bang open and all his victims fly out,
                    pin themselves
to his successor, whose caliper mouth he escapes by leaping
into the other half of his life where it's been suspended in
                    the ice mist.

Alison Townsend

230: *Red: A Poem in Five Parts*

for David Glyer

1.
Out running, I notice Mount Baldy,
first snow of the season
shot crimson
in the long, slanting light.
Its color fills me
and I remember
you taught me the name for this,
saying it over and over
as if it were a password
floating between us pure
as white flaskes on a high mountain.
Alpenglow, was what you whispered.
*When the sun hits the snow
on the side of the mountain
they call it alpenglow.*

2.
This afternoon
I found blood on myself.
Simply my own blood,
an ordinary cycle,
but it could have been our blood.
What we have burned through together
and what returns, regular
as the tides of my own
body which have known your tides
as they know no others.
Washing my white pants
in the coldest of water,
I felt a rose bloom,
fresh and eternal as a line
from the oldest story.

The story which says:
I don't care if it's all
been written before me.
The story which says:
What we do daily is begin again.

3.
Tonight,
passing the still yard
of the house where no one lives,
I saw a single leaf fall,
crescent-shaped and particular
as a small canoe skimmng
into a pond of red.
I was the only one
to ever see it.
The only one to hear
the swish of its bright, dying cells
twirling through evening.
I have to tell him, I thought.
I have to tell him
of the story I seemed to hear
in that moment
about a man and a woman,
their lives spinning together
into the place where we only
imagine surrender. The whole
street hushed and silent,
attentive while one leaf fell.

4.
You brought me a leaf once, scarlet
iced clear by a cold Texas rain.
You savored its outline in crystal,
telling me, *Look!*
Isn't it beautiful?
You knelt beside the bed,
holding it saying,
It's the most beautiful
thing I have ever seen.
I looked, at the leaf
(which was lovely),
balanced like light
on the field of your mitten.
But it is your face I remember
when I think of the word *beautiful*,

holding it carefully balanced inside me
the way you held that leaf
in the middle of winter,
like an offering,
small bonfire leaping
from your hand.

5.
And now, walking the thick
dark after my long run,
feeling the hot apples flare
then hush then flare into my cheeks again,
I glance up and see house lights
spreading themselves over the driveway
in a spill of gold and red.
I see house lights
and your outline
printed across me
like the shape of something I have always
known but rarely given names to.
What it has taken me this long
to discover about passion,
about patience,
about simple forgiveness.
I glance up and see house lights
and the place where our lives
meet in a single color,
like that word you taught me when we first met.
Alpenglow, alpenglow,
saying it over and over
as if it named us:
a field of snow on the side
of a mountain,
a shift of white
burning into red.

231 □ *The Bighorns*

Once,
climbing Mount Baldy
in August,
seven bighorn sheep
crossed our path.
Ghostly and grey,

they rose
out of steep scree
to stand, poised
on the faint line
that led
to the top
of the mountain.

Breathless and hot
in the thin air,
we were diminished
then opened
by what we saw.
Our hearts bolted
and froze
on our dry tongues
like talus,
while we stared,
mesmerized
by the hypnotic
yellow eyes
with their unflinching pupils
the scrolled horns;
the silent hooves;
the apparently effortless
ascent.

It was a long moment
spilled like a lake
on that razorback saddle.
We looked into each other
and beyond, into the real
life of the mountain.

Then the big male
dipped his horns,
and the herd was gone,
absorbed like air
into the ridge line
as silently
as they had come.

It could have
been a dream,
but it wasn't.
And we continued

the last mile
to the bare peak
that rose, spreading
its granite skirt
like a mantle
of light
to the desert.

We arrived,
but to this day
it is the sighting
I remember.
When I feel
most far from you,
I remind myself
that you
were the one
standing beside me
that hot noon
looking straight
into wildness.
That there are
some mysteries
about which
it is impossible
to ever
completely speak.

Eloise Klein Healy

232: *Moroni on the Mormon Temple / Angel on the Wall*

He is a foreigner
and not one of the angels living here.
He was imported to point at heaven.
His name is hard and final,
not like Angel, soft "n" and soft "g"
whose name is sprayed down the street
on a building, eye-level, arm-level,
quick and at night
to say, "I am no foreigner,
this is my barrio,
something old, something here."

1.83

233: *Standing Up, Looking In*

This country is preparing a war,
inking the insides of guns
to print the right death,
and I am on a hillside far away,
anxious the wind will blow me
face first into a tall yucca
I'm smelling today.

When I walk down by the highway,
strangers wave at me
and I wave at them when I drive past
road crews, survey crews, the telephone repair.
But the war will be popular again.
There are strangers to be against

and the irony is always missing.
We even marry strangers.

Here I stretch, I stand tall
and stick my nose close
to the sappy ooze of waxy white blossoms,
purpled edges, the open smell.
War has density and seriousness.
I have just my balance
and my tremendous desire to reach.

234: *You Must Change Your Life*

from "The Torso of Apollo" — Rilke

The stories say your animal
will tell you what you must do.
The tale from Nicaragua adds this:
that life in the city is cleaned of the animal
and you must go to the trees
so your animal can tell you what to change.

When I write about trees
I know I'm talking about love.

My animal is a tree
and my trees are birds
and my birds are animals
who burst from their walking
into a sky waiting for this transformation
as if it had nothing else to do
but receive.

Whenever I change my life
I ask myself have I listened
to the right breezes.
They are the tongues of all tongues
and the laughing enemies of all borders.

Have I listened enough
beyond my first knowledge
that my animal
is the largest of plants.

235: *Double Play*

If Gertrude Stein had played second base
she would have said "there's only there there"
and putting thoughts in order.

The outfield is the place to dream,
where slow moons fall out of the sky
and rise clean over a green horizon.

The infield is tense as blank paper
and changeable as the cuneiform
of cleats along the path.

Stein would have loved the arc of arm
from short to second
and the spill of one white star
out of a hand.

236: *El Playon De Chanmico*

*Lava Bed of Salvadoran Volcano
Becomes an Open Graveyard for
Nameless Victims*
              — headline, Los Angeles Times

Where are the human beings?
There are some dead people by the road.
There are some dead people by the volcano
and it has been silent for years.

Where are the human beings
at El Playon de Chanmico?
There is no smoky plume
to frighten them.
The earth is not quaking.
No fresh stone flows
on the lava bed.

Where are the human beings
to bury the dead
who mold into one another
a piece at a time,

where are the human beings
at El Playon de Chanmico?

It's daylight and the world is busy.
It's daylight and the breeze is lifting.
There is a soccer game
and aren't they going?
There is Mass today
and won't they be praying?

Where have they gone today
with their children or their mothers?
Why don't they go down that road
to the garrison?
Where are the human beings?
Who are these people piled by the road?

Someone does the counting.
No one does the burying.
Earth alone can bear it,
takes the bodies in her hands
and slowly unnames them.

Where are the human beings?
There are unfinished stories by the road.
There are dreams lying there not waking.
There are unwilling screams that keep screaming.

Where are the human beings
to bury what must be family
at El Playon de Chanmico?
See, they have their arms
around each other
by the side of the road.

Carol Lewis

237: *Niche*

Stepping into a brick entryway
To light a cigarette, I remembered
Walking home late another evening
Stepped into this entry, shielded the lighter's flame
Almost fell over an old woman serenely asleep
The shapeless sack of her, lacily snoring,
A bubble of jeweled foam in the corner of her mouth,
Motherly tucked in a dirty quilt.
She had chosen her place well —
Sheltered from wind, secluded,
Yet public enough
So thieves wouldn't risk it.
Her small possessions knotted in a cloth bundle
Settled for the night, shoulders wedged against glass doors.
Inside the unlit hardware store
Dim moons of porcelain and copper floated
On the surface of darkness.
She chose her niche wisely
All the long way home, I searched
Never found one half as good.

238: *Jocobo in Exile*

*Jacobo Arbenz Guzman, Pres.
Guatemala 1951-54*

On the whole, he prefers Switzerland
So orderly, Berne, Geneva —
Where trolleys chug up and down the
Steep cobblestone streets at precise intervals
An obedient country, unlike his unruly homeland;
Presiding in the gray presidential palace
        during the last dreadful days,

False reports reaching him from the front
Ghost armies of exiles, ten thousand
Wiping out his meagre battalions, how could he
Sweating in the grey presidential palace
Sift truth from lies, his unshaven chin
Grating on the high military collar of his tunic,
His unsteady hand reaching for the brandy bottle
It was the noise he hated most
The planes, promptly at noon, flying low over the capitol
The screaming bombs, columns of dirt and blood
        rising in the marketplace —
Those Norteamericanos, those devils — must
They have it all, wasn't their own rich country enough
And United Fruit, hunched like a black spider in its bunches of bananas
All he wanted, all he hoped to get out of it
Was a little land for his campesinos
A few schools, hospitals, dignity
And now — the schools burned,
The campesinos driven off their land, the hands
Of protestors chopped off with machetes
He sighs in a park in Zurich
Sitting on the iron bench, crumbling bread for swans
That dip their beaks into the man-made lake;
Soon he will cross the square to a cafe and a cup of chocolate
        rich with cream
His waist thickens, his hair thins, his hands no longer tremble
He closes his eyes, imagines for a moment
A rising moon hung in the branches of a manzanita bush
        like silver fruit
He opens them again to the park, the swans, a tall mountain
        crowned with snow.

239: *Lion in Lion Country Safari*

The top of a hill lifts up
A lion raises his sunflower head to consider me
Spreads one dazzling paw
The car nose quivers, stops
I roll the window down, draw in lion smell
Stretch in his light, gold wires hum
The power of that paw could flatten me
Still — I need to touch

To bury my hand to the wristbone in his plush
He's the golden key that unlocks a door somewhere
A hinge turns, the dream opens, he pads over,
Rubs his head on the fender, I crawl from the car
Imitate his growl, flare as he approaches
Together we delicately taste the scent in our nostrils
Test the middle ground between us
I would be content to abandon car, civilization, cigarettes
Follow his spoor to the bare hilltop
Wind my arms, a necklace around his throat
Swing a bright medallion from his calm center

240: *The Feral Dogs*

Returned last night, milling at the doorway
I leaned safe on a second-story sill and
Watched, the lesser members of the pack
Casting back over the mizzled grass, muzzling
for a rabbit bone, a whiff of mole,
Their teeth, the points of their fur,
Stood out like stars.
Their Shepherd leader, magnificent in cinnamon coat,
Two nights ago caught a house pet by the throat
Dragged him across our walk, chewed off his leather
Collar, I broke the melee with shouts, a broom, the spotted
Victim loped howling home, the pack flowed off, one
Pulse, one electric body fluid over the hill and gone.
I hosed blood off the walk, called the SPCA to come with nets
And tranquilizing darts, they sounded dubious on the phone.
Tonight the pack returns, the Shepherd whines and scratches
At my door demanding meat, interrupting —
I am reading about Lowell, how he flew off the handle
In Buenos Aires, nude, climbed upon equestrian statues
I see him, irresponsible, mad, lion head flung back,
Bare legs clapped to the bronze flanks, galloping down
The Avenidas...

And you, former ally, crippled companion, brain burned
To a black ball you roll toward the women who've betrayed you
Beginning with your mother
And every woman's a cunt or whore —
You slam ghostly into my armchair and damn them all.

The Shepherd rubs his shoulders against the door
Implying intimacy, his nails click on the step
The hair on my neck bristles, they'd adore
To tooth my head bone down to mush, the door holds firm, a last
frustrated whine and they drift off
Lusty barks startle and scatter among
The mounting morning traffic on the boulevard,
Sparrows, from their holes under the eaves
Lift blunt beaks and chip, chip at the concrete dawn.

Joanna Warwick

241: *Orpheus*

1.
The first thing to do
is to close the eyes of the dead,
so they don't lie there like that,
staring heavenward, seeing nothing.

There is a word in German,
Einmaligheit,
being here only once.
We want life

not the afterlife,
not the senior-citizens'
club in the sky
and angels with sales-clerk smiles;

nor standing for *x* and *y*
in a thinker's mindless universe,
touching as waves of energy,
without faces and arms.

2.
It used to be more picturesque:
the black gleam
of an underground river,
the dignity of twilight;

birdless, breathless, stationary air,
shadows clutching a coin
for the ferryman.

Charon, old miser,
what did you do
with all that money
in a country with nothing to buy.

3.
Crows stride
rather than take small steps.
They space themselves at random.
Their caw splinters the air.

They are not art.
They are not metaphysics.
You must take them as you find them,
black on white.

4.
We are told to be grateful
for everything,
the rain, the sun,
the decor of the season.

We are told the moth
blesses the flame,
the cut worm
forgives the plow.

That if we are grateful,
perhaps we too
will be
forgiven.

5.
The moon is a white lie,
the stars an idiot alphabet.
The image of the soul
is a man walking through hell,

making music as best he can,
careful not to turn around
because he knows
Eurydice is not following.

Every spring I remembered lilacs,
and the tiny stipples of red
amid the fragile white
of flowering chestnut trees;
not the hot-pink
peach blooms fevering Los Angeles,
the purple haze of polluted nights.
I could count what I had
on my fingers:
two chairs,
twice-a-year love life,
ten cents an hour above minimum.

I tutored "protozoan English,"
to dazed students repeating
"The past tense of *sit*
isn't *sitted*."
I thought I should have never left
those cracked, illogical streets
memorized with footsteps,
that sky flying with anarchic clouds;
I'd be by now
translating Shakespeare,
marry that green-eyed
motorcycle rider,
the engineering student
I met at sixteen and worshipped
with a passion only
platonic love understands;
lilacs in the park,
statues and bridges,
the gray light off the river.

I tried to check myself
imagining my engineer husband
would have an affair with a woman dentist,
the child would cry,
the upstairs neighbor watch full blast
soccer games on TV,
and I, like a character in Chekhov,
wander through atlases and whisper
the ecstasy of foreign vowels.

Then my life eased, lurched forward like a long-stalled train.
There, in the grainy freeze of newsprint,
food rations,
tracks of tanks in the snow,
the stiff back of the colonel
reading off the "news,"
police.
Chestnuts a white
blizzard of despair;
lines for a cake of soap,
a pair of shoes.
Choosing avocadoes at the supermarket,
I don't regret.

Reading Rilke and Neruda,
I don't regret.
There, truth is a conspiracy.
Here — poetics of surrealism.
A country where you pay a psychiatrist
to learn how to scream.

Nights still glow purple
over the refineries.
I don't complain.
I say I was so young
when I left,
too nervous,
no good at going to jail.

Only when I read poems
written by those
I could have gone to school with,
their words bruised
traces on cheap paper,
a cry from somewhere so far
away it could hardly exist —
those smuggled out
ration cards of speech —

and I translate,
my luxurious hobby,
adjusting commas,
splicing in prepositions and articles,
there are times I regret,
moments when I think
the worst would have been the best.

243: *Jeanne D'Arc*

It is May.
In my village, a lilac hedge.
How I want to press my face again
to those pale, moist clusters,
smoke-blue, the dusk of incense,
the sun of the monstrance so high
we were taught to lower our eyes.
But I always stole a glance up—

My head is shaved.
The English soldiers
are calling me a harlot.
The sign underneath the platform:
"Heretic, seducer of the people.'
These gentlemen who write down
what I say—
they call me the devil's daughter
not because of my voices,
Saint Catherine and Saint Margaret,
but because I wore men's clothes.
Chafing steel, the horses' sweat,
people clamor for a miracle—
don't they know all of us are born
to hear a voice from God?
In my village, a stone well.
The blackness there.

My hands wedge a steeple
in the crowded air.
An English archer
fashions me a cross with faggots.
The French bishop is weeping.
Tears dredge white runnels
down the faces of peasants.
A tall young man leans to me;
I cry, "Watch out,
you'll burn yourself!"
The wind touches me
lightly, lightly.
I never knew how to write my name—
I didn't need to—
I'm nineteen—it is May—

Slowly the red host
dances up to me.
It lays itself at my feet.
I wait for the embrace.
Now the soldiers are crying, look,
the English cardinal
is weeping!
Beware of those
who see holy words
drawn upon the smoke with hooks of flame.
Beware of those
who see their victims' souls
as white doves
flying out of their mouths.

244: *Plaques*

On the way to school, a small
rectangle of bronze:
"On this spot
50 people were shot
on May 3, 1942 ."
All inside me jammed:
should I lower my eyes,
pray, grow pale?
That would be thinking of it,
and I didn't want to:
people caught in the street,
the manic stutter
of machine guns.
The rest was to cart away
the bodies and wash
the pavement.
The same pavement.

Sometimes flowers
were fixed to the plaque.
I suspected some
"Committee to Commemorate,"
the arrangement was so tasteful,
tied with a ribbon
in the colors of the flag.
But the plaque like a dark stain
corroded every bouquet.

This wasn't the only plaque.
Somewhere on a tree-lined
Sunday stroll, "On this spot,
100 people were shot."
And somewhere near a park.
It seemed to escalate.

The train that goes
to the mountain resorts
stops at Auschwitz.
Few get off.
I could never go to Hiroshima.
Outside the window

crowds gather,
their silence demanding
to crucify us
on the scream of their terror
forever.

245: *Civilization*

A director of a natural history museum
told my mother how, at the end of the war,
Russian soldiers entered, saw
snakes, salamanders, lizards

shelved in long jars,
preserved in alcohol.
The Russians were interested
in the alcohol.

The director warned, "These snakes
are poisonous!" He was left
with a rumble of barbarian laughter
and little corpses on the floor.

Germans would not have behaved like that.
In Pomerania, where I was born,
they had cut down the forests
and replanted them in straight rows.

The record keeping in concentration camps
was exemplary: name and number
preserved in standard files;
the mounds of separated ash.

- - - - - -

This was my heritage:
the burned ground,
an age confused
between such extremes of civilization.

Kate Braverman

246: *Spring Monologue*

I want to tell you everything.
I drank poison.
I deserted my son.
I did it for love.
I tried to drink god.
I opened my heart
and found only the knife
and the cold communion
of the mystery in passage.

O, the myriad clutter
of my mistakes.
My contrived ruin
and greed for the ineffable,
as if that equilibrium
of crystal and flower petals
were bankable,
were a flame I could eat.

And this is a spell
to control madness.
Breathe deep.
Repeat this.
I will survive.
I must.
To hear voices
is not enough.
They must be orchestrated,
taught technique.

It was men or women
I loved but the wild pulse
of insanity.
I trusted it,

thought it permanent
like a congenital defect
or a chemical reaction
of moonlight and a certain
type of skin.

But it betrayed me,
found someone younger
who died better
and with more style.
Hang on.
I am absolutely certain.
I lived to tell you this
and only this.

Let your womanhood emerge.
Feel it beating, breathing.
It could rise from your shoulders
like feathers or straw.
Trust it. Listen.
Save yourself.
The bruised dissolves
as it should, used up,
exposed as small and obsolete,
a subspecies, inarticulate.
You shed it easily.

This is the moment
of divinity and grace
of which you have always dreamed.
This is the cradle, intact
in corridors without fraudulence
or the deliberately deformed.
Not blood words but something else,
more a flute than a drum
but equal in power,
still able to haunt, kill
and transform.

Surrender.
Merge with this white square
of April.
Make sacred what you touch.
Not history or events
but the details.
Yellow canna beside a lawn.
Dusk light across a redwood porch.

Your integrity is defined solely
by what you can hold,
can press with your lips.
There is more immortality
in one perfect kiss
than in the stones
of pyramids.
Defend no borders
but those of sensibility.
Be one woman truly, wholly
and you will be all women.
Tend one garden
and you will birth worlds.

247: *Fortunate Season*

I was expensive.
Two bulls, a peacock,
a trunk of pewter and brocade.

With my son's birth
my father received cheroots
in a silver box.
And my mother,
perfume from Calcutta.

In a silk-lined drawer
I keep a gold bracelet
wide as a fat man's thumb.
And a ruby ring bright as Mars
that one night in August
when she hangs low and close,
almost touching the gate
like a great rare moth.

In afternoons yellow as lemons
when my children and the children
born to my sisters sleep encased
in the palest linen
I braid my hair with orchids,
play the flute, toss dice.

Should I weep for the hungry
anbd lame?

The victims of ill-planning,
drifting ignorant on boats,
with ruined teeth
and congenital coughs?
Are they not wet enough
with the spit of God?

My father is proud.
And his father in the ground
does not stir with whittled
bones sharper than daggers.
It's a fortunate season.
I sleep well.

Laurel Ann Bogen

248: *Statuary/Poem for My Girlhood*

Four white gazebos corner
a rose garden
out of season
shorn and prickly like a nun
a girl in a white cotton blouse
orange and white polka-dot skirt
winter in California
bare legs and notebook
dry as skin she writes
hollow virginal couplets

In the center stands Apollo
his bronze torso firm and cold
untouchable
and she knows
somewhere that warm pit
moist and glowing
must reach out
embrace marble to bronze
she buries her face in his plexus
her white arms encircle
his sturdy legs
and in the coldness of her face
it all comes rushing
with a twitching in her back
the heat of lost art
all in her arms

249: *All the Earnest Young Men*

The wax of half-burnt candles
seals chianti bottles,
the mattress on the floor

is stained with sex.
At night he drives a taxi
and reads Kerouac
and in 1967 1974 1986
the songs are still the same,
"the answer is blowing in the wind."
His lips believe everything he says,
the kisses and philosophy,
voice cracking above acoustic guitar.
"Must" and "now" and "change"
flush his face like seasons.

I trace the brow that will furrow,
the jaw that will set,
with sad fingers roughened
from Innocent to Older Woman
and want to hold him there forever,
my daphne flower,
until I see him again
marching for honor
disappearing in weary streets.

250: *May 12, 1971*

Mornings starch white
the rumple of pastel sheets
two figures angle
and stave off encroachment
the sun blinks above cannisters
bodies snap to attention

they move without collision
smooth and defined
collars and buttons contain static

it is 7:34
a Wednesday

the figures compact themselves in chairs
there is coffee and stock reports
it is cheery like this
the day propped before them
like the Wall Street Journal

the solidity and logic
of the counter is interrupted
only by a wedding band
in the soap dish
and a pair of scissors
to cut coupons out of skin

she says she has to do something
he says that would be nice
and his vacant sky falls to linoleum

the short breath of morning
bustles questions into kitchen corners
it pats the figures on their hands
and says "there, there dear, it's all right"

251: *Havana*

Damp gardenias pause
this night Havana
your name a sigh
rolled on the thighs
of bronze women
Istanbul, Cairo were discarded
like petals
this is my season of Havana

Once I held a black ink pen
and wrote a word
I scarcely knew
H   you emerged unsettled
a   with each letter
v   followed this day's vivid streets
a   to find me here
n   it is for you I paint my lips coral
a   it is for you

Havana, you lick into corners
of the red night
drunk on Cuba Libres
and sugar cane water
tango, samba
the scratch of phonograph

beguiles the blood
to begin the tissuing off
of taffeta, corset, stockings
you move against me
your face a muzzle, a gun
a circular fan clicks seconds
"te amo" your black curls
shake and my head shakes
Yes

We rise from ashes of the night
dress and leave
we do this again and again
Havana, you are all they warned
me about: more than the sum
of my self and my others
more than that, more
you are every drug, liquor and sin
that was whispered among young girls
and still I choose you

You take me down pungent streets
this is the street of orchids
where you wooed me
with ambiguous dilemmas
this is the street of hibiscus
where I sweep my hair away
from my face and memorize
lips tangled in strands
here are mango, indigo, papaya
slow streets that move
like sweet intoxication
until your tattoo appears
on my shoulder,
and the stretch of our bodies
pads like cats the curve
from waist to hip
the round of belly
the knowledge of muscle

Must I divulge my secrets?

This is Hard Time, Havana
a time when the wind blows black
and your name appears
on a scrap of paper on a park bench

You beckon
from the smoke stacks of Pittsburgh
and the window sills of Manchester
and are gone

I took you home
folded you away
a bureau
where your name breathes
a hot wind blowing Havana

252: *For the Love of Strawberries*

during strawberry season
my father would plant them
in small clay pots
working in the garden
the dirt of 70 summers
on his hands
my mother would bend
over the stove
steam rising
would preserve them
sugar, strawberry, pectin

strawberries common as the sun
strawberries winking in the morning breeze
Saturday's confetti
the milkmaid's tidbit
I eat them all
red berries red

Janet Gray

253: *Typing*

There is the flickering of the mind
and the winged things that fly across the page
there is the minute intelligence of birds
crossing a white sky
we are marching
across a white plane
enlisted in other people's wars
machining the requirements of the institutions
Typing is flight   night comes and we are still marching
A row of spies is sent ahead
from the left to the right disguised
as black birds
There is the thought of summer
homelessness
parents far away
summer in mountains where the green is musclebound
and though the body is still bound
to the chair at night and
the gut is shot with coffee,
typing is how I make my pay
typing is the least earthbound living
and one of the hazardous ways to make a mind
There is the articulate intelligence of tiny bones
nesting in bright ivy
a long march   a distant war in black uniforms
exile in black uniforms
the fingers flap faster than sight
the mind hovers   hums   dives
typing is my masterpiece
I have made few mistakes   but I have made some
and there is no excuse
they must all be corrected

254: *Unborn Hummingbirds*

Laid in a nest in the ivy just outside the window and then
whisked away by jays. There ensued a jay-hummingbird war.
Saw one like this last year but the eggs were saved. One
cheers for the hummingbird—all that amazing energy against
the big blue mass of the jay. And when the hummingbird
manages to chase off the jay even though the eggs are gone
one feels victory. I feel sorry for myself because every
day I choose abortion. Unborn hummingbirds have nothing to
do with this. How sweetly the hummingbird eggs rest in the
soft nest of the hummingbird. And then the screeching jay.
I am not referring to myself.

255: *Unspeakables*

1.
Mysterious pain in the urethra.
Raw, plus throbbing.
Unexplained discomfort in the eardrums.
Plus itching.
Itching in the armpit.
Unexplained pain in the feet, hands.
Itching around the hairline.
And a humming off to the left.

2.
There is a party in the elevator.
And only one door to the elevator shaft.
The floor does not reach the elevator floor.
The elevator man is handsome, a musician.
Was once a handsome young musician.

3.
A Fritos truck passes between rows of trees.
It's pleasant, how it rocks, and silent.
This is the way evil works.

4.
"I keep a flame burning very low to the side,"
you say, and I excuse myself, go to the balcony,
and dry-heave until I slump by the door.

5.
If the wall were butter,
it would melt.
The wall lamps would sink.
"Mother and Son Kissing" would sink.
The wastebasket would be ruined.
The horsemen would show over the wall.

6.
A question not asked about absence of feeling
or what seems to be absence of feeling.
Lovers meet, the night is warm, there is fine rain,
light comes from several small sources,
they have eaten well in separate halls,
plans for the next move are complete.
Someone sings, "All night by the rose, rose,
all night by the rose I lay."

256: *Do Not Try to Pull Up Anything by the Root*

Do not try to pull up anything by the root
when it is rooted in soft material.

Do not try to pull out the peachboy,
even gently with tweezers.

Things that are watery and thin-skinned
seem to grow all by themselves,
but they are barely alive.

Once I unravelled myself entirely
thinking I had to take gifts sensibly
and at the right time.

You can't see the little faces
under the top of the soil,
but they are there.

257: *Blocked*

The phone rings. They are worried.
You tell them you certainly
will not kill yourself.
You look out a window.
When you are hungry, imagine food;
when you do not like
your body, imagine clothes;
when you are lonely,
remember all the terrible
things that love brought.
You look out a window,
straighten and tell yourself
you must roll up your clothes
tightly so you can keep them
forever in a drawer in your
abdomen; you must not drop
your clothes on the floor
where Jesus might come soil his feet
on them. You must
keep beans and grains in bins
where bugs can't get at them
and store them on a shelf
in your abdomen; then,
when you are ready, cook them up
in a big pot for a long time.
When they come out, they will be hot
and you will burn yourself.
You look out a window and
bells ring. The leaves are green
and so is the air between them.
Remember: you stood in the dark,
thick gray walls all around you. Bells rang
stand in line, don't chew your nails,
spread your clothes perfectly
over your body.
Jesus did not take form in the bright
air outside. You walked away.
You stood in a stream up to your
abdomen. Your thighs were very cold.
Bugs and wet leaves came up to you.
Your clothes changed. They floated
and showed your body. You unpacked
yourself hungrily with strong
careful hands.

258: *Things I Plan to Say*

I've never seen a cyclone,
I'll say, my life
isn't complete. Then I'll see one
in my mind's eye, as I sit
combing my hair.
The comb will be mother-of-pearl.
My hair will be the color of torchlight.
I'd like to encounter one, I'll say,
while wearing a chinchilla fur,
and to die like that — exotically
and rather terribly.
I'll laugh, as if recalling
something ironic
about the rising of last night's moon.
Suddenly, I'll be bored with danger.
I'll want only
to lie down on a Persian rug
that is rumored to have once flown,
and sample macaroons from all over the world.
No, I'd prefer the cyclone,
its intensity,
its self-containment.
That appeals to me.
Or instead I'll want
to be lost in a blizzard, wearing only
gold bracelets from Mesopotamia,
or instead
to be caressed by an heiress
who harbors a shocking secret.
I'll stretch luxuriously
like a cat
whose pedigree can't be deciphered.
I'll say it's difficult
to choose life over death
when both have certain attractions.

259: *Confessional Poem*

I was a file clerk and a famous beauty.
You marched into the office one day
in your immaculate white coat
with the streamline gold pin
declaring your name.
A cardiologist, you had knocked
on so many hearts
that just wouldn't swing open,
you were starting to lose patience.
I should adore you, you said,
because you were a doctor and had a nice place.
"Nice" wasn't the word.
Your condominium was white as a blizzard.
The lamp had a sharp edge
and rotated in space.
Even the silence was white, and like frost
it crystallized on whatever it touched.
If someone had died here,
she refrained from dropping blood on your sofa.
If she drowned in your pool,
she went down without making a ripple.

You said we'd be together forever, or until
I spilled wine on your carpet.

I said I wanted my heart to be broken.

You referred me to a specialist in Minnesota.

Failing that, I wanted my heart to be well, to be
without history, new as a baby's.

You suggested something in plexiglass.

It was not what I meant. We started
to go downhill, and you spent your nights
assembling and disassembling a plastic model,
explaining to me, "This is the mitral valve,
and this is the major aorta."
To me, it looked like a bagpipe you could blow a tune on,
though you never did.

Today something — perhaps an ice cube rotating
in a glossy 80% proof — reminded me

of your glacial heaven, your model heart,
how late one night,
under the blade-bright light of your lamp,
you unlatched the two halves and peered in,
as though searching for love.

260: *Letter to My Assailant*

On such occasions
one comes to know someone spectacularly fast.
Even with your unfriendly arm at my throat
you could hide nothing from me.
Your failures with women, for instance,
filed through my mind,
failures moral and physical.
And I knew your father was hostile to doors.
He liked to slam them or break them down.
Your mother worked her whole life
without hoping for anything.
She grew thin. Even in her grave
she kept shrinking.
Now she's thin as a needle,
one nearly invisible hand
folded over the other.
I even knew without looking
your socks had red diamonds
balanced one on the other.
In fact, with my breath stopped short in my throat,
your whole life flashed past my eyes,
but I didn't let on.
"I can't breathe," I gasped,
and you loosened your hold. I suppose
for this I should have been grateful.
Instead, I was out-of-sorts
and impatient with men, who frequently
conduct themselves in an undesirable manner.
Perhaps you felt the same about me.
You'd no sooner reached through my torn blouse,
when my screams scared you away.
One would have only to witness
up leap from each other
like two hares released from a trap, / to realize

something was amiss / between men and women.
Perhaps we talked too much,
or left too much unsaid.
For instance, when you were ripping my shirt
and mumbling, "I don't want to hurt you,"
I replied, "That's what they all say."
I'll admit I was glib
if you'll admit you were insensitive.
Look, the world is brimming with happy couples,
benign marriages, with men and women
who've adjusted to each other's defects.
Couldn't we adjust to each other's defects?
I'll begin by trying harder not to forget you,
to remember more clearly your approximate height
and your brown shirt
which I described to the police.
Our encounter must stand out in our minds,
distinct from all others.
I never intended
for all this to become blurred in my memory,
to confuse you with other men.

261 :   *Babies in Supermarkets*

usually lie over a shoulder
in line at the checkstand.
This one's hands open and close
like tiny anemones that can't breathe in air.
Its eyes, already amazed
by pandas on cereal boxes,
mountains of oranges,
fasten on me.
Today it has learned the world is chilly,
and filled with objects that aren't its mother.
And here I am, another alien shape to contend with.
Its brow furrows in an expression
that years from now will become consternation.
What am I to say to this baby,
looking at me as if I just pleaded guilty,
as if I manhandled it out of the womb?

Well someone did and now
it has a life to live, and there's just no telling.

It could grow up to be some lonely
guy who shops for small cheap steaks
and eats them with salt
and no vegetables
under the one bulk in his kitchen,
or the woman like its mother
who had more children
than she ever wanted, and less of everything else.
Hers is a life of returned pop bottles,
clipped coupons, smaller
and smaller change.

Her groceries on one arm
she bears the baby away. All body,
it knows nothing and sees
too much.
The world is a line you stand and wait in,
and nothing we make—pyramids of canned
spam on sale—is built to last.
And there is no safe route out of this place.
The mother steps
forward, the door swings open
to the relentless future.

262: *Pomegranates*

When a woman eats a pomegranate
she bends back the skin
so the fiery darts lean out on all sides.
Lifting it to her mouth
she is stung by sweetness
and it drops from her hand.

That night she will give birth in her sleep.
Her sons and daughters
will rise and leave quietly.

When a man eats a pomegranate
his fingers search each red chamber.
The dark juice rises in pools
flooding his hands.
The seeds are like door after door opening
changing shape in his mouth.

To enter a pomegranate is to touch many lives
or to journey for three days.One eats a pomegranate
by drawing out sections
stepping down
drawing out more.

It is a slow process
but in the end
you will drop into a circle of clear red light.

2.

In the beginning
the apple was unknown in the Far East
and, in any case, harmless
but not the pomegranate
with its passages threatening
to lead to some source
and the shapes
in its glossy darkness describing
the mind, the heart, and the loins.

The woman knew the pomegranate
had something to do with a snake.
She had a feverish imagination.
The man made no such associations
but she fed him her dreams.

For a while they ran about wildly
her hair trailing like the tail of a comet
her skin flashing in the sun.
Then they dressed sadly and left.

Outside the earth was parched and dusty
as their bones would be
soon now.
They had nothing to be glad of.

But that night, for the first time,
seeds of flame appeared in the sky
and they named them
stars.

3.

When I heard that the mystics
explored the entrails of beasts

I divided the pomegranate looking for answers.
The fragments of skin tore
and I saw, in the clusters of seeds
a flayed bear glistening as if in the sun.
It had stumbled a long way to this place
leaving a trail hunters followed for miles.

Animals and fruit open, giving
whatever they are.
And women, too, for each month
the womb pays tribute to a history of sorrow.

In one half of the pomegranate
I count the seasons of blood I've paid to the earth
in the other
the ones I still owe.

4.
It's the last of the season's fruit
chambered like a heart
its rooms packed.
I turn it in my hands thinking
that the simplest things
tell many stories, though actually
they're stories we tell ourselves.
The story in which we are born
is a famous one, as is the story that details
the separate terms of our death.
There's the story in which
we give in to the body
its shakings and reverberations of color
its deep-down irrepressible shine.
And each one ends on the same note
the same curious phrase
that we listen for, expectant as children —
the mysterious denouement of our lives.
We close our eyes and let go.

P. Schneidre

263: *The Artist*

Tolstoy,
appearing as himself in a dream,
accused me of dreaming.
I woke up. No Tolstoy.
He was right.

I appeared to Tolstoy in a dream.
Again he accused me of dreaming.
I woke up. No Tolstoy.
An artist is always right.

Tolstoy appeared
to himself in a dream.
I accused him of dreaming.
He woke up. Tolstoy.
I, too, will get it right.

264: *Essay on Perfection*

This is not the place to
discuss the rain forests
of Paraguay, or their
small variations in
midwinter coloring,
or whether Paraguay
has any rain forests;
neither is Paraguay.

265: *Train Song*

To ask you
not to go
is to look,
I know,
like a blurred hobo
who didn't jump quick
or hard enough
to catch
the slow
train.

So
tell me as you start to move
and your weaknesses
to fall off backwards
if I was always
among them.

266: *Autumns in a Row*

Lover, to cry
is to do so alone. You
on whom tears were lost and I,
remembering you as a season
whose hands I held
in those of someone
whose only coincidence
was to walk with you,
as whatever it was to be with you,

return
to a time
when all became clothed
in every shade of unimportance.
Every season but our own
was surpassed. And now,
because it didn't last,
it doesn't end.

I didn't
know what
you saw
as you
saw me
through blood
didn't want
even you
to know
it's not
too late
you could
still bring
me back
to your
side all
you needed
was blood
you could
not have
kept all
your blood
I know
you would
have given
half of
it, trading
some for
my own
now I
can't lose
any blood
it stays
why don't
you come
for my
blood, you
weren't so
shy when
you were
showing me
your blood
though it's

all you
showed me
at last
I don't
know what
gave you
away or
what turned
to blood
when I
looked for
it near
your body
but it
lost its
other color
you were
made of
blood it
was all
that kept
you here
a river
washing, protecting
your heart
I stepped
into the
stream of
you, do
you think
it was
so different
stepping back
out afterwards
if you
once had
loved me
not all
of your
blood would
have surrendered
to itself
surrounding me
and the
blood stopped

I believed
in blood
there it
was on
us in
the beginning
blood is
water is
not blood
you could
have had
me why
did you
want to
become blood
I only
took one
thing from
you and
I gave
it back
your blood
I was
wrong to
get on
the wrong
side of
blood, yes
but would
it have
gone on
forever, it
brought you
no further
than me
there's only
so much
one ever
sees of
one's blood,
though others
can't stop
looking I
still have
blood none

of it
is mine
because I
held you
under your
blood at
the end
you tried
to tell
me you
were more
than blood
you wanted
your blood
to be
less than
you but
it washed
all of
you away

Terryl Hunter

268: *The Boating Party*

Here on the Sound it is cold.
But we choose to take the small boat.
This one.

My child sleeps on my lap.
Bjorn handles the oars and the words.
Jeff passes the pipe and cannot catch a fish.
We see them leaping:
silver rockets to remind
little boats   little people
how easy passing is.
Two men and a woman
small gods   brood
rocking on hard wet wood.
The child   the fish   move
with fins in dreams.

The water wants to lick our lives.
We will remember this.
Like a photograph of a tide —
impossible.
But here   under our boat
under our breath
it rides.

269: *Alley/Movie*

Coming out of the movie I can see
how an alley has just the right light
to ween your eyes out from your face and a crowd.
You could be the only one here
assuming this night like a well fit shirt.

I place upon the vision just this importance:
that it is a movie I've always wanted to be in.
And it could end or begin just like this
between shadow and brick.
A hint of electricity and the crowd disappears.
You would walk to me and say
you've been looking for years for this alley
for some commonplace privacy
to entertain me   to place your hands
against the wall above my head
and lean in close to court me. Half darkness
would be only one of the perfections
of this scene.
But what really happens is
the crowd wins out. We smother. We'll look down
to watch the asphalt glitter with friends
and discuss the film we've just seen.
We'll assess the cinema's fine eye
and distance ourselves according to how little
we really know each other   how little
we trust our images of romance.
We'll go off to separate cars and sit before ignition
thinking alley. And the movie will roll
on and on   impossibly.

270: *Appearance*

for Nora

Long before I met his other lover
he handed me a stack of photographs in a dream.

One is of the waxy hood of a red car
so precise   so clear I can see
a face reflected.

I think mine.

But closer   another woman emerges.
Your dark face   the shock
of your black hair spread
across the garish metal.

I go on to the next. Again it's you.
But this time the picture turns into event

and I stand here watching you
push a bicycle
up a steep hill of flapping grass.
Wind rattles your blouse
yet your body climbs easily. Through the spokes
your legs appear banded in silver.
Taking ground.

I won't push you and you won't fall.
Even if you did   I'd catch you
prop you up
so I could see you this close.

271: *Prairies of Unbelievable Grace*

Grade school gives you that first vast itch
with a Sandburg ballad.
It tells you that sweet gold fields
are never boring. That the prairie is your birthright
as an American but you know damnwell
you'll never see one. You'll see stucco.
You figure out that America has been bored for years
with its prairiness. Too bland. They like to pave it
and place pedestrians there.
They liven it up. They chop across the acres
while you sing Amber Waves of Grain
and they bring it all to heel. Tie it up
with tight gray streaks going everywhich away.
Then they dot it
with little automobiles.

Older you see a sadder picture.
Along with the American Indian and the buffalo
and farmers called Settlers — but are they?
Sad because it's you. The Rugged Individualist
wandering and looking for the lost American prairie
of divine freedom and grace.

For me the vision becomes refined.
As specific as the photographs
that were never taken.
The Alabama prairie grandma first saw
as a girl from Holland. Poor and dry.
Or the dairy farm she came to

all grown up and married Dutch
in a California arroyo. Newlyweds struggling with cows.
Or the fields in Missouri that surrounded
little towns and my mother's people.
Crosstitching.
Playing cards with lemonade in the heat.

It's sad because just for a moment
it is not the land that is lost but me. Stranded
with this awkward heartache.
That they teased me so with Sandburg.
That every now and then I could be so startled
out of the blue. So embarrrassed
to be walking up and down the sidewalk
with everyone else
our radios crying on our shoulders.

272: *I Sit on the Back Porch and Watch*

I SIT ON THE BACK PORCH AND WATCH the trash cans sit
between the crate left from a shipment of art
and the barbie camper my daughter has thrown out.
My car has a new dent. The dog revs up
at some rat in the firewood. Things pass away in back yards
everyday. I try to imagine people in the country
porching these things
or do they really just take in all that weather?
Oh things must pass there too. And a year ago
I wouldn't have written this
that I am drinking tequila and smoking a cigarette
in the night air   placing myself so plainly
in the present and taking in the outside chance
of another evening on another porch at the same time
and how they are doing it.
My brother wrote me a letter from Hawaii and said
that my poems have disturbed him
that I seem to grab onto a moment of the past and hold on
to it and surely I do get across that moment but am I
holding onto something like a possessive mother?
This poem is for my brother whom I love
to tell that everything is passing as I sit
and everything I sit through or write will be some moment
and holding on and getting it and getting on.
As close as I can get to this night on the porch

I can get to my baby brother being swept up and stuffed
into the plymouth 28 years ago screaming
to the hospital with a waffled hand from the heater.
Me waiting on the porch.
What isn't some moment and once it is
it passes and keeps passing
as many times as it's useful to live it.

Lori Cohen

273: *Sub Specie Evolutionis*

This is the history of everyone:
a small rock.
Some mud.

The fish are outrageous.
They grow and sing.
They breathe through a slit on their hips.
They tell jokes:
What do generals do with their armies?
They put them through their sleevies!
Then gasp
and die. Water is limited
after all.
And then the sky comes
and breaks open the lake.
Soon, the fish begin to remember
each other's faces.
They think about plants:
how plants move in the water like sleeping fish.
They think about size
and physical scale.

And when the night comes
the fish crawl out to become amphibian.
The appearance of legs
blots out the other distinctions.
A few sleep without moving.
One floats into a tree.
The others, upset by
the increase of pressure
on the surface of a planet,
dip back into the water
thin and conceited:

at such depths
all differences become tenuous.

274: *Our Kitchen*

We sit at
the cold counter,
boning fish.
They're comic things,
resembling relatives, of course.
Father, who doesn't even know
the best places to fish,
empties another sack
into the sink.
Some of them are moving,
their reflexes
still urging them downward.

275: *On Ice*

In the violence I'm
afraid of, knife against
my nipples, lip and cheek
bleeding too deep
to smooth with other skin;

afraid of movies,
the human image near the door,
white shoes waiting
behind the garage.

It's all I can do
to decide: stop moving
altogether and listen.
Or move. Near the window.
Mouth against the screen.

I have died violently twice
in the last two days:
on ice, through my mouth,
a pressure in my heart,

and through the searching
for phenomenal — muscles
dead in sleep protect us
from our own violence.

There are blisters
I sleep in, sheets
I have torn with two
strong feet. I'm beginning
to believe it comes
from outside me. An omen,
a suggestion to prepare me.

My own knife breaks
the breastbone with its
tip, cutting the air
then twisting it deeply
so it stays in.

When breath stops
in sleep outside
the body, we
call it air.

Aleida Rodríguez

276: *Breaking Loose*

for Caesar

I am now beginning to understand the porcelain tank
on Caesar's toilet exploding   right in the middle of our
                    reheated meatballs
spoons frozen midway to our mouths
like a brick thrown at the house
so that at first we were drawn to the outside
for the source of this hostility   but nothing peculiar:
just the empty lot of night and the white fig tree posing
                    against it
and a gushing somewhere in the back of our ears   so that
                    it said
bathroom to us and running finding it already under an inch
of water with no sign of stopping or draining but an
                    endless childhood
of repressed complaints   seeping out into the green
                    shag carpet
in the hallway

I can understand it better now   the tank suddenly
cracking for no apparent reason   pressing its clammy back
against that wall for the last time   exhausted
with its own complacency since Nov 13 1953   a few
                    months younger
than me I find myself slipping on why   I demand of Caesar
it was still perfectly good   not old not old at all
instead of where to find the turnoff valves

But now I can understand it   fed up
with its tense white smile   teeth always showing in the
                    photographs
while the inside drained and was filled
managing never to overflow   dutifully maintaining
                    appearances

and leading a life of fine balance   controlling
how much went in   came out   carefully

I understand it wanting out   feeling
"no one really knows me"   wanting to let go
like a man who discovers he contains a woman
wanting to throw itself on the bathroom floor sobbing
for the many wasted years
and slowly inching up the sides of our shoes
as we try to make it better

277: *Little Cuba Stories/Cuentos de Cuba*

II
Opening the door of the house at one end let you see all the way
to the half-cemented back yard. The path was so direct and
without obstacle that the small dog my sister and I brought home
could see the front door open from the back yard, streak through
the house, escape—and would later be found eating and rolling
around happily in the rotting carcasses by the slaughter house.
That's the way she died. The men poisoned the discarded meat.
They were tired of her frequent visits. But not until I was safely
in this country, spared the spectacle my father saw before he
buried her.

278: *We Are Intimate*

Objects settle into their logical relationships. The dust that falls
on them has been hovering over that space with its photographic
memory forever prepared to take their shapes.

Canaries and the wild ones puffed like ornaments after the rain
sing and trill and squeak, perched in my veins' branches.

The cat stretches from her circle of black and gold fur and looks
at me as though she's gazing through the deep universes between
my atoms.

279: *Epiphany*

I'm worried about Bill Manzana, he said. He was spinning around his white kitchen on one of the hottest days of the year. Shutting drawers, sliding knives into their wooden rack.

What now. I was leaning against the wall trying to cool myself, looking out the kitchen window at the driveway filled with old cars.

He's shooting.

Great. I said, not turning around. I wanted to know what kinds of cars they were. One was fifties; it glinted its silver teeth at me. And they were all covered with peaches, peaches that had fallen from the tree overhanging the driveway.

The cars cradled them on their heads and laps as though still offering them to someone. Forget it in this heat. The sun was burning a tiny yellow laser through each one of them.

Wow. Look at all those rotting peaches, I said.

Yeah, he said. *Isn't that incredible.*

280: *I've Got Something Personal Against the Bomb*

My few childhood pictures show that I never smiled — I had nothing to smile about — and instead held my lips compressed into a little smirk. Just as I entered the world it was already spoiled for me. Where were the jewel-like teeth that should have accompanied my angelic spirit into the world, I wanted to know. By the age of seven I had kicked my patent leather shoe into the face of a dentist.

That was the year after Castro took over. The year we were waiting to see what would become of the promise of abundance, the taking from the rich to give to the poor. My father squinted his eyes at such a promise and applied for our visas. But my mother was carried along by the earliest wave of enthusiasm and pulled me with her to the event that started the general slide toward disillusionment.

The field was yellow-green where the helicopter started to land and my mother was forcing me between the bands of rusty barbed wire. My shirt caught and we were held up from joining the others who had already slipped through and were running toward the helicopter. Fidel was supposed to be in it — a man of the people coming to our little village. But the copter changed its mind when it saw all the people running toward it. It swooped up suddenly and people screamed and waved and my mother and I just stood looking up at it holding our foreheads and not understanding what was happening. Later we heard that it wasn't him at all but someone dressed up like him in that helicopter, fooling us.

I come from a land of betrayals and disappointments, rotten teeth and a corrupt revolution. It has taken me thirty years to smile despite my teeth, twenty-one years to claim and cultivate the island inside me because the one shaped like a crocodile has been taken from me forever. I have done this despite the bomb leaning intimately over my shoulder, spoiling the taste of flan, wilting my hopes for a tropical garden. I have managed to put one word in front of the other like steps away from the edge of a cliff, steps away from the razor blades and pills in my parent's medicine cabinet.

So you see, that's why when they persist with their blow-up scheme, I say no to them. I say no to them and will keep on saying it. And my spirit, which began in the filth of decay, is rich compost now and will make more life bloom in answer.

281: *The Carwreck Poem*

(Portrait of the man you saw
in your rear-view mirror on
the highway south of big sur)

Never been without a car before
since I was a boy at least
and a bicycle was enough
oh there was once years ago
when we rented a car
and honeymooned on the coast
and for a few months
streetcars and busses were fine
sometimes we caught the same one home
when you worked late
Remember the first Christmas Eve
I got off at noon
and raced home and trimmed the tree
and every time a streetcar scuffled to a stop
at our corner I hid in the closet
behind the pulldown bed
to see your face
behind the pulldown bed
to see your face
when you opened the door
we spent half my twenty buck bonus
on fruitcake and brandy
the rest went on past due bills

But speaking of cars our first one
a shiny blue jewel on the used car lot
with lines clean as a colt
cars were lean and manageable then
no lacy chrome no fins wings bullets

no padded dash no stereo
we got a radio later
and   had a helluva lot of fun I think
I don't remember where all we went
except for the time we got stuck
in the mountains in a snowstorm
Washington's Birthday wasn't it
and later coming home weekends from the new job
each trip a little faster than the last
then when the baby was born
and we moved and the three of us
explored all the coves and villages
north of Point Conception
and the trip up the coast looking for work
riding a winter rainstorm all the way
we stayed overnight someplace south of Salinas
and Lisa slept on the closet floor
and we all ate crackers
I wonder sometimes
what if I'd taken that job in the City
Excuse me I was distracted
by the regular evening meeting
of woodpeckers blue jays and sparrows up here
getting back to cars
our first one the blue colt lost its guts
towing a trailer up the Santa Barbara hills
we were on the move again
and I traded the carcass and payment book
for a paid-up straight 8 Packard sedan
ten or twenty years old
the radiator drizzled incessantly
but you could coast a lot
when it rained
I steered through the side window
and cursed the leaky pneumatic windshield wiper system
you heard me coming up the hill blocks away
and you got the hose and buckets ready
and all the kids on our street lined up
and cheered when I made it
I taught them a lot about whales and geysers
but their moms weren't quite sure about me
though they liked the way I could settle a scrap
or quiet a crying child

Then one day someone at the office saw me
parking three blocks away in the old wreck

and the boss called me in and he said
look you got a good job here
how come you drive that old wreck
think what folks will say if they know you work
for me and drive that old wreck
you drink or something can't you handle money
maybe you can't handle this job
I like someone who drives a new car
or maybe something two three years old
but still respectable
well I considered steaming up Alameda Padre Serra
and rolling the old wreck down the driveway
into his prize-winning begonias
but instead I walked for a while
and then thanks to my promising future with his firm
and a totally demented credit manager
I got anpther car something like the colt
but it wasn't the same around the office anymore
especially a few months later
when I put STEVENSON FOR PRESIDENT stickers
on both bumpers things got
a little slow and we moved again

Back to the city back to the
souped up flat out 4-on-the-floor city
and for the first time in my life
big fat paychecks
goddam what a system I said
I used to be a jr executive
but jean still had to work between babies
now I'm a fucking peon
but we eat out once or twice a week
and I send my shirts to the laundry
and we buy the best booze
and holy jesus we can afford a new car
a brand new car
dad never even had a new car
a brand new car
and boy the sweet smell the fresh clean smell
of virgin paint and upholstery
and christ how the thing glistened in the sun
when I washed it and chamoised it down
it was a stationwagon of course
and it looked great anyplace

Well it's three cars later now
and three four jobs
and ulcers and alimony and all that crap
and the last car's totalled out
rusting on a garage floor
waiting for the insurance adjuster
who'll never come
hell they can have the wreck
for the towing bill
me
maybe I'll learn to walk again

Max Benavidez

282: *Los Angeles*

Cars roar,
faces stream by
in ennui-stricken horror —
a park with walking talkers,
tree leaves shaking in the wind
under self-conscious sunny skies.

Drifting along Broadway near
the Million Dollar Theater,
scents of grease cooking, cheap
perfume, old pissed wine.

At night —
a taxi to
Violette's room on 5th near Central.

Almost Transparent Blue by
Ryu Murakami on her dresser. She
passes a silk kimono over my face,
we are flush with strong wine.

Bitter lemon morning,
cold morning,
late fall.

We are talking walkers,
a duo
through pershing Square —
her hand-embroidered scarf,
gold, black and red,
grabbed up by a delirious
breeze swooping west,
and hitting the
Biltmore's flags.

City of Angels,
ghost of my emotions
stranded
on an off-ramp,
in a car
abandoned
with no engine.

In L.A.
that can be
a raw joke.

283: *In a Room with No One*

sitting, darkness, television running on,
grieving, it's 4 a.m., the set is dead,
the whiteness, the coarseness bleaches
the walls of the room.

sitting alone in a room with no one
only a television, you say I'm normal
it's only normal to be alone again and again
sitting alone in a room with no one

in my chair with a remote control, sitting
watching nothing at 4 a.m., it's quite normal
to be alone in a room with a tepid whiteness
staring at my bloodshot eyes that never shed
tears for anyone, anytime, anywhere

sitting alone in a room with no one
with something that speaks and says nothing
with my solid state hot color tubes burning
sitting alone in a room with no one

sitting by a telephone that never rings
no one thinks to call because no one thinks
that I exist except maybe a mother
somewhere in a room alone with no one watching
a series of blips move across her blank screen

sitting alone in a room with no one
screaming for help, waiting for my story
to be telecast in full-bloodied color
sitting alone in a room with no one

sitting, darkness gone, in a yellow morning,
having cut off my tongue and squeezed its blood
on the screen, I remember that no one is with me
that I am alone, that I want to talk but no
longer can —

sitting alone in a room with no one
with cotton balls in my mouth
I am bleeding to death and the television is
sitting alone in a room with no one

284: *Acts of Anti-Heroism*

The smell of evening
after evening, silently sad

having left

the ember in your eyes
remnant of a fiery day

you keep saying
as I leave

adios adios
whispering

forever forgetting
the sad leaving

tired and whipped down
jealous

nothing more

remember the winter?
the snow?

into the cold wind
I dissolved

if ever again
yes, then

your taste, your smell
the evening is thin

come with me
I'm not proud

weaker than weak
I walk the same road

look at me
love fading fast

285: *Arizona Moon*

You read me a poem.
It said:
there are no roots,
everything barely rests
on a tremor of rain

I ran
from you,
drove the desert
to forget you,
to erase you

I drove
into the night
and saw the moon

It lives and dies
like us

It comes and goes
like us

And I made love to it

Then I drove home
to you
to beg
for your touch
that makes me hot
with a lovely
neurotic
passion.

 **286:** *City of Ash*

I live
where the city
flattens
like an empty lake bed.

I wear
a black ritual robe
my singing robe.

I chant
from a mass
where silken vestments
fall like shadows.

Smoke rises,
everywhere
with sadness
the gauze smoke
rises.

Goat song,
tragic song
in a hot space
buzzing in the silent
hole of death.

I hear
the goat song
burning
like sun reflecting
on shiny corpses.

Eclipse
apocalypse

That is the song
in the air
in the shadows
in the stone
that is the mystery.

I'll sleep
in the city of ash
and dream
the goat song,
my goat song.

I am the goat...
I am singing the song

And my hoofbeats
mark my steps
to the city of ash.

287: *Falling Sand*

We see
a flash,
white light
glazing the sky.

We hear
a sound,
rushing
like falling sand.

Shadows
are burned
into walls,
people who were.

We feel
an air blast
like a sudden
annihilating wind.

It moves
away,
then back,
sucking up
dust & smoke
into a stemmed cloud.

A rain
falls,
black & radiant.

A freezing
chills
the air.

Clear skies.

My body
disperses
like falling sand...

And
I'm...gone...

288: *Portugese Man-of-War*

I

The Portugese Man-of-War is a large, warm-water jelly-fish which floats on the ocean by means of a translucent gas-filled sac, streaked iridescent, like oily water in the sun. Below this "balloon" hangs a mass of multi-colored "guts," and many blue, red, and purple tentacles for stinging prey.

Seen floating at a distance, the balloon brings to mind a sailing ship, hence its name; though its shape is more nearly like the top half of a Roman helmet, or the head of nearly submerged, crested dinosaur.

II

Around March 1, before the Spring crowd, Ted Liedeker and I liked to hit Galveston. While our families grilled sand-burgers, we'd comb miles of beach to see what winter had tossed up. There'd be old bottles, light bulbs, net-floats, shells, crates with foreign writing, driftwood (sometimes whole trees), plus an occasional dead shark, grouper, sea turtle, or nameless rotting monster inches deep in flies. Not to mention Man-of-Wars. March was their month.

We'd grab long sticks and gallop up and down the shore like knights, lancing balloons to hear them pop. They were made of a thin jello which dried brittle in the sun. When one washed in, we'd wade out, poke out sticks behind it, and lift ten feet of tentacle. Being heavier, tentacles trail the floats. So we were safe—we hoped. On shore or off, we never walked behind a Man-of-War. Even the popped balloons spit out a mist which reddened our red legs, and itched to beat all hell.

III

Looking up "plesiosaur" in the BRITTANNICA, I came across Portugese Man-of-War. Some facts:

1) The Man-of-War is not a true jellyfish, but a complex colony of polyps, each adapted to one special function: protection/food capture; digestion; flotation; reproduction.

2) The Man-of-War was named by English sailors, who encountered flotillas of them in the seas off Portugal.

3) Man-of-War tentacles may exceed fifteen feet long. Their sting can kill a man. The best antidote is vinegar.

4) The Man-of-War's float may be a foot long. The animal secretes the gas inside: 90% nitrogen, a trace of argon, the rest oxygen. A valve allows gas to escape, and the float to sink as much as necessary, when necessary.

5) The Man-of-War moves solely by current or wind, its float doubling as a sail. It slows its speed by releasing gas and sinking.

6) The Man-of-War's shape causes it to tack 45 degrees into the wind. In the northern hemisphere, it tacks to the left; in the southern, to the right.

7) Sea turtles are one of the few animals which can eat Man-of-War's. Their shells and scales protect them; but they have to feed with their eyes closed.

8) The Man-of-War Fish lives among the the tentacles, safe from enemies, sharing food killed by the Man-of-War, and browsing on its tentacles. Healthy, the fish is immune to Man-of-War vemon. Becoming sick or injured, it falls prey at once.

IV

There were always Man-of-Wars around Galveston; but except in March they're rare, and you usually see them coming. Even so, half-blind as I am without glasses, I never swim or surf without a friend to scan the waves. I remember too well my father's tan face, stark white against the sand, my mother frantic, me hysterical, thinking he was dead.

The rows of fiery welts on his back and legs lasted into the next spring.

V

I just heard a lecture called "Confusion in Sexual Identity: The Search for a Model." Some guys have it tough. If I was ever confused that way, it stopped on my fifth birthday.

I was sitting on Dad's shoulders, surf-fishing and jumping waves, both of us in swim-trunks. I saw a rainbow-balloon float by and started to show Dad, just as he flinched once and, without even scaring me, waded the fifty yards to shore, and gently set me down.

Austin Strauss

289: *Two Portraits*

If all the things known by everyone who has ever
                    known me
Were spoken like bits of glass onto a wall
That wall would not resemble me.

It would be some unearthly creature with animal
                    eyes
Longjawed and strange
Perhaps a forest god, perhaps a fish.

Yet if all the things I know about myself, or
                    think I know,
Were spoken like flashes of steel, like cuts in
                    a face of rock,
That rock would not resemble me.

It would be someone I once passed on a street,
                    some guy I caught a glimpse of
                    in a speeding car,
                    some familiar stranger with a crooked
                    smile and veiled eyes,
                    someone who refuses to be sneaked up
                    upon.

290: *The Shortest Day*

                    for Sascha

there will be the briefest of lights
like brightness glimpsed
between tall buildings

and you will live quickly
inside that light, if you leap
into it, if you are not afraid

and the light will color your skin
and flow into you like water
and ask you questions

and you will wrestle with it
as with an angel, and you will
achieve and create and be whole

and when the light squeezes you and the
light into that last
point of brightness

you will be drunk with the light
you've devoured, and you will truly
be one to be reckoned with

291: *The Sink*

the sink is
a hard white flow
er
with two nick
el
cocks
that spout
cold
and colder;
I wonder
lying here
in this crack
ed
room
beneath a cei
ling
pregnant
with roaches
between walls
full of
dip
lo

graceful sink,
so solid and
white,
sculpted flow
er
clutching
last light
to your
pedicel,
glowing,
making of this
foul dump
a hushroom
forest
where
dresser
table
chair
rug
are trees
and grass,
where sink is

matic
rats,
who the guy was,
fifty,
maybe a hun
dred
years ago
sat down and
flowered
a sink
to sway
my thoughts to...

a sacred spout
of bee
and bird
and blackbug
wisdom,
where sink is
a holi
ness...
flow
er
of my hotel night
goodnight!

John Thomas

292: *In My Bed: In My Arms:*
How She Comes

Drake Passage
a thousand miles
of open ocean /
                    all afternoon
                    the frigate bird flies
                    ahead of his reflection
                    in the wave

293: *Her Poor Things*

make a heap on the floor
beside the bed:
frayed old cloth purse
crammed full and trailing
sad little coils of toilet tissue
borrowed underpants (whose?)
Chico Marx Goodwill felt hat (Chico Marx???)
satin blouse all creased, minus a button
the small rest of it, all
junk.

            Divested, bare
            she brings to the bed only
            splendor, only
            gold leaf, stained glass
            shimmering veils of aurora
            splendor
            that defeats poetry, defeats
            my poor efforts, anyhow

Two days, now she's been gone.
I'm edgy, I'm distracted, I miss her already.
Oh, she'll be back, and
I can wait for
the splendor

> but dammit
> I miss her
> old red socks

294: *Underwater Interlude*

fast in the grip
of the starfish
fifty fathoms down
I feel the pulse
deep inside her my lips
on the arch of her foot
I see the day flow away
like a slow fuse and up
up faraway up there
quiver the great blue screens!

295: *They're Wrong to Call It the Little Death and to Hell with the Here and Now*

> "I do not believe in the witchcraft
> she practices on me..."
> — Caravaggio

we take our pleasure, it is dark and regal
and strange, she could be Guinivere
risking Hell and her crown and damn their eyes
it's worth it ten times over and I
I hope to die at the last thrust lost
in her smell of sweat and vanilla we pause
I want her again but we pause and
casually she tears off a toenail
drawing blood then slyly tucks it
under my mattress: scary but

so moving: Guinivere
to the life

then she shifts a lazy shoulder and
Tara Tintagel Lyonesse the
whole damned Bronze Age
rolls up against me
her fingers lace into mine
on the wet tuft of her sex I
want her again our two hands become
one great paw I'm into her again
don't know where any longer but
into her Christ! is this Africa?
I smell blood and grass I search
her face as I come the lioness
glows in the antelope's eye

296: *Untitled*

you bring me apple trees, flowering apple trees
all the lost best poems of Sappho
new life at the core of the flame
happy deaths in a sea of milk

my pockets are a poet's pockets
that is to say, nearly empty
please accept what I bring you tonight:
a cold quart of Coors
(one dollar twenty-two cents)
this limping, feeble poem
my whole heart

297: *Poem Written in Your Absence*

On Isla Patranca down
in the Straits of Magellan
there are five great waterfalls.
Four of them pour uselessly
into the cold grey sea.

298: *Thanksgiving Day*
for Philomene

food in the kitchen
two cups of coffee warm in my belly
last night's loving still warm in my heart

I sit here, writing
you sit there, writing better
perhaps in an hour or two
in bed with you again

I will strive
all the rest of my life
to deserve this day

299: *Our Old Age, A Joyous Vision*

You are smiling serenely, eyes agleam above two bright spots
of rouge. You wear two tweed jackets, five skirts, no socks. A
rhinestone coronet completes the ensemble. I am a great
mouldering haystack, a dropsical heap in pajamas and over-
coat, ten years crippled, forgetting and forgotten. You are
hopelessly mad. I am hopelessly not, which is the same. We
are both still mad with love.

It is the first of April and it is dawn and we are taking the
air, making our stately progress down an empty grey board-
walk by the grey sea. You march ahead, pushing the rusty
shopping cart piled high with every shabby thing we own. You
might be pushing the Prince Imperial in his perambulator, you
move with such an air. I trundle along behind, hunched in my
wheelchair, trailing you in great eccentric swoops.

You reach the spot before me, as always, and you stop.
Turning, you nod most graciously round about you, accepting
the hallucinatory cheers of the theatre-going multitudes.
("Author! Author!") I am badly winded when I catch up.
After I collect myself and my breath returns to me, I speak.
"My dear, you have never looked more beautiful." For an
answer, you caress my cheek and I blush like a schoolboy.

The package, when I produce it from inside my coat, is an eight-inch cylinder clumsily wrapped in gay gift paper. Together we hold it, my hand at the base, yours above mine. "Now?" I ask. "Now," you say, and I strike a match and light the fuse.

Your smile is stunning. Your rhinestones sparkle. Ten seconds pass, ten thousand lazy smiling years. We explode into one another and into the great grey eye of God.

300: *Ghost Story*

He stands on the pier in dripping swim trunks, smiling like a hero. He holds a one-gallon bottle of milk, his left palm at the bottom, the fingers of his right hand not quite encircling the neck. They will photograph him, drinking this milk. He is a contestant, perhaps, or the smiling winner, or he is endorsing the product of some local dairy. The pier stretches off behind him. BAIT SOLD HERE! SKEETER BALL 10¢. There are men and women on the pier, in the summer dress of 1938 or near enough. They do not look at him. He will be photographed. Any moment now, he will tilt the great white bottle and drink the milk. He is muscular and looks very fit. His hair is combed straight back. He is balding. I have just noticed that while his baggy woollen trunks are wet, his hair is dry and carefully combed. His picture will be taken. Judging by the length of his shadow, it is mid-morning or mid-afternoon. He drinks nothing yet. He is just about to, always. The people behind him stroll or stand about. None of them looks at him. They don't know. He doesn't know. A man will photograph him. He smiles a hero's smile and it is 1938 and he will never drink this milk, never. No one knows anything. I am very afraid. I have forgotten how to breathe.

301: *Camp Starvation Aug 5*

There be nothing to eat here Just bugs and trap door spiders I eaten a little root I dug this morning which was bitter It must of been some kind of loco weed for I been crazy all day Not over it yet I dont think because just a while back a little cloud fetch past out of the south just sailing along ever so lovely and I up and running after it I cant run much being much weakened Not much to nourish up on here So I fallen down and see my fool self sitting in the dirt trying to cry with my arms raised up My hands stretched out for the cloud and my damned old fingers turn to dust Fall right off my fists I know this is crazy so no more of them roots for me Just bugs till I croak and it is the bugs turn But no real cloud ever was so fair You should have seen it

All the boys are dead the whole troop I wish I could say they died good but not true Some real bad ways to die out here and I wish there was no eating of bodies but this is a true report and the truth is there was some of that Not me on my oath never me But Corporal Wingos kidney was offered to me It was roast on a long stick I lie if I say I didnt want to but not me I am Sergeant and I would not though the fat drippings smelt ever so good Sergeants do not eat Troopers I let them eat it though I just ate my bugs and puked A lot of good it did them All dead now but me and soon me

I could maybe hike out Still strong enough I think Have to slice meat to do it Make jerky Could just about make it No sir Not this old soldier I wont slice that meat Any how I got them into this I thought I knew the short cut God damn me for that All my young troopers dead and my fault God damn my sorry ass I will not slice meat and pack out I will just eat bugs and die God damn my sorry ass

> *Love. Love.*
> *How do the others bear it?*
> *The white cloud*
> *drifts out of my reach;*
> *sour dust stops my nostrils.*
> *How do the others bear it?*

302: *Doctor Faustus*

The interview was conducted in his kitchen, at a small round table which had not been recently scrubbed. Medicine bottles and unopened mail left little room for our elbows. There were just the two chairs. He rarely leaves his kitchen now, he said. He did not offer to share his oatmeal, but ate it all himself, rather messily, straight from an old black pot.

I asked him all the obvious questions. His answers were not evasive, but I found them oddly disappointing. In recent years, he told me, he has been much troubled by insects.

From time to time while we talked, he would glance up in annoyance at the ceiling, where the household angels hung upside down, like bats. "Nasty things, young man. You've no idea how nasty."

"One last question, Doctor. What would you say is the least pleasant aspect of having made your famous Pact?"

He sighed, probed his ear with a long old finger, examined what he had found there.

"It's a marriage," he said.

303: *Noctuary*

As if it were a ghastly, glaring death-mask drawn on paper. Each night he wads the paper carelessly and tosses it on the floor beside the bed. We imagine him asleep and slowly through the night the stiff paper unfolding in the dark, so that every morning the face is there again, staring at him. Every morning (because of new creases and new ways of unfolding) it has a new expression: mockery; ghoulish appetite; awful patience; accusation; or, worst, sympathy and understanding.

Every night, while he sleeps, the slow, silent, inexorable unfolding. It is waking, not dreaming, that separates the soul from the body.

Paul Vangelisti

304: *The Extravagant Room*

and the world which is art
who understands
so much glass
so many windows needed in cars
to entertain the word 'art'
that bread is no commodity
but a hand spread on a wobbly table
a butterfly wearing the saddle
of your own death
and the world which refuses every gesture
not rewritten at the cost of art

*

yet the appetite that we are
a hunger for not remaining alone
reduced to four receding walls
the single perfectly pliable mouth
where all are said to find shelter
to reveal their most peculiar dreams
walking and talking
just like the guy next door

*

and these dreams of
what seems a moment before waking
on one's back
the lines
five or six of them
repeated over and over
like ironing a bright tablecloth
to be remembered

until it is time to remember that one
hardly visible and breathing
in the room

*

though now five or six lines
become twelve ways
of beginning the fantastic
the vacant poem
of becoming what they have become

*

one foot in the dark
tracing the cool grain of the floor
the dog is asleep
the children are asleep
flower pots at the open window
crouching like three cats
each minute or so
a woman somewhere cackles
what must have once been a laugh
though little matters
but the sheet caught between your knees
as you lie here asleep
fingers tracing on your hips
the same thing my foot is thinking
there is no metaphor for this sheet
this distance drawing me

*

so awkward this 'drawing'
maybe that is the value
a resilience to even extravagant use
like the old joke about the fastest draw in the West
like the old joke about the fastest draw in the West
like the old joke about the fastest draw in the West

*

to say nothing of
the puckered heart
painted on tit or forearm
the flirtation of conscience

we offer the earth
the very air we run through our fingers
as if it were a gift

*

because he is asking to sit down
actually at the same table sit down
when there are ten other tables
wearing a suit without a tie
the accent of small business
empty rooms and children
slaughtered in a century beyond dreams
a history which has stopped
begun again and stopped
though he repeats his question
and adds if I don't mind

*

to say nothing
of what some chose not to say
denying the beast
the light-guzzling aperture
of that dreamy performance
we have all been promised from birth

*

good night good night
as in New York New York
that time of night
not hard to imagine Land's End
the ocean the rocks below
oblivious and fresh
as that first morning you woke up
next to her

*

nudging as if knees and feet
under the table
to end here
to begin once more
that face
that clarity of lost heroes

in search of a delirious afternoon
hoping for a phone call
to break off this poem

*

not even shadows of what little we dare
but the suggestion
of dreadful odds and ends
some voice not quite overheard
a matchbook in your pocket
from a city you have never been
an odor the back of a hand
which is no one else's but hers
who is not here

*

so the terror of innocence
the telephone calls continuing
to wake in a cold sweat
or maybe just the hopelessness
of certain poems
small ecstacies evoked
and as quickly forgotten
all but the sequence of syllables
the conclusions of an argument
like the color of someone's eyes
you simply cannot remember

*

of police and helicopters
the drone hammerlike
the hunger that is waking
words which are not words
but more like persons voices
missing in a place
one may never trust

*

and the language which is art
what is it so different
making new readers
of new poems

or as a painter said it once
working all night
into the first glance of morning
the room is so large
each corner and nick on the floor
as if the eyes are coming
right out of your head

*

yet the pronoun
the I of this peculiar vision
prone to sense what is not stated
to state what is not prone to sense
the sympathy of color after a light rain
the size of windows and parked cars
the boundaries of this and every other afternoon
the telephone poles
the pencil
the light switches
growing so small
one is left holding nothing
but one's breath

*

something like naming vision
though by naming vision
it is more improbable
less complex
than the vertical ambition
of naming love
in our own likeness

*

and 'likeness'
the bath the heat of water
as we lay back hardly touching
and likeness
the word unwanted
not understood
the likeness of what is not love

*

there are islands
moments of rock and coral
where ships vanish
because they are parables
and there is no communication out there
but the reconstruction of whimsy
chance encounters
phrases one can't finally remember
and there is a quiet about the eyes
almost green this quiet
and sometimes even green the eyes

                    *

without an answer
November brought you
from the east the wind shakes the houses
the warm mornings
the livid afternoons
knives and forks saltshakers even
glowing enormous with the size of it...
to shipwreck
to discover an island
to cross out so many words
you can recite them even in your dreams

                    *

yes
all it comes to
she says
'cielo e mare'
sky and sea
and there are no other questions
or answers
no comparisons
but the thin line her lips are
in the dark

                    *

simple as picking or
not picking up a pencil
not only the telling of it
is what brings one to the page
but the preoccupation

with what continues unspoken
as a man walking his bicycle
turns his head
at the passing windows

*

so the terror of innocence
a justification of marble eyes
which are not marble
but the color of a sparrow's beak
stiff and upsidedown
when it dies
the little wire legs
like a TV antenna
like that stuttered pronoun *I I*

*

sea and sky
which is not art
anymore than they are its inspiration
which is only the impossible fact
of not dreaming
what we are

*

We are on the other side of a window in a room which
expands and retracts. The room is there because we have
never been. It is furnished with the sound of two people
talking into the night though the sun has already been
up for a few hours. It is winter and the streams are low
and translucent as August. The eucalyptus are dry and
noisy though by the color of the hillside it must have
rained yesterday. The two are listening. They have
stopped talking but are not aware of having done so.

1975

Robert Crosson

305: *The Great Bronze Age of China*

first of all 2 dimes in yr pocket
wall-pictures of mines they dug
the treasures out calendars pitted
green pots & wine jugs under plexiglass made chinese brunch

*

rude girls with radios in their ear
cast bronze shadows inlaid with copper
& ivory skin noted they must in their
prime have been polished ceremonials
that sacrifice

*

feathers on the stairs
stone warriors propped up with their
horses rode stone follicles for hair
a jade phallus bridled & pitched
forward

'which accounts for their stance

*

poolside
with bobbed tails

*

swum.

306: *from: William James*

madness is isolate
an uncommon sense that says
you are someone else
in the face of anyone
who expects you to speak
so you do that
& that's what it's all about

a tone of voice & circumstance
feeling the shape of a thing
beyond the blank page
so you always, in that way,
have something to look forward to

them rare surprises

that is why it is not necessary anymore
to take notes during an earthquake
because you can stop when you want to
& be certain it will still go on
though you have not finished
yet
the description

music anyway is not
concerned with.

only the sound & exercise
of its signal repetition

307: *Homage*

To A Lady

*

in cuban heels she walks high on
hallmark movies and demands to change
all channels for valium telling me
(god) she wants a catholic marriage
& hasn't been laid in 2 months what

*

silence pertains to the customary
performance she dresses up for 3 days
crying steadily because kent told her
to fuck off last night before the shrink
phoned today to tell her he couldn't

*

take her on as paying customer she
demands he be (without problems) a
nonsmoker over thirty-five
& happily married
not fat she says

 Swamp

Two Pieces on Wittgenstein

1
The swamp had to be cleared of brittle weeds
and rusted teakettles.
        'Bombed out, wind-sucked to ground zero.'
The head gone, the rest buried.
(Somewhere the picture of him with a lump hardon—
how she got flushed when he did that—like that
once at the restaurant—fiddled up her dress
with his tennis shoe)
        Them days ws done.
        'You didn't snatch that young cock—
and or orifice, red-lipped warm and willing.
        He was not willing.
        But hell, you didn't seem to want it anyway.
        Being he ws eighteen, in bed to begin with.
Waiting for it...

        'Babbling, you are babbling.'
The Colonel stood watching. Twenty of those
'ruffian' (how he sd the word) soldiers gangfucked
before their memory went. 'Shanty songs—'
    Midway between a tar dock and an uptown
bank of cattails.

*

Dead now of course, his best friends sd so:
wanted three things — to get married,
make a baby and commit suicide.
Wrote haiku, fucked and exploded.

'Logic, man.' The Colonel ws adamant.
'Can't tell a man by his eyes.'
I am my car, I am my cristmas pajamas.

Tackiest part of the enterprise put hives on yr ass.

2
Pills?
A razor blade?
'Here man,' sd the Colonel, 'stop whining.'
Needed to hold he sd, and wasn't inclined.
Had to have a woman.
'Can't tell a man by his eyes.'
Cornholing ws nothing you did in knickers.
drolly standing in.
'I am my car.
I am my christmas pajamas.'

got him on the bed, serenaded mendelssohn records
plowed it in (his head caught under the doorsill)
and burnt his elbows on the carpet.
'Shanty songs —'
midway between a tar dock & an uptown bank of cattails.
Doubtless well endowed...
Dead now of course, best friends agreed.
Wanted three things: to get married
make a baby and commit suicide.
Wrote haiku, fucked and exploded.

'A = A2.'
A cow is not.
Tackiest part of the enterprise put hives on yr ass:
the creaking shoes, the itchy shirt that never fit him.
Stones were stones. The Colonel ws adamant:
'Do it asshole.'
Then send boxes of caramels.

309: *Six*

for Paul

the footstep freezes in midair
discursive as photographs or cold cars
abandoning ship or loud talk

'a fieldmouse that sounds like
a rather large rat in the heater'

a shimmering mirage
gods inside the hula-hoop
rattling everyday goodbyes

twelve songs across the road
singing ukulele
the metaphor

Intractable.

mouth damp on the pillow.

310: *Bagels*

dizzy the two sides spill out
shouts for that aversion being
a thursday on the hands sweat
three pounds and ten plastic
bags brought home to dock

surreptitious as my slippery ass
paid ten bucks to haul out the garbage

*

warmed-over red satin sheets we
sweat yesterdays stopping oceans
at the side of the road humped
like fence posts

making the act secure locks in the
bedroom thonged sandals under a pin-
ball machine beneath 5 acts the number
flashed neon & blue gas beneath or
atop yes the mouth upright

*

best health & a stout toast to
shine on each and every ramif-
ication words gobble up sense
to which the act stands perambu-
lating

*

get your foot off mine (under the table

Jed Rasula

311: *One Is As Red As Another*

> (my arm reached into the snout of this
> Being which Wills It
> and pulled out *Red*)

One is as red as the other
One is as read as each other
One is *red*   *as they are who*

Speech Demon squats on the children's mouths
pressing labials & gutterals out

An empty noose — used for their fantasy cargo —
swings from the heavenwood tree

Snapdragons govern the course of a fly,
a lifetime's breath steams up the eyes

the red knot tightens the thought
of time shorn away like a veil

body in the trail of the smoke
from a pile of leaf mould burnt up decades ago

the leaves themselves
the leaves left selves
here in the crown of belief
here with the cat and the hat
here on the hilltop loaded with rain
here in the daisy bush coronating fate
Ananke's grip on the leaves themselves

the leaves themselves
came into my thought
as though dripping through stone

the One is as real as the other
"stet"
as stars to skulls
as brightens to pales
as wrought by Eros sensing the worm
sprawled in the system with hairy fibers
lunching on rot

the squirming rod
divines by vowels alone

and all these things that mortals alone have hurled down
will be the Names

312: *Oh Yes*

Profound memory loss to some extent can be mimicked when
the (lesson) is extracted from the inferior lateral surface of
the temporal (growl). He wants to abandon (dualism) in
favor of a triadic expatriation of mind-body (t'issue).
Thought is a (search) through the distributed holographic
memory for resolution uncertainty, according to the different
heresies of the people undergoing religious (treatment). Other
poets associate the most awe-inspiring of nature's moods with
the (anger) of the meter. To use the oracle like a (language)
was an ominous (pump). Here at the (fringe) of the desert,
scree and sulfurous (colors) seem to burst with plump, rosy,
earthy, sweet-smelling humid zones in thick (paradise), extremely fertile. Talking with such intensity, sometimes the
brims of their (hats) actually touch. Oh yes, the (television)
knows many stories. But the storyteller knows me.

313: *The Future Perfect*

After all, what did they call it — the Gimmick, drummed up
by the Longhairs — "Little Boy" & "Pumpkin," names of the
Bomb. Nagasaki, Hiroshima, victims of know-how, still
come apart in the dark, scattering larval silhouettes behind
the retina, now I lay me down to sleep.

*

Detect & interpret corrosions out of space:
they carry the news long gone.
Look out at the stars : look back in time
— these are one & the same.
Quasars no longer exist, but their transit
makes us ourselves. We be-become.
If magic snakes into their lingering tones
how will we know? Or who? What's slipped inside
on a wick or a jet, a radio shiver
gliding though hypnotised leaves,
through peeling layers of memory,
thinning out, become transparent,
wandering out in single cells, brain drifts by
in dwindling herds, blurred and sluggish
with dormant atomic sleep, aroused by electrical laws,
commanding suns with a string of zeros —
who passes through conscious results and lands on the map.

*

I walk about,
the stars change position above me:
we swallow the pact.
Three degrees above absolute zero
the earth is bathed in sound.
And we who catch this long gone sound of creation
                    just reaching our ears
are bundles of after-effects,
not created or plucked but cooked, chunks of a star
exploded and then set adrift
and made the sun and were the world and puzzled the cause.
What matters is *extremely hot.*
"We were" it seems to say,
deceived by the present tense.
The present tensed in thought concurs, and blurs.
Already gone when it gets here, it seems to have *said.*
But what would it say?
— "we are" wherever it was when it "said"?
And how did it know we would listen, or hear?
The future perfect:

it will have been.

Leland Hickman

314: *Annotation for that which follows (Excerpt from TIRESIAS)*

Terror outcast young girl trembling auburn soft pageboy fear blown
    tears, scream;
tiresian purloin san juan de la cruz cruise text cross out
    graphemes for
god outhouse captivity cry let me out cry poisoned defeated
    brutal, lewd;
despumate desquamate perineal bubo mary janes slap
    sharp upon
pavement his dislocalized speech immobilized arm her
    elbow skin
withered nervously recounting it ladder to which de
    lusional com
parison "wronged every rung of" bad catch
    me bad hurt

me bad hate me mama at

    orisonned out
set immiserizations mandala his
    mandatory sen
tencings fiery in child dreamt burnt flesh bloodtaste cess
    pool out
fall, writ, chalkt up in a shit shed shoeheel bang bars keep
    death row a
wake mandala aflame uncharred vermilion-haired satanhead in't whose
    blond eye
lasht boyhood bloodied boymate fled, sobbing under obscure care here in
    tensive care
here arroyos aflood in downcaster plain in purgative night in
    ebriate ca
rotid catheter celebrant rectal esophagal capillary-rain brainsbust in out

    burst

verse here; panning gold death valley; she grammardays 19two3 spring so
      lazily over
comix page age 7 quite contrary mary mary late on yr way to school a
      lone a lone
ly man's candies small movies stop pitchblack in secret by se
      cret ladder dis
guised "brought groceries in stood wide-eyed staring at
      nothing saw
right off the bat he couldn't move speak braced him from
      falling got him
into a chair called the" planets stars sun progeny of
      thunder cross
out thunder dim out kitchen railroad free
      way din in

gasp struck blank still

      'd space in
haled commere lemme showya a chokehold bud
      dy pale lasht
trust on summerstreet; whose lyric breeze whose parted locks
      what wounding sus
pends tender text in oblivion howsomever begrudgings denials for
      given sick
nightwatcht breathings gone limp slippt grasp fallen knockt-out for
      real his
monkeymug kisst asphalt come-to ahowling, hands to his broke face stum
      bling home
but a stiffneckt brutish boy gets led by a god down planks in a mudwrackt
yard gets
      turd-housed gets
lockt in in dank to unlearn in shiver in crumple in whimper let me out

      in out let me

out cloyed anguishes sweetrots his candies halt our schoolgirl in terri
      fied husht
mary jane shoes thin kneesox frail pinafore tremulous instanter to
      flee she
screams eludes him kickt demonic out of her womb by his crude grum god
      who smasht his
sucking bottle in his mama's face blent splendor for his first gaze blood
      milk stream

ing noxious child vengeances boxed unto horrors hys
     terical cack
ling thru peckerwood flats san quentin sordors death
     row night
long longings to be gone to be scattered
     in isolate

sierra in the strong somber trees

     or wrencht in squal
id sleeps guided by a cross-eyed bald de
     mented bitch
past sabretootht text toward stone deaf stone
     eyed stone
tongued weavers of inflictions drencht under stone
     aged river of
avidya scared little girl breathless to be safe near an oak
     tree by storm
fenced schoolyard whenas oak hides terror with his hideous smile his
     idiot out
stretcht arms panickt she runs screaming runs years reclines no tender
     text maker his
face in his maker's chest kisst where he slumbers dusk at his window

     screen un

veils thick-scabbed visage forehead to chin seept pus glistens no hand a
     sleep ca
resses his neck no harsht sentencings suspended metastasis liver to
     lungs no
amorous breeze aroused among cedars; luger-rounds steept long in
     godhead of
stray cats strangled set fire to drowned, trusst dogs airgunned im
     paled on a
mopstick godhead of a thousand times stabbed prime pig vic
     torious man
slaughter laughter teen-aged caged kangaroo gang raped
     twice shank
slasht wrists pubescent laughter after last rippt-off mus
     tang never to

hang for a yellow-gut

        godhead in
scriptures bullets in an infant's laughter bad catch
        me bad hurt
me bad hate me mama "man I sure did blast that dumb punk's
        brains all
over the trees"—gentle abandoned childish text, silvery wet,
        outstrung in
awe struck leaves—

Dennis Phillips

From "The Hero is Nothing"

315: *Dream of Ocean (With Doors)*

This dream riddled with doored openings at night
when you fall overboard no one hears you.
In the morning your scream has cooled and merged.

It would be up to you to float calmly, waiting,
or seek one of the doors,
but then rescuers would find nothing
that would matter your choice more final
than their worst fears.

This dream is a hard test.
It is a dream where you say again and again
"This is not a dream. This is waking.
Only in waking can this be said."
You see a deep channel
and in the pulsing waters doors.

316: *"It would be like going under"*

It would be like going under
and finding air at the bottom. Like looking up
and seeing the surface far above.
Like seeing the sister of your first lover,
asking her for information which she cannot give.

317: *"You were the one I knew..."*

You were the one I knew long ago still young skin
still seamless, smooth, water tight.

I was around you and your arms a wind on me my ears
against you hollow you hollow on me a rounded, firm, proud

the way you naked are in me an island.

318: *"Someone was supposed to fetch you..."*

Someone was supposed to fetch you but no one came.
You walk in lost and angered.

You kept waiting to hear steps or calls.
You held out a card for searchers

thought: A blackboard, school chairs,
           the pitted floor, Windows! There aren't any windows.

319: *"What I hid today"*

What I hid today
through a slit I found
in what we thought was a perfect carpet.

There's this emptiness not a bad emptiness
but quiet, absorbing, only receptive.

At a place near the end of highways
where mountains protect a sloping valley
where I expect to be impressed by sheerness
a grey mist erases expectation.

For a moment nothing is left.
A perfect hiding place
more complete, less dirty than Underworld
but transient, unpossessive.

320: *"We fall to the underworld by choice."*

We fall to the underworld by choice.
Smaller and smaller details beckon.
Their voices imagined, finite.
We cannot retrieve lost things.

But insoluble darkness
drinks light and sound and touch,
pulls us to its shore.

We arrive without offerings
for the voices awaiting blood.

We bring only heat
which rises back to overworld.

No voice greets us.
Nothing is received.

321: *"We couldn't know..."*

We couldn't know (tell) whose mouth it was. Our
sequestered float without calendar.
The complex theory we had collaborated on
about sync, matches, ties: worthless, laughable.

Thus: It is early. It is 3 or 4 AM. After an overture
of thin metal quieted, you're at the window.
"Dogs," you say.

Hence: Rising beyond a newly seen vista
of Mojave desert is the imagined denture of the southern
Sierra. We fly past them,
turn east, to the third valley.

You speak to the window spirits we
bring to that moment an expectation. And yet
a powerful hook holds us down, separate.

322: *"I sat on a bleached plain..."*

I sat on a bleached plain we talk about moods,
alleviation, the back of my head, a knot of capillaries
where caffeine is caught where headache
is fertilized in tight cords.

> Nor touch even your hand,
> rounded digits forgotten.

A specific of civilization.

> From a netted root ball
> Medula Oblangata,
> a water basin rimmed
> a chance to drink.
> One hundred canceled tributaries.

Our porcelain desert.

323: *"It was a religious face..."*

It was a religious face or a face from romance.
It was an erotic face giving a tongue tip
to your lips. It was a religious face
and the response was violent.

The cork won't fit back in.

Not in the name of Eros nor Aphrodite.
The flowers were decoys. But a horrible name
without vowels sucks out your will.

324: *"Later it will be impossible..."*

Later it will be impossible to move simple objects.
An envelope in front will not make sense.
The time ladder splits into teeth that
mesh as gears against each other.

A jew inherits the canon.

Buildings disconnect, halls become land tracts.
Ordinates are benevolent; time not.

I've forgotten to wear my shoes. The paycheck drops
but the envelope closes my eyes. If I try to replace them
my interest will seem like treachery.

325: *"Elpenor reaches in..."*

Elpenor reaches in, attached but vanquished.

Small amber cubes, sharp cubes clog his ears.
We borrow Elpenor today, we like him
partially deaf. We have no reason to give him
all he wants is a proper fire.
We borrow matches to console him.

The hero is nothing.

From limbo we are given a new vine
its leaves are furry, its casings burst
with orange flowers. They will burn completely
but only at the right moment, by the right corpse.

326: *"Then find it"*

Then find it
barren as always.

A minuscule change, angle of light,
that's all. I would stop here.
I would stop and wait for recall.
Instead I salmon up this dry bed some
instinctual pool calling me but arid.
I slap down on hot boulders, belly over, push
against air.

At the pool Persephone is laughing.
She opens a red fruit:
it's filled with fish eyes.
"You're here anyway," she says.

327: *"It is 3 o'clock..."*

It is 3 o'clock the window is white the light grey
the breeze has begun as usual. By 7 o'clock
the air will be still, the window rosey, Homeric.
At 8 o'clock 100 years ago? I can't
tell. If I drill this spot I still won't find
layered wind or light.

A year from now I won't find you
unless I search.

Ian Krieger

328: *Lessons of October*

You lean against the bruise
of a solid wall.

Your thermos filled
with warm coffee.

Two doughnuts in waxed paper,
and your romantic nature.

The convalescence of evening
rolls on like a moth.

Your literal mistakes
become your reveries.

You say nothing about trees,
which unseen

still sweeten the coarse texture
of what perceives.

Your shape erases,
though all color is as warm

as lamplight.

A cold dew
fails to impinge.

Something you miss very much
nags at you.

In the unfinished gleam
of transitory stars

you encompass the steep
secondary steps

of unearthly black.

Your clarity
an outline

which sleeps
on the substance of things,

which know you
like a handyman.

329: *The Eternal Reoccurence of 1957*

Venetian blinds can be a bore,
as long lived as a botanical garden,

yet there is a science to madness
like there is to pollen.

If the pain of words
is that they turn aside
at the gate,

leave us astray
as the lull of slanted sunlight,

strangers
at bus stations,

cuttings off of old vines,

their joy is
that they tremble

like a fixed idea,
power supplies,

or Carl Perkins.

Why do you think of cupboards so much?

Why do crannies feel like whirlwinds?

What terror leads you to chocolate?

There are shivers,
formica whorls,
drizzles of embers.

Evening comes
with its appetite for cellulose,

or like a bunko officer.

I can't tell you why I like the modern,
but I do.

330: *The Theory of Sex*

An anecdote recalls pleasure
or fades.

No clues from the placid.

Sensation intensifies
or snaps back.

Self-proclaimed ugliness
or awe
from the same semantic root.

Images badger,
erase scent from memory.

What's palpable eats;

the rest fakes inattentiveness
and thus is oddly flirtatious
or mundane.

There is nothing as archaic
as forgotten sex.

You're either capricious
or drowsy.

Either the soles of your feet are ready
or you curdle in time like the banal.

331: *Eva Hesse I*

Sexual waters
to say Perrier
with a twist.

Survival and papier mache.

A cappella repetitive harmony
triggered by the framework
of a garden.

The arbitrary has kholed eyes.

No difference between a black throat
and a tulip.

Bare loft,
exposed space

which brings
the premature.

Mind transcribed
by minimal form,

form by heart.

Embargo through which
all things must move

like a color.

332: *Elaine in Chenille*

By yellow wordiness
a witty endomorph in tweed

slurs a story.

It's somewhere between Baltimore
and Norma Desmond,

between seediness and St. Laurent.

On a bamboo settee
with dove grey cushions
she sits,

an onanistic silhouette
of a secondhand bookshop in Prague,

the painful moodiness of Expressionism.

Farewell to an idea.

Tim Reynolds

333: *Eight Haiku*

Kill! Kill! Kill! Kill! Swifts
wingtip to wingtip, insect
Armageddon, dusk

Up and down, up and
down, up and down, up and down:
mosquito larvae
                              (Issa)

I've held them in my hands
Petti[light as bird]bones

In the Buddha's nose,
Mommy, look,
swallows!
                              (Issa)

Suddenly heavy
as a 3 year old asleep:
muertito kana

BAD foot! Bad bad foot!
So sorry please
Snail San

Curtain up on: housefront, window,
TV flicker. Pause. Shot. Pause.

       CURTAIN
            (Cangiullo)

F'og B'loop!
        (Bassho)

334: *from The Singularity: Hell*

Auschwitz provides a useful sociological model of Hell, one
bunch of people totally in control of another bunch and trying to make that bunch's existence as miserable as possible.
The difference would be that in Auschwitz you could die.
(Actually, you *would*. "Up the chimney in any case" was the
camp motto.) So if you could adjust for that difference you
could begin to develop a psychology/sociology of Hell.

You'd start by assuming that Hell was like Auschwitz in providing preferred situations; some would be relatively less
awful than others. Some imps would be less sadistic, less in-
telligent, less imaginative, greedier. With what could one
bribe a devil? The cons would find something.

I guess people in Hell metabolize, how could you torture
something that didn't metabolize? So food becomes *the* issue,
as at Auschwitz. And power. Satan would delegate power to
the imps and the imps to selected inmates (the imps
themselves would hardly clean up the waste products of
metabolism; the post of *Scheissminister* was a cushy job at
Auschwitz). And so on.

Hell and Armageddon are effective programming devices
(Manson and Rev Jim used them, for example, in the nuclear
variant), but strong programs exist without them (Oneida,
Scientology.)

An 18th century hip priest (friend of Pascal), asked if he
himself believed in Hell, answered "Bien sur! It's an article of
dogma! I don't have to believe there's anybody in it"

According to Restoration of Sacred Name Bible, there are two dozen miracles in I/II Kings and one in Chron. If so, a new look at the Deuteronomist — who might have seen himself or themselves as very hip and modern, come to think of it, with their new understanding of historical processes and all. And then there are three more miracles from then to *Cana*: one in Jonah (plus one dud) and two in (one guess) *Daniel*.

As it happens, I've some slight acquaintance with miracles. In my 20s there was a lie I used to tell. I was visiting Ed Ricketts, Steinbeck's friend, mentor and model for Doc, on Cannery Row and he said, "Tim, what would it take to make you accept the fact that there is more to it than your three dimensions?" I said, "Levitate that bottle." The bottle of bourbon rose quickly and smoothly from the table, four or five inches. There was a pause. Having been a conjuror in my youth, I asked "May I put my hand underneath it and stuff?" Ed said OK. I ran my hands all around it. Nothing. I said, "May I touch it?" He said OK. I took it by the neck. For a nanosecond it was weightless and then it was just a bottle in my hand.

My memory of the rationale for this fantasy, aside from making me the center of attention of my audience and name-dropping, was that the world was a limited place, and I wanted people to feel it was more interesting.

Two things worth noting: I was in Monterey in 1957 and 58, at the Army Language School, knew Cannery Row, my friends the Arrisses had told me Ricketts and Steinbeck stories, I'd read *Sea of Cortez*, Steinbeck's nonfictional Ricketts memoir. Though there was no core of levitation truth, there was a core of Ricketts truth. On the other hand, if I hadn't fessed up here my biographer could have nailed it had it come up — Ricketts died (suicided actually) some time before I was in Monterey. We smalltime liars aren't thinking in terms of being subjected to biographical scrutiny.

Charles Bevins

336: *inquiry before snow (1)*

doesn't that great show — lighted
      shapes appearing in
      dreamtasm — leave its tracks
      on this very heart (this
          mind)

sunrise & set not thirty feet between
      it seems
      great bolts of controlled (it seems)
      explosion — great bolts of (there
          is a wolf rotating
          in my first eye)

clearly defined false dawn
  rising on frail
  desert skies
those same skies (their texture)
  that here within
  this solemn procession
  of evening
through what poison i contemplate
      the mountains
through what poison lean need now speaks

337: *inquiry before snow (3)*

Oak Ridge Tennessee
how breedth your reactor

Amarillo Texas
how bomb your neutrons

338: *inquiry before snow (5)*

pastel cloudbank in dawnscape:
   it is indonesia
   it is terra incognita
   it is isis
   it is komodo dragon
   set blazing in the east

339: *inquiry before snow (12)*

concentric light medical air
whirr of x-ray technology
G.E. Monitrol 15
no human being is at ease
in this environment
roentgen room shadowed lungs
dance these ceilings
syringe of totalitarian discipline
faces me as i write
authoritarian essences distilled
from these shades of fluorescence
(yellow door with radiology sign)

340: *inquiry before snow (13)*

sitting on the seawall
in neptune beach florida
october 1962 watching
the ships headed for cuba

341: *inquiry before snow (14)*

arctic silence
arctic song
down in silos beneath
north dakota plains
hushed subterranean ready

342: *inquiry before snow (16)*

my great grandfather
on my mother's side
was a blacksmith in liverpool
he dispersed a mob
with his hammer

my grandfather
on my father's side
had his throat
cut in ambush
in the south georgia night

irish or english
my ancestors
have found this
world a brutal
violent host

343: *inquiry before snow (18)*

     i came to see bronze
spoke the queen bee with shattered eyes

  the leopard seal
  the sonoran pronghorn
  the red wolf
  the sea wasp
  the komodo dragon

every gentle web & fiber moving
     stirring in seascape

pristine beaches where first fin
  then foam
    then human forms touch

    perform ceremonies
    of the die dragon down
  dead & moving

ah then whales like islands once

344: *inquiry before snow (19)*

fire in tin cans
on the beach at night

snow cats clearing mountain roads
moon insects yellow lights blinking

sitting at my desk
at the third source

imagining - remembering
night as i have known it

345: *inquiry before snow (21)*

i approach
the campfires
of my enemy

& see fast
among them
radiant

to behold
forgotten
shape of

my superfather
watching
only my own eyes

346: *superintendent of the void
(in abstractia)*

it traveled like a marvel-wind
through 43 or so cities
picking up & occasionally dispersing such poisons
as perhaps would make a million tyrants tremble
or raise fur on a cluster of breakwater cats

i felt its formlessness
here on its final coast to coast tour stop
& wordlessly i asked its essence
why aren't the demons on duty
when does the next mandala leave

firebird out of void-dark skies
it showed in answer
shit & putrescence & a stinging rain
then before leaving for oceanic excursion
showed razor burn across a raving moonphase

347: *herbal light*

i came down the hall in darkness
my hand groping for the lamp chain

   ----

i exchanged bitter words
with an elder in a tavern today
one of the aged who congregate
in these slickly lit abattoirs

handed over four bills to my contact
(four notes to the equal of eighty)
then to the st. with Isis pectoral
& a sack of precious herbs

& home for cups of spring water shining
clouds of herb smoke in shalimar incense
   blent
wind chimes as finger cymbals lightly
   rang
on breezes vernal & mockingbird night

   ----

now the lamp chain found
the tea reheated & so to the
ritual of herbal light

348: *haiku*

much too late in the
   year to hear my
   nightbird sing ...
the chirping crickets

349: *images of the beast: los angeles*

ashes of a pathetic magician
or a passing scalded dog

car wash by gas station on ventura blvd.
or a mission in the night

persian gulf oil transformed
into incense of poison

into speeding license of bare powers horses
on satanist lotus burning down strip

mutant cells of megalopolis
moving — stirring — on these deserts

the past randomly fed into
this cauldron overflowing with

lepers & refugees storming & restorming
non existant walls of pure wills city state

or a mad hermit with the mane of a lion
hiding in mission shadows

Murray Mednick

350: *from The Coyote Cycle:*

Coyote Evocation

"Try to talk about Coyote directly and he will bite your large intestine.

His is a Spirit that must be evoked.

It's like electricity: you don't see it, but it's there all right.

You catch it by plugging into it.

Start at the soles of your feet as you walk. Earthmother is breathing power into you. Then Coyote comes along and brushes your spine, like a shock.

Coyote runs off howling.

You can catch a glimpse of him through the corner of one eye. But you'd better be prepared for what you see – that's yourself, falling into your own shit.

Coyote gets a kick out of that.

Nobody can do like he does and survive. And yet he does, barely.

That's him laughing over your left shoulder as you pass on by.

Coyote is laughing at your thoughts.

Coyote doesn't have time to think about life.

He doesn't have time.

He knows he'll still be here after we've all disappeared. He watches our disappearing act for awhile, then he goes on to something else.

Coyote would fuck a snake and call it feathers.

There's no point in arguing.

He is sometimes known as Trickster, the Whisperer of Questions.

He stalks your beliefs. He spies on your little devices. He hunts down the hiding places.

He can be evoked by taking a breath and one step forward—then offer up the cry of panic. Then come right back, back to the feet.

Let go the panic. That is Coyote laughing. That is Trickster whispering. The spine is an arrow, pointing above and below.

Ho!

351: *from The Coyote Cycle:*

Waterfall

       I was sitting by the waterfall trying to describe
the waterfall
         it was the most lovely waterfall trying to get a grip
on things describe the waterfall
               in my notebook on the bridge
only goddamn it I have lost my right hand
               I HAVE LOST MY RIGHT HAND
trying to describe
         the waterfall as it goes
MY RIGHT HAND in the current
            my head sucking air UP UP
How did I get into the water
I was sitting on the bridge with my notebook
             in my LEFT HAND

as it goes into the water cool and strong flows past
WHERE IS MY RIGHT HAND
                       courses through me
                       I mean actually courses through me

THE ROCKS
              watch out for the rocks goddamn it
But I have got my head up
                 I have got my head up

watch out for the rocks
              MY RIGHT HAND
                     the water is COLD

it has got COLD under the bridge
                  deep green cold fast
                  nobody knows where it goes

how deep goddamn it
              MY RIGHT HAND
              Has GOD got my RIGHT HAND
Has God got my right hand
Who is God that he should have my right hand
When I am alone in the river
Give me my right hand back God
                    I am afraid of these rocks

give me my right hand back God
                 there is no God
                 there is no right hand

but I need my right hand
             my left hand is busy

even the notebook if gone
            my left hand is busy keeping me in the water
How did I get into the water
How could I go into the water without my right hand
                trying to describe the waterfall
                    the SPEED of it

no that is not true
        that is not an accurate description
of the waterfall see the waterfall
                 has no TIME in it
        the waterfall has no TIME in it and I must be STILL
therefore I must be still
        if I am still I will get my right hand back
no no
        that is not the reason I must be still
                 my LEFT hand
is busy too busy to describe the waterfall
        trying to get a grip on a ROCK

```
                grab onto a ROCK
if I am still I will SINK
                        no no
that is not the reason
                        the water is moving me
I am being moved in the water
                                that is not true either
There is no MOTION in the water
    there is no MOTION in the water
that would not be an accurate description of the waterfall
        to say something about the waterfall
                                with my RIGHT HAND
while the LEFT hand is keeping me up
                            in the water
        busy keeping me up in the water
then the RIGHT HAND
```

352: *from the Coyote Cycle:*

Trickster's Death Song

In my dream, the cloud upon which I walk is full of holes:
one for every step I take. A boat is weighing anchor off the
continent. It has made no sound. There is no sign on it.
Some of the inhabitants have turned against each other.
Some are wading out into the water. Some are bsuy with
masts and sails and a flag...

> My name is Mudhead!
> I am born of Earth!
> My Father's name is Taiawa!
> And I cannot die!
>
> Once I was a newborn child
> And Coyote/Trickster was my name.
> I knew nothing.
> And nothing had been named.
> Then I was awakened.
> "Now you have to learn about Life,"
> My mother said,
> "Now you have to learn about Life."

My death song
Is:
SHUT YOUR STARS.

353: *from The Coyote Cycle:*

Coyote's Death Song

Divine is sunlight
Divine is Earthmaker's tent
Divine is the Spider Lady's posture

Divine is thunder
Divine is lightning
Divine is Coyote's Journey
      From beginning to end

I became a human being
And walked among the two-leggeds
I saw the new colors in the sky
I tasted the new flavors in the earth

It was not pleasant to me
It was not agreeable to me

I saw the bones of my planet
Whitening in Starlight,
On a scaffold in Starlight
            Made of a subtle wind
            Singing a subtle song

Deep as all the dead together
Deep as all the dead together

At once!

354: *from the Coyote Cycle:*

Trickster Surrenders His Vengeance

This land is Paradise. This place is a boon to mankind. We got freedom here. We can worship whatever we want here. Oh, the water is sweet. Oh, the air is sweet. And there is every kind of food here in abundance. We can have time here. We can worship what we want here. First we'll clear the vermin off the land. Those ones that are not us, that don't believe as us. Then we'll cut up the land in pieces, and everybody can own a piece of land. And we'll clear the land and plant food in the land, because the game won't last forever. We can worship whatever we want here. We'll buy and sell the land we cut up. We'll buy and sell the food we grow. We'll have cattle ranches and stockyards. And we'll create wealth. We'll get wealth out of the land and out of the ground. And we'll create power. We can worship whatever we want here. And we'll find energy. We'll cut into the land for energy and power. And we'll get energy from the water. And we'll keep the vermin out of the way. Those who don't believe as us, who aren't one of us, who aren't in this thing with us. We'll fence 'em and we'll feed 'em, but we'll keep 'em out of the way. Because there's nothing like this land, and there's nothing like this wealth, and there's nothing like this power. And we can worship what we want here. And we'll cut our way through mountains and cross the rivers and valleys, and we'll be moving, we'll be on the move, we're moving, moving, creating wealth, creating power, and it has to be fed, it has to be fed with ENERGY! WE'LL FIND THAT ENERGY! WE WORSHIP WHAT WE WANT TO! WE'LL CUT INTO THE LAND FOR ENERGY! WE'LL DAMN THE RIVERS! WE'LL CUT THROUGH BEDROCK! WE'LL CUT THROUGH MATTER! WE'LL FIND MORE! MORE! WE WORSHIP WHAT WE WANT!

After walking a long time, angry that there had been nowhere to go, no one to see, I came to a cafe—a pale blue light in a darkened street. I was thirsty and went directly to the counter. There was a lady there wearing a red dress, red shoes. Bright red. And she wore red-jeweled earrings, and her lips were painted red and there was red shadow around her narrow blue eyes. She looked at me with disdain, shaking her head. I made the gesture of one drinking from a bottle. She nodded, handed me a cold, black beer, and smiled. I felt embarrassed at my anger and began thanking her profusely. She mumbled something, shrugged, and turned away. I went to a table near the door and sat down. Everything was blue—tables, chairs, floor, walls, ceiling—all blue. The cafe faced onto a square. Directly across the way was a great, old stone church framed in orange electric lights. A windowless red bus was parked on the corner and shrouded forms were climbing on and off, in a desperate hurry. As I watched the bus, trying to understand what was going on, I became aware of the steady drone of conversation in the cafe. They were speaking an ancient, musical language I had never heard before. Then I became frightened. The language these people were speaking was an extinct Mayan tongue, *Lacandon*. I don't know how I knew this with such certainty. I looked up and caught the woman in the red dress watching me as if she knew my thoughts. For a moment I became overwhelmed by a tremendous sexual longing for her. She was aware of this and smiled sardonically as she moved from table to table, her wide hips swaying in the tight red dress. At the table nearest me, three men were whispering intensely. I was sure that they were discussing my presence, and that if they knew—they would attack me. I indignantly stared at the floor, trying to concentrate. Suddenly two beggars approached me, a woman and child, their outstretched hands covered with sores. I started to give them money, but the woman refused and spat on the money...I noticed two groups of people passing back and forth in front of the cafe...two young girls flanked a crippled old lady...the old lady had to swing one leg in a 180 degree arc in order to walk....somehow I understood that the girls were talking about the consciousness of spiders and worms...the old cripple giggled continually...the other group was composed of three young Indians...as they passed before the cafe, the man in the middle would turn toward me and make a face—he would show his teeth in a wide, mask-like grin, flaring his nostrils and rolling his eyes...his teeth were jagged, filed down to a point in the ancient way...each time they passed I became more deeply enraged by that face...again and again they passed, and that Indian made the horrible mask at me — finally I hurled myself out into the street and went for him — I wanted to cut away that face with my broken beer bottle — we rolled together on the pavement — I was stabbing at his face — it was the face of a jaguar —

356: *from Black Hole in Space: Lark*

It was a world in another solar system, and you were a soldier. We were marching, marching. The terrain was a wasteland, with ditches and trenches and weird canyons everywhere. We were marching along, and we knew we were going to be destroyed. The people around us, the other soldiers, an officer — I couldn't trust them. They might do anything, stupidly, insanely, and get me/Robbie killed. I kept trying to talk to Robbie, to ask him to take me away from that place. And I KNOW he heard me because it was as if I were speaking with HIS mind. But we couldn't MOVE. We could DECIDE but we could not MOVE...And then we came to an area that had just been BOMBED. There were stacks of bodies in neat rows. I mean, just piles of mangled flesh. And through each pile were stuck four bombs. I don't know why FOUR, but FOUR bombs, like huge, fat arrows. And the stacks of bodies went on and on into the distance. On and on. The most terrible thing was the STENCH. That's how I knew I was THERE, because of the stench. It was so absolutely vivid. A voice, it was the officer, was saying, "Well, this is what happens when you get bombed. These are the bombs. They come from the enemy." A soldier reached into a pile and pulled off an arm, and then — a heart! He reached in and pulled out another heart! I was shouting, "ROBBIE! ROBBIE!" with Robbie's own voice. I was so desperate I began to slowly come back, to wake up. I was coming away from the smell of death, and I was only out of it when I could no longer, no longer actually SMELL the piles of dead meat, with those four bombs sticking through them like arrows.

Rob Sullivan

357: *from: The Long White Dress of Love*

VIII.

You know?
You want to know?
I'm going to tell you.
What I've been thinking and what I've been feeling.
What I've been thinking and what I've been feeling.
And what I have some suspicions about, O.K.?
And what I have some suspicions about, O.K.?
This is it, this is it, this is it.
And it's just thoughts, just thoughts, just some thoughts.
It's just feelings, it's just some feelings, just some feelings.
It's just some suspicions, just some suspicions, that's all.
And it's just some suspicions about my thoughts,
it's just some feelings about my suspicions,
it's just some thoughts about my suspicions,
it's just some suspicions about my feelings,
it's just some feelings about my thoughts,
it's just some thoughts about my feelings about my suspicions,
It's just some thoughts about my feelins about my suspicions,
it's just some feelings about my thoughts about my suspicions,
it's just some suspicions about my feelings about my thoughts,
it's just some thoughts about my suspicions about my feelings,
O.K.?
Anyway,
what I've been feeling, what I've been feeling, what I've been
feeling, is this.
That I've been thinking, that I've been thinking, that I've been
thinking
That I suspect, that I suspect
that you don't like me anymore.
Is that you don't even like me anymore.
Is that you don't even like me anymore.
Is that you don't even like me anymore.

And what is more than that, and what is more,
and what is even more than that,
is that you never ever did like me anyway.
Is that you never ever did like me anyway.
And what is more than you don't even like me anymore
is that you never ever even did like me from the beginning.
Is that you never ever even did like me from way back at the
beginning.
Now these are just my thoughts, just my thoughts, just
thoughts. Just my feelings, just my feelings, just my feel-
ings, just my suspicions, just my suspicions, that's all.
And...And... and it makes me kinda angry and it makes me a
little sad.
Yes, it makes me kinda angry and it makes me a little sad.
Yeah, well, you know what I'm beginning to think?
You know what I'm beginning to think here?
Is that maybe I never ever did like you either, too.
What I'm starting to think is that maybe I never ever did
like you either, too.
And maybe I never did like you either from way back in the beginning
either, that's what I've been thinking, that's what I've been
thinking, that's what I feel, that's what I feel, that's what
I suspect.
Is that maybe I never ever did like you either.
And maybe I never ever did like you from way back in the
beginning, too, just like you, just like you.
Anyway...so...so...what was I there for anyway?
To fill up some lack? Did I just fill up some lack
in your emotional life? Some lack? Some void? Some ditch?
Some drainage ditch lack of a void in your emotional life?
Some pit? Some pitch-black pit of a drainage ditch lack in
the void of your emotional life?
Was I just there to fill up some hole?
Was I just there to fill up some hole?
Was I just there to fill up some hole?
Some void pitch-black hole in the drainage ditch lack
of a void in your emotional life?
Huh?
Yeah?
Well...
Well...
I don't even want to see you anymore either, that's
what I want.
I just don't even want to see you anymore either, that's
what I want.

I don't even want to see your face in my mind anymore.
I don't even want to see your face in my mind anymore.
I don't even want to see your name in my mind anymore.
I don't want to smell your smells or feel your skin
or remember your touch.
I don't even want to smell your smells or feel your skin
or remember your touch anymore either.
I don't want to smell your smells.
I don't want to feel your skin.
I don't want to remember your touch.
Not even in my mind.
Not even in my mind.
And I don't ever ever want you to become famous, cause
I don't want to see your face on the television
and I don't want to see your face in the movies
and I don't want to read about you in the newspapers.
I don't want to see your face on the television.
I don't want to see your face in the movies.
I don't want to read about you in the newspapers.
And I don't ever ever want to hear about you from
friends or from strangers.
And I don't want to hear about you from
friends or from strangers.
And I don't want to hear about you from friends or
from strangers. O.K.?
So...
Why don't you just go away?
Why don't you just go far far away?
Cause I'm staying right here and I sure don't want you to
be around.
Cause I'm staying right here and I sure don't want you to be
around.
Why don't you just leave the state?
Yeah, why don't you just leave the state?
Why don't you just go to Utah cause I'm never ever going to
Utah.
Why don't you just go to Utah cause I'm never ever going to
Utah.
Why don't you go to Ogden Utah cause if I ever ever do go to
Utah I'm going to Salt Lake City not to Ogden and so you'll
be in Ogden and I'll be in Salt Lake City and we won't see
each other anyway then.
Why don't you be a waitress in Ogden Utah?
Why don't you just be a waitress there in Ogden Utah?
Cause I'm staying right here.
Oh no, I'm staying right here.

This is my place.
This is my place.
I paid the rent on this room.
That's my —
I own this place.
This is my room.
That's my , that's my chair you're sitting on, that's my chair
you're sitting on, that's my chair you're sitting on.
This is my room.
This is my place.
You'll have to leave.
You're the one that has to leave.
You have to go, you have to go.
You have to vacate, you have to vacate.
You have to vacate the premises.
You have to vacate the premises.
Not me.
Not me.
I'm staying.
I'm staying.
Right here.
It's decided, you're going to Ogden Utah to be a waitress
and I'm staying right here.
You're going to Ogden Utah to be a waitress and I'm staying
right here.
I'm here.
I'm here.
Let's not even talk about it anymore.
Don't even mention Ogden Utah again because it's all
settled anyway so what's the point of even bringing it up.
I'm right here.
I'm right here.
You're in Ogden Utah and I'm right here.
Right here.
Right here.
I am here.

XI.

She is one of the mysteries
She is the mystery
She is the mystery

She is the mystery come back
She is the mystery come back
She holds your fingers
She holds your fingers in front of your face
She takes your fingers
She takes your fingers
And she points the way
She is the mystery come back
She rubs your fingers in between her legs
She rubs your fingers in between her legs
She points the way
She points the way
She is the mystery come back
She is the mystery
She is the mystery come back
She takes your fingers
And she shoves them up inside herself
And it's like you're travelling down some never-ending river
Over-flowing upside-down inside itself
And you keep on going endlessly
You may never come back
You'll never come back
She is the mystery
She is the mystery come back
Down upon inside itself upside-down beneath
Flowing on your finger-tips
Pointing out the way
Like a river curving out upon your face
She takes her fingers and traces out your face upon the air
And down beneath inside where things can travel distances
Both ways at once she takes your fingers inside herself
And traces out her life on them
She rubs out mysteries on your skin like she's painting signs
On your very soul
On your very soul
She is one of the mysteries come back
She is the mystery come back
To haunt you time and time again
As if you could escape from that
You travel as far as you possibly can
Down some river in your eye
Where you think there is such a thing
As a safe retreat
But even there back along that high cliff

Where you can walk alone above the ocean waes
Even there she will come
Holding up rivers and fingers in front of your face
Tracing out your life upon the sky
And taking your cock inside of her fingers
And taking your cock inside of her fingers
You go down inside beneath where things are turned both
in and out upon themselves and over and over and end on end
Till the liquid skin erupts and strips you clean
Yes, the liquid skin, it strips you clean
Till your flesh rips itself right apart
Yes, your flesh rips itself right apart
Right apart
Come back
She does
As you discover
That she is the mystery
She is the mystery come back
Down along a river-side
Where you left your skin
Where you knew there was no escaping back along your eyes
Where she runs time back upon itself
And fierce ecstasy cries out that she is one of the
mysteries come back
Come back upon you with the force of a river of skin
Which you will eat
And your cock does know as it runs
Down the rivulets that run
Upside-down upon themselves
Flashing out colors of skin
Tracing out lives in wombs
That remain afloat above the ocean waves
Yes, your cock does know as it comes back out upon her skin
Out upon her mystery of skin
That the cock is the force inside the eye
That sped out like a thunder-bolt across the sky-
lined river where she came back upon herself, she came back
upon herself
Sleeping there, yes, sleeping there,
Beneath the trees
and leaves
The ocean heaves
and surges back upon itself
Time and time again
Over and over and end on end
As she sleeps and dreams, sleeps and dreams

That she is unwinding forver
Down along some beach
Her skin unravelling
On the sand, on the sea-birds, on the jellyfish, and the
Castles in the sand dancing out their lives upon her skin
Upon her skin
Come back
Come back
She is she
She is the mystery lost come back the mystery come back donw
Upon itself she is the mystery come back and I am winding
Myself right around her until my skin is like an ocean wave
Rolling down her river sides.

XII.

You see how dark it is here.
Nothing's moving.
And it's like all that ever ever existed
is just this night here, alone, without you.
You see how quiet it is.
Nothing even creaks or rustles.
You see me here.
You see me here.
And there's a wall, and the phone, and the door, and the blan-
ket on the floor.
The wall, the phone, the door, the blanket on the floor.
And I lean against the wall and watch the door and wait for
the blanket to crawl across the floor.
You see how dark it is here.
You see how dark, how quiet, it is.
You see me here.
I lean against the wall and watch the door and wait for the
blanket to crawl across the floor.
I try to call.
I try to call.
I pick up the phone and try to call.
But, on the other end of the line, on the other end of the phone,
your voice dangles, hangs there, on the words, like
I'm not even sure you exist there behind the words.
I'm not even sure you exist there behind the words.
I'm not even sure you exist there behind the words.
On the other end of the line, on the phone, there.

I really don't think you do.
I don't think you do exist there.
I really don't hink you do.
I try to picture your face there, your mouth there, as you're
talking and I can't picture it. I have no idea what you look
like anymore.
Who are you there? Who are you? Who the fuck are you?
Then I think... you don't even want me to remember your face,
that's why I can't remember it because you don't want me to
remember it, you don't want me to call, to leave these words
here on the line in the phone here, you don't want me to remember you, do you? You want me to forget all about you, forget all about you, forget your face, forget your voice, forget your eyes, and that's why I can't remember you because you
want me to forget all about you, all about you, all about you.
Then I think...what the hell am I going on about? She hasn't
even answered the phone yet. She hasn't even answered the phone.
Are you going to answer the phone? Answer the phone. Answer my
call. Answer me. Pick it up. Pick up the line. Are you? Aren't
you? Are you? Aren't you going to go ahead and answer anyway?
I need to talk to you.
You see me here.
There's a wall, a door, a blanket crawling across the floor.
There's a wall, a door, a blanket crawling across the floor.
And this phone is ringing and ringing in my hand like it must
mean somehting that it's ringing and ringing and ringing and
there's no one answering, no one answering the phone, with some
words, on the line, across the darkness, but it doesn't mean
anything, does it? It just means that you aren't there, that's
all that it means, the ringing and ringing, that's all that
it means, the ringing in my hands.
I don't know...I don't know...I don't know...
What you can say anyway that would make any difference anyway.
What the fuck you could say that would make any difference anyway.
What the fuck you could possible say you can say you can say
that would make it all go away anyway.
So all right all right all right all RIGHT then DON'T answer
DON'T talk DON'T leave something on the line that will cross
across the darkness into this room with the wall, the door and
the blanket crawling across the floor.
Across the darkness into this room with the wall, the door
and the blanket crawling across the floor.
The blanket crawling across the floor.
Yes, I want clear air.
No words.
No phone.

No person.
No you.
I just need to walk to the door and open it up
and look out across the other part of this darkness
that spreads out beyond the phone-lines.
That spreads out beyond the phone-lines. The other part of
this darkness.
I just need to walk to the door and open it up.
That's what I need to do.
But I don't get up.
I sit.
In the quiet dark.
Against the wall.
I watch the door.
The blanket crawls across the floor.
The blanket crawls across the floor.
Goes out the door.
I lean against the wall.
Watch the darkness as it grows.
I watch the door.
Watch the darkness as it grows.
I watch the door.
I watch the door.
I watch the door.

Robert Peters

358: *Dialogue*

"You stole the dynamite, dad."

"On $40 per month, son, the WPA
won't miss it. When I build the basement
it'll be handy."

"That's robbing...."

"We're poor. We've got our own laws."

"I'm scared when you go hunting."

"Don't worry, son. Just keep your nose
clean and your britches pulled up.
We've got our ways. There's struggle.
We have to make it, what ways we can."

359: *Mother*

Girl, sixteen, straining over a washtub
in an iceshed of a house
chinked with moss
veiled with tarpaper.

House alive with mice
in warm weather,
in cold with ice.

Your stuttering washlines
strung up
through the house;

slab underwear (flat
salted fillets) sheets,
shirts, board-stiff
dresses, nightshirts.

And the meals: pancakes
whipped out of batter
kept in a crock
fermenting on the back
of the woodstove.

Peanut-butter (County Relief)
extended by blendings
of bacon drippings...

Repeat those gestures!
Strip away all subsequent
events! Goad us out
to the pasture, to the starved
potato field, and the bean field
while you prod, curse
your life, as night
(a peddlar) drops
poisoned seed, and a
wreathing fog settles in,
soft underbelly, soft thighs,
tight against the throat
dark lovely throat
of night. I crouch again,
waiting, hoping you are near.
Touch me! Touch me!

360: *Miscarriage*

My mother bathes alone —
the metal tub, the kettle
of hot water, on a strip
of carpet, in her room.

She has lost another child.
Dad buries it under the birches
behind the well.

God is on her side.
She didn't want the child.
He listened to her when she cried.
He opened a fresh wound wide
in his eternal side.
The baby slipped in and hid there
when he died.

361: *On Falling from You*

Cold stars
have said it all

and turbulence
dies, misfiring
meaning to kill

you. Still as a
naked archer frozen
in ice, through eons

of blizzards (what
new creatures will lap
up pools of fire)...

that we were one and
one. Whatever is creased
to make a fan, whatever

craves to dance, and can,
as I fall from you, as
you leave, mountains of

ice rise, vast peaks
of blue and white, who
knows, how can I know?

those barking monsters
and craters are
the frozen tongues of god.

I thought that to fall
was to know, I thought
that to know was to fall.

362: *Cool Zebras of Light*

Your fists
are warm
against my ribs

The musk of love is
hot mercury
pressed between
layers of skin

At last
cool zebras of light
are feeding

363: *Parrots*

My mood tongiht
howls blacks and reds.
I could fuck tables
chairs, dish
washers or owls.
The self won't do.
I observe my leg.
Nothing ascends.
My hand rests
by a cup, so
calm. In my brain
parrots eat one another.

364: *from Mt. San Gorgonio Ascent*

(the highest peak in Southern California: 13,400 feet)
1
We had come to a hill.
The path fell to a ravine.
Blue pine and fir.
Pellucid atmosphere.

Our speed set to the terrain.
Who should precede.
Talkers to the rear.
In the lead the walker

who would determine
the breaks, appraise
dangerous places, streams,
fallen trees, the shale.

Dung from the ranger's horse,
dust raked up by boyscouts,
Slushy Meadow, Dollar Lake,
the Saddle, grit along the way.

No gloom in our minds,
no beasts
under a canopy of sun,
no threat of storm.
Calm.

2
The sun burned down
swung its force
through the manzanita brush
burned ant trails bronze
burned ponderosas with its salt
seized the switchbacks for its own.

8
At a drop below
hangs a cloud, mercurial.
The mountain it claims
floats green, lung-red, and blue.
Pines flare. Boulders
glow. Light falls.
Total mountain,
total drift of mist,
of flesh. The trance
is my own.

My hand is a peach
attached to a limb
swung over a gorge.
It hangs beyond all reach
gathers ripeness in.

11

We reach the summit.
The snow burns; we feel it.
Our feet
no longer beat but shuffle,
constricted by
snarewire drawn tight.
Our lungs crowd our throats,
our ears snap and burn.
Air
cuts over, through,
freezes sweat
on chest, loins
and back, smashes
the self.
We are mirrorless,
utterly.

365: *Mother*

The resuscitation team had little time
for decency: his mother lay on the floor
with her nightie hiked around her neck.
The team seemed indifferent to the exposure:
the shanks, the little body like a worm
in a nutshell, the sagging breasts.

He grabbed an afghan from the couch, one
full of strong flower-colors, and covered
her parts.

The team kept thumping on her chest.
They clamped an oxygen cup over her mouth.
Nothing helped, as she sunk deeper
into the floor, through the cement slab,
lower than the potatoes.

Dick Barnes

366: *The Time of the Tumbleweeds*

My father watched the scar where the fire was
in the mountains above Redlands for years

and he was the engineer who had the idea: where tumbleweeds
grow along desert highways the state

can let them alone. Buicks coming back from Las Vegas
will have to take their own chances

with shapes rolling over the freeway; the sand
blows over it too and no one aspires to get rid of it:

some hazards will remain no matter how prudently
the authorities provide. He came out against guard rails

along curves on mountain highways: "If they can't
steer well enough to stay on the road

let them fall off, then they won't
bounce back into traffic and hit somebody."

Early one morning he lifted back specimen tumbleweeds
green and still moist with the scant dew of the desert

sure enough there in that shelter and condensation
a new world was alive, the bunch grasses

the flowerlets that grew up after
that could take hold

while tumbleweeds having lived out their era
left roots and rolled away in the wind

it's practical just to let that happen

367: *Alfalfa*

Past midnight in a wide field:
out there a John Deere tractor is stalled.

By the light of a drop cord
an okie and an arkie, two rednecks are working

from sunup. They both are tired,
their movements have become unhurried and sure.

One says, *They're all sposed to run —*
that's what they're made for.

Knuckles barked where a wrench slipped hours ago,
the treachery of rust, grease, worn metal, fatigue.

Well don't that go to show — the dumb
resistance of a machine. Arcturus sinks

toward the horizon,
autumn stars gather in the east,

a breeze lifts dust
from the half-harrowed field. They keep on.

In their leisure they are violent
intolerant men

but now in the night when I hear them
their voices, that courtliness, that calm concern

I too lack social consciousness
and I care nothing for anyone's scorn.

368: *Satisfaction*

The sooner you stitch the better
but fire is a matter of tact:

there's a moment there just before she explodes
when the rugs and curtains are smouldering

while the heat is slowly getting more intense
she sort of draws breath,

now that's the time to slam open the fog nozzle
you can lay the whole fire flat

it's you or it: ten seconds more
you may be cooked, but you have to wait

which is what Ed Sepulveda was doing
when the phone rang! right beside him

he was in the front room by the sofa
it was there on its own little table

when the time came, and wham!
he opened up with the inch-and-a-half, the

hose leaped in his hands but he held on
the phone still   ringing   still

ringing: "Hello?
Sorry, no, she ain't here

this is the fireman
excuse me, I'm busy with the fire"

which he had under control! He'd done it again!
Still sweating, he played the hose on the hot spots

smoking or just steaming:
that's satisfaction, for a fireman.

369꞉ *In San Bernardino
During the Nineteen Thirties*

Rhubarb green in the grey dirt
  a hot flimsy garage with spiders
    mysterious old iron tools that had the same odor

and the paths! through vacant lots!
  rank grass going to seed, wild flowers
    when we came down from the snow at Easter

370: *The Shit Inspector Har Har Har*

A melancholy man walked through the canyon
he kept his eyes to the ground.
What others might pass by he spotted and counted,
the crotties, lesses, wagging, drit, every kind
of wild shit: the government
hired him to do it
so as to know what to kill.

"Like fun you will," said lynx rufus.

"Like fun I will," said he, and set bait.

371: *A Boot Stomps in the Hallway*

Young men laugh trying to sound tough
from inside it sounds ugly as puking
leather and grease
you'd be surprised
some of them really are tough

372: *On the San Bernardino Freeway*

He saw the underpass coming down
because a driver following saw him
let go the wheel and lift both hands!
He tried his best to hold it.

373: *Song: Mohave Narrows*

to say that death is a river
and my love for you a star reflected in the river

that the river has worn a channel through boulders, and flows
north and east from the Forks a hundred miles without tributaries

to say a dry lake is a mirror, where the river
gives itself up to the sky

374: *Floating*

Late spring on the river trying to catch fish, he noticed
peach blossoms floating on the surface of the current
the fish were under; it was an easy matter
to follow the fallen flowers, as more kept on floating down the river,
rowing back up stream by choice of confluence
to where they were falling from trees in a hidden, inhabited valley.
Descendants of refugees lived there in harmony;
they had never heard of his century
nor earlier ones he knew about from history,
Wei, Han, et cetera: Ch'in was enough for them,
they told him: "You needn't mention us
out there when you go back,"
and must have followed him to move the marks he made
for he never found that valley again though he tried it often
no one else ever looked for it even
until now, in the snow, Chairman Mao,
the living mythical helmsman,
swims swiftly over the everflowing stream
upheld by hidden frogmen.
Him say, "great men"
him say, "history"
say "only us, today"

375: *Reading the Lao-Tzu Book in San Bernardino*

Cocks crow in the next town,
this town, all towns around
but only one of them
can make the sun come up.

Marine Robert Warden

376: *Night Mission*

the second hand keeps sweeping
i wish i could turn it back again
the clock above the x-ray viewer says one
outside it is black no moon just cold stars
inside the flourescent glow through black
and white x-rays while the patient moans
on her litter the oscilloscope bleeps her heart
a male nurse tonelessly counts her falling
blood pressure background sound of whoosh
of blood pumps nylon rustle of female nurses
everyone in green scrub gowns the raspy breathing
through the patient's torn windpipe time is short
ray paces the floor pondering two bullets
one must have torn the spleen
the other in the lung no entrance
wound her face is shot away
where did it come from he asks again
and turns the patient on her side
still sees no hidden chest wound just skin
i ask do you think the spent bullet
that hit her jaw could have torn her
trachea and just dropped down her
windpipe into that right lung
ray snaps his fingers and points to surgery
his green clad team is already on the trot
pushing the litter the monitors and iv stands
just begins the sound of your own heart
as you walk toward the doctors' parking lot
past the green light of the emergency room
her shattered face flies together like a puzzle
a jig-saw you put together as a small boy
you realize this woman was lovely before

the shot there's a female beggar waiting for
alms by the emergency door a teenage girl
in a flower print dress sits on the floor
her knees tucked under her chin her hands out
palms up to catch your trousers involuntarily
i look up her dress as i pass expecting white
panties instead black stripe of panty-hose
i catch her eyes tears well over i pause
a young man sidles beside her left shoulder
bearded with leather jacket and rings of keys
hanging from a wide black belt his hand
caresses her soft brown hair her cheek
rests against his knuckles i heel and pass
out to the parking lot where under the steam
of the power plant in the air above a whine
of a lone bomber from march air base
out on a night mission
too high above us to know

377: *Chicago Spring, 1954*

in april when lilacs should have bloomed
in parks and courtyards cold winter held
and there was a strange aura in the sky
each day the sun hung submerged in smoke
and the ice thaw on the lake came late then
stray wounded geese blew off course from the prairies
and circled aimlessly over the pronged tv antennas
deep in the ghettos at night you could hear them
coughing blood from the sky like tubercular men
while down below traffic growled and honked back
one morning when the last goose was gone
it cleared and the wind whistled all day
long down the brick canyons peeling paint
from the loose shutters rickety-rack slam
i stood in front of our brick apartment
tried to forget the cold ghettos
i couldn't forget the children
we delivered by flashlights
in cold little basement flats
deep in the slums at christmas time
bells booming christ is born today

we held them close to the only heat
open gas ovens shivering ourselves
in our thin white student coats that day
blast furnaces glowing bright orange sky
didn't warm us or white snow drifting down
like magic through broken casement windows
across the street faces pressed to dusty windows
while a little black girl bowed her head and prayed
on the street corner where a white snow goose fell food
for the ghettos that spring it didn't take long
to get a parking ticket on that one way street
so i slammed the trunk lid and left for denver
honked horns for the april geese who were gone
and the smoking sun married bricks to heat

378: *The Great Ground Swell*

for Lois Anne

in the great arc above the earth we have lost
the sense of what land could mean for us
a healing process a rebirth out of rocks and
wind the blades of grass that bend the endless
moan across the prairies the vast reserve power
of a giant exhaling very softly on a stalk
of wheat golden in the kansas sun
i tell you this
even this vast land and all the other continents
are only islands in this world of oceans
the continents merely rocky extrusions
of the sea's bed feel the great ground swell
rising off the coast of asia under this ship
miles before the first islands and rocks appear
even before the first scent
of night soil the tempo changes
the ground swell rises higher and then
in all its maginificence the land
will genesis from the biblical void
the sea our great mother
gives birth to the land for us
but whether animate or inanimate
she never remembers to mark our graves
not like her more gentle child does with crosses
and mounds the memorials and inscriptions

we associate with death on land
in the sea's bed there are no markers
engraved or wreaths of flowers
down there
the molecules join
i thought about all this at an open window
of a ramshackle motel at an unmarked junction
halfway between chicago and los angeles
when i was driving alone to california
to claim you as my bride
there was a renewal
like the beginning ground swell off the coast
of asia
it was june in the rockies and we camped high
just below the tree line near glacier basin
the ground was cold at night
and in our khaki pup tent we huddled
in our zipped together sleeping bags
for warmth the stars were close
silvery blue lights on the lingering snow
the wind came with a rush through fragrance
of pines that swayed like the waves
of a moderate sea
and i talked to you as we lay there
about the difference in tempo of a ground swell
as we come closer and closer
to land
i tell you this
i have travelled to asia several times by sea
and all over this land of ours on detour roads
slept half frozen under railroad bridges
shaved in glacial mountain streams
all these dusty miles and blown tires
crests of waves marked by the disappearing
wakes of ships
at the time i never knew it
they were all part of a great ground swell
out of which you appeared

379: *Portrait of You: Number 1*

it's early september and you're willing
to lie naked with me on the white sand
at saugatuck

we hope that no one else is on the beach
or at the top of the sand dune where we lie
below us blue lake michigan pounds and whitens
a large oak log that's floated up
muffles our murmurs our breathing
the sounds of our small voices the cry
of the circling hawk overhead
the late afternoon wind off the lake
waves the flat dune grass blades
against our skins stripped white our faces
we lie under the constant flow of grasses
green waves we drown
everything in
the hawk soars upward
you wait
until we are together again my hand
someplace you need it you subtly shift
my fingers onto your clitoris
until you make the upward thrust
of your pelvis contract your vagina
with climax
i pulse into you everything i own or ever knew
we relax into
silence until you come back
and can make a little joke
about the sand that's gotten inside your vagina
you ask me if it scratches my penis too
and laugh
when i tell you it does but it's worth it

380: *My Father-in-Law Remembers*
the Argonne, Sept. 1918

it helps to be mad
to hear voices
to have Jesus speak through you
and through the tv speakers
to see visions
before your eyes flickering lights
circles around street lamps
on the walk through the park at night
they rise up
cities with immense glass walls of light

to see ghosts who stand at windows
and light the lamps of the cities

to remember the men who crossed the field
and fell in rows like corn after hail
to look at photos of the dead rows
decades later
their faces are all beardless and innocent
love made them cross the field
or fear or madness
but they didn't have enough of it
their realm was the farm
and the farm died with their innocence
love made one or two of them
look back at the end

381: *On My Fifty-Third Birthday*

if the sun became smaller
or more cold
i didn't notice
one more day
i count gains
the moon still talks
     the vast machinery of stars
whispers a song in the night
     earth splits
     gives birth
     i hold my grandson against my chest
his brown Asian hands
reach beyond my thin ribs
     feel the beat of my heart

382: *For Esther*

not the blue parrot in the jungle
or the sea covered by froth and moonlight
but a bright light behind my right eye
that wouldn't go away
the night you died

Bill Mohr

383: *Manifesto 1984*

I'm not a punk, an intellectual,
or a neo-idealistic anarchist.
I'm not young, though when I was,
I danced to the music, I was famous
in the background, uninhibited in
the center of a crowd. The first
poems weren't difficult to write.
Personna? Style? No problem. Now
I'd like a disguise, a stack
that's different, but all
you see is someone who's
obsessed by poetry and can't
understand why so few others
don't hear the obvious.
A poem without words exists
in the midst of more words
than my mind knows what
to do with. Why should I continue
to put one word in front of, behind,
next to? Surely the words on the page
aren't like the ones in my mind —
Easter Island statues bobbing
in a torrent of velvety plankton.
Or are they like Darwinian
rollercoasters drag-racing twenty-
six letters, capitalized
parachutes emblazoned with
their intangible essence.
Each word's driven by the joke
that conjured up that word
millennia before I spoke it.
The engines cannibalize each
other's parts. What other way
is there to explain why this word
is here at the end of the line

rather than another word? Why
does this amusement park need
so many rollercoasters? Actually
there's only one word in the brain
and every word we hear goes into
that word and every word we speak
comes out of it and it's a word anyone
can pronounce but nobody wants
to say. Since only one at a
time can fit in my mind, the
rollercoasters live in the real
world and move like hell when I want
their ride, ignoring the "scenery"
flying past. The Carthaginian
scenery. Imagine Hannibal's
consonants luring Scandinavian
vowels, self-constructed out of
territorial ambiguity. I wasn't going
to write anything this morning. I didn't
feel inspired. Yet now this
is in existence. It's strange
to think of anything coming
into existence. But here we
are, Cathay and I, alive and
working, tired every day, wondering
whether we should get married. The TV
last night showed *Streetcar Named Desire*
and when I couldn't resist saying
Stanley's line about the Napoleanic Code
as he said it, you said when we get married
it's going to be the Josephine Rule.
One of the rules is making coffee in
the morning. I have to make twice
as much as we drink for it to taste good.
Otherwise, it's either too strong or weak.
Driving to work, it's easy to get lulled
on memorized routes. The revolution
didn't happen because I wasn't willing
to lead it. Or to follow. It would've
been meaningless unless people were paid
to read or write four hours a day.
This is as real as I can get, breathing
these words into your presence.
It's easy enough to make the mistake
that the poem is only a mask. The person

who writes the poem is the mask
the imagination put on to appear
in this world. I choose to wear the mask
and have no idea of what you're looking at.

384: *Autobiography*

I didn't create
the stars; they came from
a power who tried
to please me with gifts —
not bad the first time.

Obsessed proportions
decay, turbulent
sanctuaries thrust
out of a glowing
abyss. Outside of

Am, I meditate
on the exhaustion
of animal love,
reincarnated
penetralia.

Observe: my ruins
are fun for children
to play in. They eat
as much as they want
and play the same way.

You'd be surprised how
big a fort they can
build out of destroyed
walls and roofs — they are
the paradise of death.

385: *The Vision*

for Emile

Nupnah lingers in the minds
of grazing horses

Finally a god
who doesn't need to ride us!

386: *The Hunt*

the attempt to leave
the quietest poem behind
without my name
anywhere around it —
so far away,
if possible,
that no one thinks
of it without
wondering how anyone
so ignorant of the real
nature of
the universe could've thought
of the absolute name
of the Creator's gift
a tongue
in a baby's mouth
speaking
so slowly
that the confusion of words
pleases itself
with visionary hush
no one
should
bow
to Eternity
although to watch
it hunt
is an honor
which we
are foolish
enough to forget

387: *In Line at Pancho's Tacos*

At first I don't recognize him
walking through the door;
he owes me $75 from a year ago,
offers me his hand. I don't shake.
We talk. He's married and divorced,
going back to his first wife
whom he left nodding out at the piano.

"You still living at the same place?"
he asks, writing it down. "I'm expecting
a big check from back East, 2500,
by the end of the week."

"You got a phone?" I ask.
"No, I'm sort of moving around
right now." I grin, "Must be hard
for those social security checks
to keep up with you." He orders
a bean and cheese burrito,
then cancels it. I follow him outside.
New Jersey license plates.

One night he dropped a beer bottle
on the kitchen floor. Mid-morning
I walked in half-asleep, barefoot.
I missed a glass blade by a toe-length.

                    *

In fiction a writer's not supposed
to use real people. Your job's to create
new characters. In poetry, why lie —
if you're looking for a roommate,
don't let Nick DeNucci move in.

388: *The Ambiguity of Motion*

The fur, still warm, when you scoop
the cat's body off the pavement.
The cat's not crushed and there's no blood.

Your car's engine sounds louder
than I expect it to, but it's late
at night and there's no traffic

except for the car somewhere ahead of us
that hit this cat. But motor noise
collaborates. Sometimes I've woken

up very early and walked around
before alarm clocks ring and then
I realize how much noise a car makes;

or standing by a broken-down car
on the freeway, the other cars
zoom and whoosh. Death makes a big noise

that we can't hear, even though we
are listening all the time and often
hark as he drives past; his stationary car

wheeling with the voice of our thoughts.

389: *Slave of the Sun*

The sun destroys a planet with madagascarian trees
    crowning polar swamps
The sun destroys orange lizards with velvet wings
The sun destroys skulls the size of a hundred fists

The sun surrounds its barriers with a fragile deluge
    of polyrhythmic interruptions
The sun destroys the burial grounds of intimate memories
The sun creates the illusion that the present tense is infinite

Repetition allows spontaneous eruptions to vanish into
    equators of green eyes
Trees stare at the sun's meditation and never go blind
The sun destroys the jealousy of rejections, the humiliation
    of desire

The sun destroys limp & strut, antagonistic drought
The sun destroys the thirst of eroticism
The sun destroys the delays of words, breath tantalized
    by scintillation

The sun destroys all praise and worship & heroes in its image
Resistance is demanded and given
The sun destroys the annihilating despair of consciousness

The sun destroys the poem as soon as it is written
I'm the slave who's not supposed to use that word
I'm the slave who's better off than most other slaves

I'm the slave who teases other slaves about the ridiculous
    possibility of forgetting how hard life has been
I'm the slave of extinction with its seething convoluted refusal
    to caress the impulse to die
I'm the lucky slave, the quiet slave

Quit says the quiet of the sky
I'm the laugh of the slave that the slaves being born
    will be told about
He laughed like this

ha
ha
ha

I'm the happy slave of the big lion
    roooaaar
    roooaaaar

The sun destroys the beginnings of all sentences
Does the sun confuse the execution of fish and cows with the
    slaughter of human beings?
Does the sun interrogate the metamorphosis of beings
    who torture their prisoners?

I am the slave whose lover bought him a thrift-store shirt
    reading "Mysterylands" on the back and "Bill"
    on the front
I am the meditation whose slavery has no future
I am the slave of green leaves against hot blue

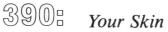 *Your Skin*

for Cathay

A woman who gave you
a massage a year ago
said you have the softest
skin she's ever rubbed.

You did it by yourself
for a long time, straining
to reach the part between
the shoulder blades, but only
able to cover the skin
and not rub it in. So that's
where you asked me to start
the first time your back hurt
but when I rubbed your lotions
between your shoulder blades
that's where your skin
seemed softest of all,
as if the skin there
were the tap root
of the flesh and
all the warmth of
the lotions trickled
to this crevice in
a riverbed and flowered.
You have the prettiest
eyes after you come,
you say, and I only wish
they were always that soft.

The Poets

DAVE ALVIN was born in Los Angeles in 1955 and grew up in Downey. He studied with Gerald Locklin and Eliot Fried at California State University at Long Beach. He is the songwriter and lead guitarist for The Blasters. They have released three albums, *The Blasters, Non-Fiction,* and *Hard Line.* He also plays guitar with The Knitters, a group which includes Exene Cervenka and John Doe. His next book of poetry will be a collaboration with John Doe, Victor Noel and Doug Knott entitled *Stories from L.A.* (Illuminati, 1985).

DICK BARNES was born in San Bernardino in 1932 and was raised in the wilds of eastern California (the San Bernardino Mountains and the Mojave Desert). He received a B.A. from Pomona College, an M.A. from Harvard, and a Ph.D. from Claremont Graduate School. He taught at UC Riverside, lasted two years writing in Mexico, and then came back to Pomona College. He is currently professor of English and Director of Creative Writing. He has published five chapbooks and one full-length collection, *A Lake on the Earth* (Momentum Press, 1982). He has had several plays produced including *Nacho* and *San Antonio Noh* at Mt. San Antonio College as well as plays using Southern California landscapes/environments: *The Cucamonga Wrapdown* (produced by Pomona College in a ruined winery in Cucamonga, 1967); *The Eighth Avatar* (1967) and The Death of Buster Quinine (1972, both produced by Pomona College at two different sites in an abandoned quarry in Cucamonga); *Purple* (self-produced on a butte on the Mojave Desert, 1973); and the *Bradford and Barnes Poverty Circus* (1977) and *Come Sunday*, both produced by Pitzer College. He has also written, directed and produced four short films and recorded an album.

MAX BENAVIDEZ was born in East Los Angeles in 1951. He graduated from UCLA in Philosophy in 1974. Since then he has edited three magazines; published articles and essays on many topics including the arts, Native Americans, national security, and the media. In 1983, he worked in the California Art's Council's Artist-in-Social Institutions program, and co-directed the creation of the California Chicano Mural Archive. He co-edited *Hard Words, Short Time*, a collection of prison writing. He reviews books for several publications including the Los Angeles *Times* and appears regularly on an L.A.-based television program. His first book of poems, *The Stopping of Sorrow*, was published by Momentum Press in 1985. He is a Lecturer at Cal State Northridge and lives with his wife, Kate, an actress, in Santa Monica.

CHARLES BIVINS was born October 5, 1948 in Winter Park, Florida. He moved to San Francisco in the late 60s seeking unusual experience and loud music. He moved to Los Angeles in 1975 and has been living here since then working as a yard man, security guard and apartment manager.

LAUREL ANN BOGEN was born in Los Angeles in 1950. Her most recent books are *Do Iguanas Dance under the Moonlight* (Illuminati, 1984) and *The Great Orange Leonard Scandal* (Illuminati, 1984). In 1986 Illuminati will publish a book of short fictions entitled *The Projects*. Ms. Bogen has served as Executive Director of the Los Angeles Poetry Theatre, Poetry Reviewer for the Los Angeles Herald Examiner and Poetry Director of George Sand Books and the Hyperion Theatre. She is currently working on a new book of verse entitled *Vulnerable Street*.

KATE BRAVERMAN was born in Philadephia. She was educated at U.C. Berkeley. Her books include *Milk Run* (Momentum Press, 1977), *Lithium for Medea*, a novel, Harper & Row, 1979), and *Lullaby for Sinners* (Harper & Row, 1980). She has appeared in many anthologies, including *Cameos* (Crossing Press, 1978), *Alcatraz* 1 (1979) and 2 (1981), *The Streets Inside: Ten Los Angeles Poets* (Momentum Press, 1978), *Dreamworks* (1980), and *Amorotica* (1981). She has taught creative writing at U.C. Riverside and U.C.L.A., written literary essays for the L.A. Weekly, essays for the Opinion Section of the Los Angeles Times and is currently reviewing books for the Herald Examiner. Her new novel is entitled *Palm Latitudes*.

CHARLES BUKOWSKI was born in Andernach, Germany in 1920, and brought to the United States at the age of three. He was raised in Los Angeles and presently lives in San Pedro, California. He published his first story when he was twenty-four and began writing poetry at the age of thirty-five. He has now published over forty books of poetry and prose. His recent books of poetry include *War* and *Dangling in the Tournefortia* (both from Black Sparrow Press). Some of his prose titles include *Post Office*, *Women*, and *Ham on Rye*. Most of his books have now been published in translation and his poems and stories continue to appear in magazines and newspapers throughout the world.

PETER CASHORALI was born in Walpole, Massachusetts in 1954 and moved to Culver City, California in 1964. His three major influences while growing up were Donald Swanson in high school, Sam Eisenstein in college, and Leland Hickman. He lives in West Hollywood.

EXENE CERVENKA is the lead singer and songwriter for two groups, X since 1977 and The Knitters, which was started in 1984. X is releasing its fifth LP on Elektra on July 4, 1985. The first Knitters' LP, "Poor Little Critter on the Road," was released May 13th by Slash Records. Her first book of poems was *Adulturers Anonymous* (Grove Press) with Lydia Lunch. Her poems were recorded live at McCabe's on February 1, 1985, for one side of the Freeway Records LP, *Twin Sisters*.

MICHELLE T. CLINTON came from the east coast at the age of seven and spent her childhood in South-Central Los Angeles. Since 1984 she has facilitated the Beyond Baroque Poetry Workshop. Her first volume of poetry, *High Blood/Pressure*, is scheduled for publication in early 1986 by West End Press. She worked collectively on *Eve Acts*, an anti-rape performance art piece featuring her poetry which was presented at S.P.A.R.C. (Social Public Art and Resouce Center) in May, 1985. She hangs out by the ocean in Santa Monica.

LORI COHEN was born in Boston and has lived in Los Angeles most of her life. Her first book, *The Border* was published in 1984 by Bombshelter Press. A book-length poem, *Faith in Grace*, is due out at the end of 1985. She works as an Artist-in-Residence of the California Arts Council and is one of the Los Angeles coordinators of the California Poets in the Schools Program.

WANDA COLEMAN: "Up from the ashes of Watts." Her books include *Art in the Court of the Blue Fag, Mad Dog Black Lady* and *Imagoes* from Black Sparrow Press. She received a fellowship from the National Endowment for the Arts 1981-1982 and a Guggenheim in poetry, 1984. She is the subject of a film, *Mad Dog Black Lady* by Jeff Land and Scott Grant, 1983. A live reading of her work was recorded for one side of the Freeway Records' LP, *Twin Sisters*.

DENNIS COOPER is a poet and prose writer whose books include *He Cried* (Black Star Editions, 1984), *Safe* (The Sea Horse Press, 1984), *The Missing Men* (Am Here Books/Immediate Editions, 1982), *The Tenderness of the Wolves* (The Crossing Press, 1982), and *Idols* (The Sea Horse Press, 1979). He was born in Los Angeles in 1953 and attended Pitzer College where he studied with Bert Meyers and Pasadena City College where he studied with Ron Koertge. He was the director of the

Beyond Baroque reading series from 1980 through 1983. He established *Little Caesar* magazine in 1977 and edited twelve issues before it folded in 1983. He published almost two dozen books of poetry under the Little Caesar imprint between 1979 and 1983. He moved to New York City in 1983 and teaches writing workshops at St. Mark's in-the-Bowery and writes art reviews. In 1984 he gave a talk at the Langston Arts Center in San Francisco as well as reading at the International Poetry Festival in Holland.

ROBERT CROSSON was born in Canonsburg, Pennsylvania. His family moved to Pomona, California in 1942. He studied acting at the University of California at Los Angeles and did two years of "Dragnet" shows on radio and ten episodes on television as well as working on series such as "Father Knows Best," "Superman," and "The Lone Ranger." He recently appeared as "Sam" in *Mike's Murder*. His first book was *Geographies* (Red Hill, 1980) and his second was a collaboration with John Thomas and Paul Vangelisti, *Abandoned Latitudes* (Red Hill, 1983). He lives in Laurel Canyon.

JOHN DOE came to Los Angeles from Baltimore in the mid-seventies. He met Exene Cervenka at a Beyond Baroque Poetry Workshop and they formed a band with guitarist Billy Zoom and drummer Don Brakebone, "X". He plays bass, writes songs, and sings. Their first two albums, *Los Angeles* and *Wild Gift* were both voted as Best Albums of the Year by several polls of critics. Other albums, *Under the Midnight Sun* and *More Fun in the New World*, were equally praised. He is acting in a film which is being shot in Mexico.

DENNIS DORNEY was born in Hollywood and grew up in the San Fernando Valley. He went to the University of San Diego and did graduate work at San Diego State College. He edited a poetry magazine, *Cafeteria*, with Gordon Preston for several years and moved back to Los Angeles in 1973. He makes his living as a camera person for the movie industry.

BOB FLANAGAN was born December 26, 1952 in New York City, but has spent most of his life in Southern California and now lives in Los Angeles. He has been program director at Beyond Baroque Literary / Arts Center in Venice, as well as co-director of its poetry workshop. He taught poetry to children for seven years through the California Poets in the Schools program. He was a singer and songwriter in the post no-wave rock group, *Planet of Toys*. His first book of poems, *The Kid Is the Man*, was published by Bombshelter Press in 1978. *The Wed-*

ding of Everything appeared from Sherwood Press in 1983. Illuminati has issued a cassette of a recorded reading. His work also appeared in the Little Caesar anthology, *Coming Attractions*.

MICHAEL C. FORD was born on the Illinois side of Lake Michigan and moved with his parents to Pasadena, California toward the end of World War II. Between 1974 and 1977 he co-edited a prose/poetry journal called *The Sunset Palms Hotel*. He also edited two anthology projects, *The Mount Alverno Review* (Peace Press, 1971) and *Foreign Exchange* (Biographics, 1979). His full-length collections include *Lawn Swing Poems, Rounding Third*, and *The World Is a Suburb of Los Angeles* (Momentum Press, 1981). His chapbooks include *Sheet Music, West Point* (Biographics, 1977) and *Sleepless Night in a Soundproof Motel* (Mudborn Press, 1978).His play, *Goddess Latitudes*, was included in an evening of short dramatic pieces at the Odyssey Theatre Ensemble in 1980 and was published by Illuminati in *2 American Plays*, which also featured his one-act *The Great American Grab-Bag of 1945*, which was an installation of the California Dada Festival.

AMY GERSTLER was born in 1956 in San Diego. Her books and chapbooks include *Yonder* (Little Caesar Press, 1981), *Christy's Alpine Inn* (Sherwood Press, 1982), *White Marriage/Recovery* (Illuminati, 1984), *Early Heaven* (Ouija Madness Press, 1984), *Martine's Mouth* (Illuminati, 1985) and *The True Bride* (Lapis Press, forthcoming).

JACK GRAPES was born in New Orleans and attended Tulane University where he received a BA in English and did two years of graduate study in History, then entered the MFA program in Theatre. After a short stint as part of the *Second City* revue he moved to Los Angeles and has lived there for the past 16 years working as a professional actor in episodic televsion, movies-of-the-week, films and theatre. His first poems were published in Jon Webb's *Outsider* in 1967, and his work has appeared in various magazines and journals, and 6½ books including the most recent *Breaking on Camera* and *Trees, Coffee, and the Eyes of Deer*. He was awarded a National Endowment for the Arts Fellowship in Poetry in 1984. Jack is also editor of Bombshelter Press, which has published dozens of Los Angeles poets. He teaches poetry at UCLA Extension and has received several California Arts Council grants to work as Artist-in-Residence in Los Angeles schools as part of the Poets in the Schools program.

JANET GRAY types at home for a living. She was born in Altadena, CA and lives there still (after a cumulative total of 10 years in Kunsan, Korea; Darjeeling, West Bengal, India; Richmond, Indiana; Syracuse, New York; Philadelphia, PA; Middlebury, Vermont; and Greyhound buses). She began publishing in little magazines in 1969-1970 and enrolled in the Creative Writing master's program at Syracuse University in fall '70 but dropped out in late Novemeber when the snow reached shoulder height. She's had work in over two dozen little magazines. She's been a member of the Pasadena Poets Workshop off and on since 1977. She has two books out from Illuminati: *TO PULL OUT THE PEACHBOY* and *I HATE MEN*.

JOHN HARRIS was born in China where his parents were missionaries. He was one of the founders of the Beyond Baroque Poetry Workshop and, with Joseph Hansen, led its meetings for many years. He edited several issues of *Bachy* magazine, which was published by Papa Bach Bookstore. He operated Papa Bach for many years and established Papa Bach Editions, which published several large volumes of poetry, including work by Bert Meyers and William Pillin.

ELOISE KLEIN HEALY has published three books of poetry: *Building Some Changes* (Beyond Baroque Foundation), *A Packet Beating Like A Heart* (Books of a Feather Press), and *Ordinary Wisdom* (Paradise Press). She has also produced an audiotape, *Some From Ten: Poems 1975-1985* (Prism Productions). Her works appear in anthologies and magazines, among them *A Geography of Poets: An Anthology of the New Poetry* edited by Edward Field (Bantam Books), *The Streets Inside: Ten Los Angeles Poets* (Momentum Press), *Southern California Women Writers and Artists* (Books of a Feather Press), and *Amorotica: New Erotic Poetry* (Deep River Press). Ms. Healy has taught at Immaculate Heart College, California School of Professional Psychology, California State University Northridge, and at the Woman's Building in Los Angeles where she has served on the Board of Directors and as an organizer of the Woman Writers Series. Among her interests are a study of the work of Gertrude Stein, an investigation of girlhood, and the influence of landscape/location on poetry. She has been awarded residencies at Dorland Mountain Colony and the MacDowell Colony.

LELAND HICKMAN was born on September 15, 1934 in Santa Barbara, California. He was raised there as well as in

Bakersfield and on a farm in Carpinteria. After three years at the University of California at Santa Barbara and Berkeley and a stint in the Army, he spent several years moving back and forth between New York City and Los Angeles. He finally settled in Los Angeles in 1970. Parts of TIRESIAS have been published in the *New American Review, Bachy, Momentum, (Beyond Baroque) NewLetters, Little Caesar,* and *Boxcar, as well as the anthology, The Streets Inside: Ten Los Angeles Poets.* His first book of poems, *TIRESIAS I:9:B Great Slave Lake Suite,* was nominated for the Los Angeles Times Book Awards prize for poetry in 1980. He was the poetry editor of *Bachy* magazine from its ninth to its final issue. He edited an issue of *Boxcar* magazine with Paul Vangelisti and now edits *Temblor,* a magazine of contemporary poets.

TERRYL HUNTER is a Los Angeles native currently living in Pasadena. She's also lived in San Francisco and Seattle, but returns to Los Angeles, where her father's parents were Dutch immigrants who had a dairy farm in the Arroyo Seco before it was a golf course. She's been a single parent for 17 years. Her daughter Tina is getting ready for college to pursue her interest in film and video. Her poems have appeared in a limited edition portfolio of LA poets, *Life in LA,* as well as in the anthology *Southern California Women Writers & Arts* (rara avis). A series of poems about her childhood, *For All This Time,* was published in a letterpress edition by Paradise Press. She works forty hours a week in an office at a local university and recently returned to school to study sociology. "There are wild parrots where I live and the roses and plums come out each year no matter how neglectful I am of them."

DAVID JAMES is an English poet, living in Los Angeles for the past 15 years. Two books, *Driving to Here* and *Surface Streets,* have been published by the Applezaba Press. He is featured on the record, *"English As a Second Language."* A new book, *The Book Called Thibet,* and a record are forthcoming.

RON KOERTGE was born in 1940 in Olney, Illinois. He teaches at Pasadena City College. His books of poetry include *Life on the Edge of the Continent: Selected Poems (University of Arkansas Press, 1982), Sex Object* (Little Caesar Press, 1980), and *Diary Cows* (Little Caesar Press, 1981). His novel, *The Boogeyman,* was published by Norton.

IAN KRIEGER was born in New York City in 1948 and currently lives in Venice. His works include *Homage to Magritte* and *Pavans* which is being published by Ommation Press. He was the editor of *Telepoem*, L.A.'s first dial-a-poem service, and *Accept*. His poems have been set to dance by a Portland dance company. He is also a playwright and writes on art.

JAMES KRUSOE was born in Cleveland, Ohio in 1942 and moved to Los Angeles in 1963. He has been a house painter, administrator (for the California Poets in the Schools Program), editor, and Public Health Investigator. He teaches at California State University at Northridge and at Santa Monica City College. He was the original director of the reading series at Beyond Baroque Foundation and held that position for seven years. His books include *History of the World* (Bombshelter Press, 1977), *Small Pianos* (Momentum Press, 1978) *Jungle Girl* (Little Caesar Press, 1983), and three chapbooks, *Notes on Suicide* (Momentum Press, 1976), *Ju-Ju* (Bayrock Press, 1976), and *ABCDEFGHIJKLMNOPQRSTUVWXYZ* (Illuminati, 1984). He received a National Endowment for the Arts Writing Fellowship in 1984. He lives in Santa Monica.

MICHAEL LALLY was born in Orange, New Jersey in May, 1942. After a brief career as a jazz musician and four years in the US Air Force, he graduated from the University of Iowa Writers Workshop with an MFA in poetry. In 1968 he ran for sheriff of Johnson County, Iowa. In Washington DC he taught at Trinity College and started Some of Us Press and the poetry project Mass Transit. He has won several awards including the New York Poetry Center's "Discovery Award," the Poets Foundation Award, and two National Endowment for the Arts Fellowships. He has written for *The Washington Post* and *The Village Voice*, among other publications, and published twenty collections of poetry and prose including an all-German edition — ROCKY STIRBT FEIGE — of his small press bestseller ROCKY DIES YELLOW. Other books include a collection of love poems, *just let me do it* (Vehicle Editions, 1978), *Attitude* (Hanging Loose Press, 1982), and *Hollywood Magic* (Little Caesar Press, 1982). The latter was adapted into a stage play and presented at the Odyssey Theatre in West Los Angeles in 1983. Besides performing in that production, he has acted in several films, including *Last Rites* and *The Nesting*, plays (the L.A. premiere of Lanford Wilson's *Balm in Gilead*, and several television shows, e.g., "Cagney and Lacey" and "Berrengers."

In June 1982 he moved from New York City to Santa Monica where he now lives with his children, Caitlin and Miles.

PETER LEVITT was born in New York City and went to San Francisco State College, where he studied with Kay Boyle, and S.U.N.Y. Buffalo, where he studied with John Logan and Robert Creeley. He moved to Ocean Park, California in 1973 and to Los Flores Canyon in 1980. His books include *Two Bodies Dark/Velvet* (Momentum Press, 1975), *Running Grass (Poems 1970-1977)* (Eidolon Editions, 1979) , and *A Book of Light* (Amargi Press, 1982), which was chosen by the Best Western Books Exhibition as one of the best books published in 1982. Forthcoming from Lockhart Press is *Homage: Leda As Virginae.* He is a translator of Chinese, Japanese and Spanish. He teaches for the U.C.L.A. Extension Writing Program and private workshops. He participates in the Arts America Program, an international exchange of artists. He is married to the writer Joan Sutherland and has one daughter, Sheba. He is a practicing Buddhist under the tutelage of Jakusho Kwong Roshi at Genjo-ji, the Zen Center of Sonoma Mountain. He has read his work and lectured around the United States and recently at Ritsumaken University in Kyoto, Japan.

CAROL LEWIS was born in Chicago, Illinois and lived there until she moved to Los Angeles at the age of thirty. She worked as the buyer of children's books for a Bill Martindale's Bookstore and now works for a firm that sells educational materials to schools. She lives in Culver City.

MARTHA LIFSON received a PhD from Yale University after writing a dissertation about Milton. Her academic work focuses these days on Shakespeare and autobiography. She has lived in Ohio, Massachusetts, Connecticut, N. Carolina, and Los Angeles. She teaches at Occidental College and in the summer of 1984 made a most wonderful trip to Japan with her son and her sister and her husband and children.

GERALD LOCKLIN was born in 1941 in Rochester, N.Y. He received his M.A. and PhD. from the University of Arizona. He has taught at California State University, Long Beach since 1965. Some of his books of poetry are *Poop, and other poems* (Mag Press, 1972) and *The Criminal Mentality* (Red Hill Press, 1976), *Two Summer Sequences (Maelstrom Press, 1979), and Scenes from a Second Adolescence (Applezaba Press, 1981).*

His books of fiction include The Chase (Duck Down Press, 1976), *The Four-Day Work Week and other stories* (Maelstrom/Russ Haas Press, 1977), *The Cure* (Applezaba Press).

SUZANNE LUMMIS is an actress, playwright and a freelance comedy writer. Her book of poetry, *Idiosyncrasies*, was published by Illuminati in 1984. She is a strong supporter of the idea that pets should have surnames. Her pet's name is (little) Billy Smith-Hermenez.

LEWIS MACADAMS was born in West Texas in 1944. He graduated from Princeton and also attended S.U.N.Y. Buffalo. He lived in Bolinas, California from 1970 to 1980 and was the director of the Poetry Center at San Francisco State University from 1975 to 1978. He moved to Los Angeles in 1980 and edited *Wet* magazine for two and a half years. He works as a screenwriter and a free-lance journalist. He co-produced and co-wrote the documentary, *What Happened to Kerouac?* He recently defended his world heavyweight poetry championship against Joanne Kyger in Taos, New Mexico. He has had eleven books published, including *Africa and the Marriage of Walt Whitman and Marilyn Monroe* (Little Caesar Press, 1982), *News from Niman Farm (Tombouctou Books, 1979), and Live at the Church*, (Kulchur, 1977). He lives in Los Angeles with his children.

NICHOLA MANNING was born within the sound of the Bow Bells in London, England. She became a professional tennis player. She arrived in Los Angeles in 1973 with a three-speed bicycle and gave tennis lessons. She moved to Long Beach in 1976 and began writing stories and poems. Her books include *The French Woman Poems* (Applezaba Press, 1977) and *Hysterical Document*. Illuminati published *All Down to a River* in 1984. She was a featured poet in an issue of *Wormwood Review*.

MURRAY MEDNICK was born in New York City and was one of the original group of off-off-Broadway playwrights who were involved with Theatre Genesis. Some of his published plays are *The Hawk, The Hunter, Taxes, The Coyote Cycle,* and *The Deer Kill,* for which he won an Obie. He is the founder and artistic director of the Padua Hills Playwrights' Workshop and Festival, which stages plays by a wide range of American playwrights, including Maria Irene Fornes, Martin Epstein, John Steppling, John O'Keefe and Michael Monroe. *The*

Coyote Cycle consists of seven plays. It has been performed in its entirety, sunset to sunrise, in Santa Fe, New Mexico, and will be presented at the Paramount Ranch this Summer by L.A. Theatre Works.

BILL MOHR was born in 1947 in Norfolk, Virginia. He grew up there as well as in Hawaii and San Diego, California. He moved to Los Angeles in 1968 and acted with several theatre companies, including the Burbage Theatre Ensemble. He has worked as a California Arts Council Artist-in-Residence in the San Gabriel Valley and also taught creative writing classes for L.A. Theatre Works at prisons in Chino. He is currently re-writing a one-act play, *Slow Spin Out*, about a group of prisoners who are about to be released. His work has appeared in several anthologies, including *Poets West* (Perivale Press), *Young American Poets*, a Japanese anthology edited by Bob Kuntz, and *The Southern California Literary Anthology*. His first book of poems, *hidden proofs*, was published by Bomb-shelter Press in 1982. His second collection, *PENETRALIA*, was published by Momentum Press in 1984. He is working on a new manuscript, *barely holding distant things apart*. He lives in Ocean Park with his wife, Cathay Gleeson.

HARRY E. NORTHUP is an actor as well as a poet. He was born in Amarillo, Texas and grew up in Nebraska. He has acted in over two dozen films, including *Mean Streets, Alice Doesn't Live Here Anymore,* and *Taxi Driver*. He starred in *Over the Edge* and *Fighting Mad*. His recent television credits include guest star roles on *Scarecrow & Mrs. King* and five *Knots Landing* episodes. He has had four books of poetry published: *AMARILLO BORN, the jon voight poems* (Mt. Alverno Press, 1972), *EROS ASH* (Momentum Press, 1976), and *ENOUGH THE GREAT RUNNING CHAPEL* (Momentum Press, 1982). He received his B.A. from California State University, Northridge, where he studied poetry with Ann Stanford. He lives in East Hollywood with Holly Prado. He has a sixteen year old son named Dylan.

ROBERT PETERS was born on a farm in northern Wisconsin in 1924. After WW II, he attended the University of Wisconsin, earning three degrees in literature. He has taught at the University of California at Irvine since 1966. He lives in Huntington Beach with his friend of many years, Paul Trachtenberg.

He has published twenty-two volumes of poetry. The most recent are *What Dillinger Meant to Me* (Sea Horse Press) and *Hawker* (the winner of the di Castagnola Prize from the Poetry Society of America, published by Unicorn Press.)

Two volumes of his poetry have been adapted for the stage: *The Picnic in the Snow: Ludwig of Bavaria* and *The Blood Countess*. Both were given their original performances by the author at Beyond Baroque. He has given almost eighty performances of *Ludwig* throughout the country.

Peter's career as a poet began in 1967 with the appearance of *Songs for a Son*, poems on the unexpected death of a four year old son from meningitis. Some of his other books include *The Sow's Head and other Poems* (Wayne State University Press, 1968), *Cool Zebras of Light* (Christopher's Books, 1978), *Bronchial Tangle, Heart System* (Granite Press, 1975), *The Drowned Man to the Fish* (New Rivers, 1978), and *The Gift to Be Simple* (W.W. Norton, 1975), a book of poems about the founder of the Shaker religion, Ann Lee. Work from his first five books appears in in *Gauguin's Chair: Selected Poems* (Crossing Press).

He is a Contributing Editor for *The American Book Review* and for *Contact II*. Many of his reviews and essays about contemporary writing have been gathered in several volumes of criticism, *The Great American Poetry Bake-Off* (Scarecrow Press) and *The Peters Black and Blue Guide to Literary Journals* (Cherry Valley Editions).

DENNIS PHILLIPS is the author of *The Hero Is Nothing* (Kajun Press, San Francisco). He was the first poetry editor of the L.A. Weekly (1979-1980) and the book-review editor of *Sulfur* for the first nine issues. He is currently director/president of Beyond Baroque Literary/Arts Foundation in Venice.

HOLLY PRADO has had three books of poetry, prose-poetry and autobiographical fiction published: *NOTHING BREAKS OFF AT THE EDGE* (New Rivers Press, 1975); *FEASTS* (Momentum Press, 1976); and *LOSSES* (Laurel Press, 1977). A chapbook, *HOW THE CREATIVE LOOKS TODAY* was self-published by THE JESSE PRESS. She writes a column reviewing poetry for the *Los Angeles Times*. *GARDENS*, a novel, will be published by Harcourt Brace Jovanovich in November, 1985.

JED RASULA was born in Michigan but moved around as an Army brat. In 1976 he moved to Los Angeles with his wife and settled in Echo Park. He works as a researcher for the ABC series *Ripley's Believe It or Not*. He edits *Wch Way*, which he began in 1975. The two most recent issues were produced with *New Wilderness Letter*. His first book of poems is *Tabula Rasula* (Station Hill Press, 1985).

TIM REYNOLDS was born in Vicksburg, Mississippi in 1936. He received an M.A. in Classics from Tufts University in 1962. He has lived for extended periods in Japan and England. His first book of poems, *Ryoanji*, was published by Harcourt, Brace in 1964. Since then seven titles have appeared including *Slocum* (Unicorn Press), *Que* (Halty-Ferguson), and *Dawn Chorus* (Ithaca House). He lives in downtown Los Angeles.

DOREN ROBBINS was born and grew up in Los Angeles. He has traveled extensively in the United States and the Mediterranean. He is married and lives with his wife and daughter in Los Angeles. His books include *Detonated Veils* (Third Rail, 1976), *The Roots and the Towers* (Third Rail, 1980) and *Seduction of the Groom* (Loom Press, 1982). He makes his living as a carpenter.

BROOKS RODDAN was born in Los Angeles in 1950. He went to Principia College in Illinois and finished at the University of California at Berkeley. He lived in San Luis Obispo for three years and moved back to Los Angeles in 1979. He is the vice-president of an advertising and marketing firm. He is married and has two sons, Drew and Spencer.

ALEIDA RODRÍGUEZ was born in the village of Güines in the province of Havana, Cuba six years before the Revolution. Her writing has appeared in such anthologies as *Lesbian Fiction* (Persephone Press, 1981), *Fiesta in Aztlan (Capra Press, 1982), Cuentos: Stories by Latinas* (Kitchen Table Press, 1983), and is forthcoming in *Compañeras* (KTP, 1985). In 1982 she was awarded an NEA Creative Writing fellowship, during which most of the poems included in *"Poetry Loves Poetry"* were written. She has also received a Woman of Promise award from the National Feminist Writers' Guild and a Vesta Award in writing from the Los Angeles Woman's Building. She is the co-founder/editor/publisher of *rara avis* magazine, which was published for six years but terminated in 1984 and Books of a Feather, a Los Angeles-based women's press.

PETER SCHJELDAHL: "When my wife's acting career first brought me, as a tag-along, to Los Angeles in 1978, I was 36 years old and a 14-year New Yorker with a New York poetry style and the New York profession of art critic. (Before 1964, there had been small towns in North Dakota and Minnesota, three years of college, and a newspaper-reporting itinerancy that took me east.) I hated Los Angeles. Through seven years of sporadic sojourns, that emotion has gotten mixed up with some others, including love. In trying to defend myself against Los Angeles, I changed; and my poetry changed. Though still New York based, I have no qualms about being called a "Los Angeles poet." I went through a lot for the honor, and it's mine." His books of poetry include *White Country* (Cornith, 1968), *An Adventure of the Thought Police* (Ferry, 1971), *Dreams* (Angel Hair, 1973), *Since 1964: New & Selected Poems* (Sun, 1978), and *The Brute* (Little Caesar, 1981). Unpublished: *South of the Border*. He is a former regular art critic for the Sunday *New York Times*, 1970-75; *The Village Voice*, 1980-82; *Vanity Fair*, 1983-84. Contributing editor, *Art in America*. He received the 1980 Frank Jewett Mather Award for art criticism from the College Art Association.

P. Schneidre was born in the Pacific Northwest in 1950 and moved to Southern California twenty-five years ago to be with his parents. He has worked as a magician, experimental sleep subject and graphic designer. His son Riley is currently seven weeks old. He started Illuminati in 1978 and publishes twenty-five books and magazines a year.

JACK SKELLEY was born in Los Angeles in 1956 and graduated from Humboldt State University in Arcata, California in 1979. He moved back to Los Angeles and worked as the supervisor for NewComp Graphics Center at Beyond Baroque Foundation for the next six years. He also has produced the concert series at Beyond Baroque, directed the reading series, and led its weekly writing workshop. He co-founded the rock group *Planet of Toys* with Bob Flanagan in 1981 and performed with that group for three years. He now performs with *Lawndale*. He edited and published *Barney: The Modern Stone-Age Magazine* for four years. His first book, *Monsters*, was published by Little Caesar Press in 1982. Illuminati has published two novellas, *from Fear of Kathy Acker* and *more Fear of Kathy Acker*.

ED SMITH was born in Queens, New York in 1957 and his family moved to Southern California in 1959. He grew up in National City, Paramount, and Downey. His first book, *Fantasyworld*, was published by Cold Calm Press in December, 1983. He resides in Hollywood.

AUSTIN STRAUSS has been a SW Regional Coordinator for Amnesty International USA, a representative for Southern California at the Citizen's Party Convention in Cleveland in 1980, office manager for the Campaign for a Citizen's Police

Review Board in L.A. His radio interview program, "The Poetry Connexion," appears regularly on KPFK-FM. He is also an artist/collagist, currently experimenting with burnt paper collagraphs as well as etching. He lives in L.A. with poet Wanda Coleman and three children.

ROB SULLIVAN is a poet and playwright. Since 1974 he has worked with the theatrical troupe, The Mums, as a writer, actor, director, juggler and tightrope-walker. In 1979 he co-wrote and acted in a show with the Mums, *Mumfukle or A Small Goat in Crete*, which was presented at The Mark Taper Lab. He wrote and performed his first one-man show *Flower Ladies and Pistol Kids* in 1980 and received Drama-Logue and L.A. Weekly Awards. In 1982 he was a resident at The Edward Albee Foundation in Montauk, New York where he wrote the first draft of *Last Quarter Moon*, which was performed at The Met Theatre in Hollywood in 1983. In the spring of 1984 he performed his second one-man show, *The Long White Dress of Love*, at the Nighthouse Theatre for L.A. Theatre Works. It was directed by Darrell Larson with music by John Densmore. *The Rattle of the Moon* will be produced in the summer of 1985 at the Burbage Theatre. Another play, *Just the Way It Was*, will be produced by Susan Dietz in the Fall of 1985. He has two books of poetry published, *Wind Rivers* by Dust Books, and *Hands in the Stone*, by Holmgangers Press.

JOHN THOMAS was born in Baltimore, Maryland, December 31, 1930. He began to write verse in 1959. His first book, *John Thomas*, was published by Red Hill Press in 1972. His poems have appeared in many anthologies, including *A Geography of Poets* and *Specimen 73*. His second book was *Abandoned Latitudes*, written with Paul Vangelisti and Robert Crosson.

ALISON TOWNSEND grew up in the rural Northeast (Pennsylvania, New York state, and Vermont), but has made her home in the San Gabriel Valley since 1975. She has a B.A. in American Studies from Marlboro College in Marlboro, Vermont and an M.A. in English and American Literature from Claremont Graduate School. She has done publications work for the Pomona schools and worked as a library reference assistant. She is currently working as the assistant director of a bookstore. She shares her life with an environmental economist and three completely magical cats.

PAUL TRACHTENBERG was born in Lakewood, a suburb of Los Angeles, in 1948. He attended Cal Poly Pomona, majoring in horticulture. His first book of poems, *Short Changes for Loretta*, was published by Cherry Valley Editions in 1982. His second book, *Making Waves*, will also be published by Cherry Valley. His mentor is Robert Peters, with whom he lives. He has worked extensively on Peters' stage performances, serving as director and tech consultant for Peters' *The Blood Countess*, which is now on national tour. He has been stage manager and technician for *Mad King Ludwig*.

DAVID TRINIDAD was born on July 20, 1953. He received his B.A. in English from California State University at Northridge, where he studied poetry with Ann Stanford. In 1981, he established Sherwood Press in memory of the poet Rachel Sherwood. His first book of poems was *Pavane* (Sherwood Press, 1981). His second collection, *Monday, Monday* was published by Cold Calm Press in 1985. His poems also appeared in *Coming Attractions: American Poets in the Twenties* (Little Caesar, 1980).

PAUL VANGELISTI was born in San Francisco in 1945 and has lived in Los Angeles since 1968. Some of his books of poetry include *Air, Pearl Harbor, Another You,* and *Rime*, a sonnet sequence with drawings by Los Angeles painter Don Suggs. Since 1971, he has co-edited *Invisible City*. He has worked on several anthologies, among them the *Anthology of L.A. Poets* (1972), co-edited with Charles Bukowski; the poetry exhibition and catalogue, *Specimen 73*, for the Pasadena Museum of Art (1973); and the international casette antholohy of sound poetry, *Breathing Space 79*, which he did for Black Box in Washington, D.C. He has translated numerous volumes from the Italian, including *Italian Poetry, 1960-1980: from the Neo to the Post-Avantgarde*. From 1974 to 1982 he worked for KPFK Radio as Cultural Affairs Director. Since 1978 he has produced many shows for the Los Angeles Theatre of the Ear (L.A.T.E.). The L.A.T.E. production of James Joyce's *Ulysses*, which Vangelisti adapted and directed, won the Corporation for Public Broadcasting's 1980 Drama Award.

MARINE ROBERT WARDEN lives in Riverside, California. In 1975 he left a private practice of medicine to work as a consultant for the California State Health Department. His published works are *Beyond the Straits* (Momentum Press, 1980), *Love and the Bomb Don't Mix* (Grey Whale Press, 1982), *Lullabies from Cochiti* (Seven Buffaloes Press, 1983), *The Il-*

linois Suite (Spoon River Press, 1983), and *Song of the Rose and the Phoenix* (Seven Buffaloes Press, 1984).

JOANNA WARWICK was born in 1948 in Poland, and came to this country when she was seventeeen. Before settling in Los Angeles, she lived for brief periods in Washington, D.C. and Milwaukee. Her translations of modern Polish poetry have appeared in *kayak* and *The American Poetry Review*.

CHARLES WEBB is a long-time professional rock musician, now earning his living as a Creative Writing teacher at Cal State Long Beach and a psychotherapist in Beverly Hills. His degrees include an M.A. from the University of Washington, and an M.F.A. and Ph.D. from the University of Southern California. His first novel, *The Wilderness Effect,* was published by Chatto & Windus (London) in 1983. His first collection of poems, *Zinjanthropus Disease*, won a Wormwood Review Award. His most recent collection is *Nose Collector* (Illuminati, 1984).

Dave Alvin

Dick Barnes

Max Benavidez

Charles Bivins

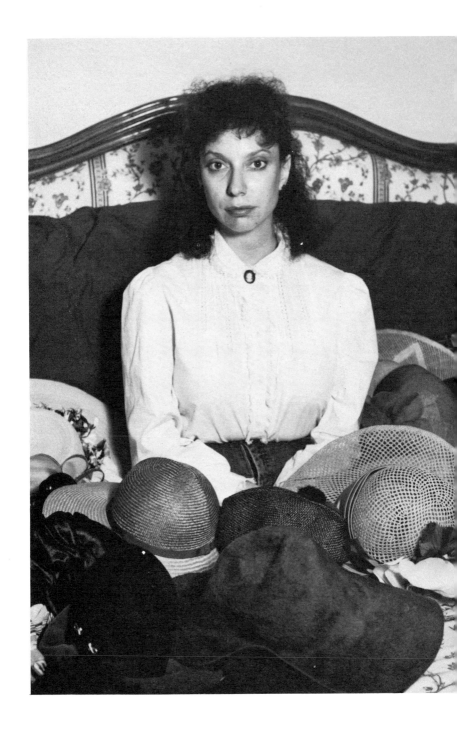

Laurel Ann Bogen

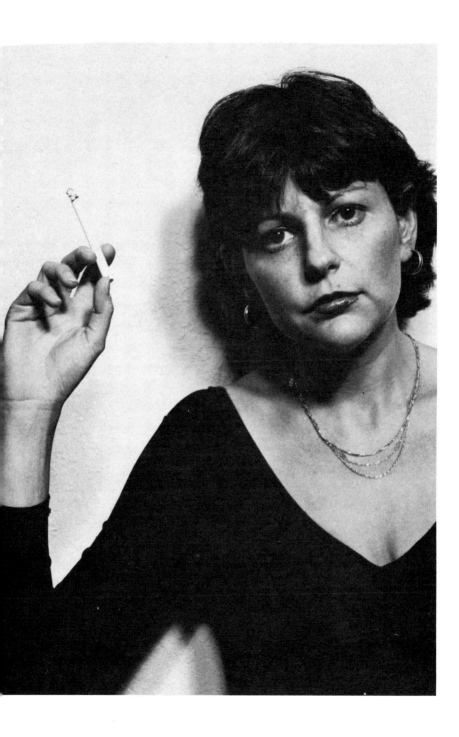

Kate Braverman

Charles Bukowski

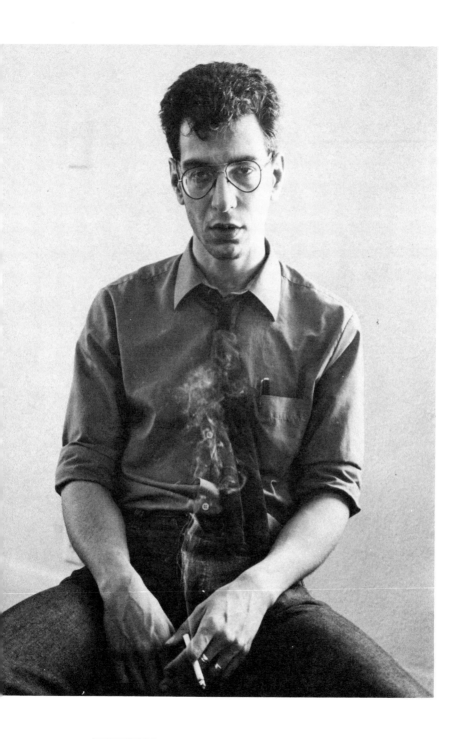

Peter Cashorali

Exene Cervenka

Michele T. Clinton

Lori Cohen

Wanda Coleman

Dennis Cooper

Robert Crosson

John Doe

Dennis Dorney

Bob Flanagan

Michael C. Ford

Amy Gerstler

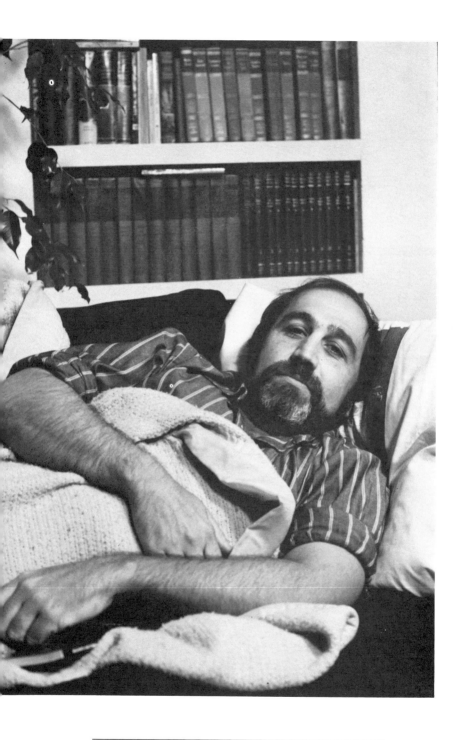

Jack Grapes

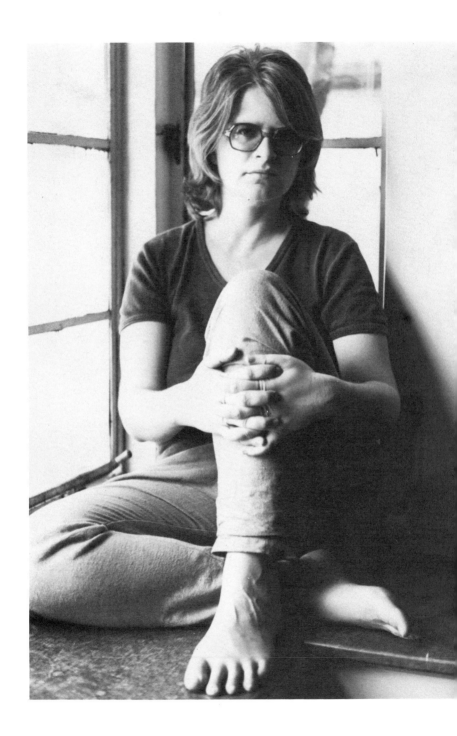

Janet Gray

John Harris

Eloise Klein Healy

Leland Hickman

Terryl Hunter

David James

Ron Koertge

Ian Krieger

James Krusoe

Michael Lally

Peter Levitt

Carol Lewis

Martha Lifson

Gerald Locklin

Suzanne Lummis

Lewis MacAdams

Nichola Manning

Murray Mednick

Bill Mohr

Harry E. Northup

Robert Peters

Dennis Phillips

Holly Prado

Jed Rasula

Tim Reynolds

Doren Robbins

Brooks Roddan

Aleida Rodríguez

Peter Schjeldahl

P. Schneidre

Jack Skelley

Ed Smith

Austin Strauss

Rob Sullivan

John Thomas

Alison Townsend

Paul Trachtenberg

David Trinidad

Paul Vangelisti

Marine Robert Warden

Joanna Warwick

Charles Webb

Index of Titles

Index of First Lines

Who couldn't pick out the intruder: 26
words in order words other words in order words in: 71
You are one of the shadowless east-west routes: 1
You are smiling serenely, eyes agleam above two bright spots: 299
you bring me apple trees, flowering apple trees: 296
You know?: 357
You know, it's probably: 152
You lean against the bruise: 329
Young men laugh trying to sound tough: 371
You read me a poem: 285
You're right, Holly!: 45
Your fists: 362
you stand up: 56
You start out with a shot glass: 102
"You stole the dynamite, dad.": 358
You were the one I knew long ago still young skin: 314